Filming Shakespeare's Plays

The Adaptations of
Laurence Olivier, Orson Welles,
Peter Brook and Akira Kurosawa

Anthony Davies

The right of the
University of Cambridge
to print and sell
all manner of books
was granted by
Henry VIII in 1534.
The University has printed
and published continuously
since 1584.

CAMBRIDGE UNIVERSITY PRESS

Cambridge
New York   Port Chester   Melbourne   Sydney

Published by the Press Syndicate of the University of Cambridge
The Pitt Building, Trumpington Street, Cambridge CB2 1RP
40 West 20th Street, New York, NY 10011, USA
10 Stamford Road, Oakleigh, Melbourne 3166, Australia

First published 1988
First paperback edition 1990

Printed in Great Britain at the University Press, Cambridge

British Library cataloguing in publication data

Davies, Anthony
Filming Shakespeare's plays: the
adaptations of Laurence Olivier, Orson Welles,
Peter Brook and Akira Kurosawa.
1. Drama in English. Shakespeare, William.
I. Title
791.43'75

Library of Congress cataloguing in publication data

Davies, Anthony, 1936–
Filming Shakespeare's plays: the adaptations of Laurence Olivier,
Orson Welles, Peter Brook, Akira Kurosawa / Anthony Davies.
    p. cm.
Filmography: p.
Bibliography: p.
Includes index.
ISBN 0–521–33508–6
1. Shakespeare, William, 1564–1616 – Film and video adaptations.
2. Film adaptations – History and criticsm.   I. Title.
PR3093. D38 1988
791.43'75–dc19   87–37377

ISBN 0 521 33508 6 hard covers
ISBN 0 521 39913 0 paperback

SE

To Professor Winifred Maxwell and Professor Guy Butler,
consummate sharers of enthusiasm,

and to my mother and friends,
whose generosity and encouragement
kept this endeavour alive through three winters.

Contents

Illustrations

Preface

The films of Olivier, Welles, Brook and Kurosawa constitute the most important material upon which this study has been based. It is only right, therefore, to point out that certain variations were noticed in the prints available for viewing. Not only were there omissions which reduced the duration of most prints from the advertised time lengths, but in some cases sections of film had been replaced in the wrong sequence. Only once was it possible to see a print of Kurosawa's THRONE OF BLOOD which included the prolonged and very significant sequence of Washizu and Miki (the respective Macbeth and Banquo figures) as they ride into and out of the forest mist early in the film's action. One print of Olivier's RICHARD III was 18 minutes short of its advertised length. These variations had to be accepted as inevitable disparities.

Welles's MACBETH and OTHELLO present special difficulties because Welles does not seem to have declared one particular version of either film to be definitive. The original version of MACBETH is believed, according to the Folger Shakespeare Filmography, to have had a running time of 105 minutes. That original 1948 version was withdrawn because of its faulty sound-track and re-released in 1949 and 1950 with a recorded sound-track and a shortened running time. Copies of the film available on current distribution have a running time of about 86 minutes, but the BBC screened what was termed a 'newly restored' version of MACBETH in May 1982, which ran for 108 minutes.

There are no fewer than six versions of OTHELLO catalogued in the British National Film Archives, and the version screened by the BBC (also in May 1982) varies significantly from the version available from the British Film Institute Library. The print of the version screened by the BBC (NFA Catalogue no. 900112 E) is dated 1953, the year after the film's copyright was registered with the Library of Congress in Washington. The version currently in distribution is dated 1955, and it is clearly this latter version which is referred to in all extant critical literature. It has not been possible to trace a review of the film which is dated before 1955. The version televised by the BBC differs from the more widely known version of 1955 in having no printed credits (all credits being spoken as 'voice over' by Orson Welles), in omitting the narrative introduction which establishes the dramatic situation, in curtailing the closing sequence of the funeral procession and Iago's imprisonment, and in placing the montage of ship-rigging and water-reflection shots among the opening sequences of the film. As well as being 216 feet shorter than the 1953 version, it is described in the NFA catalogue as 'having footage unique to itself'.

The available film scripts have been examined, but for two reasons the scripts have been of only limited use for this study. Firstly, a shooting script does not describe in detail the composite image framed in a shot, nor does it take into account the editing of the shots and their ultimate duration. Secondly, two distinctly different kinds of film script emerge, one a proposed shooting script whose details are often changed in the process of shooting, and the other a release script composed only after the film has reached its final form. The latter document is therefore little more than a written record of what can be observed in the film.

In order to distinguish reference to a play from a reference to a film, all film titles will be printed in capitals. OTHELLO will therefore refer to the film; *Othello* to the play.

While this study does not set out to compare the dialogue of the films with that of the plays, it has been considered helpful to indicate the placing in the play texts of important sections of film dialogue quoted in the chapters below.

Acknowledgements

I owe thanks to many, but especially to Ralph Koltai and Richard Pasco of the Royal Shakespeare Company, Charles Barr of the University of East Anglia, John Wilders, Literary Adviser on the BBC Shakespeare Television Series, and to Peter Brook, all of whom found time to discuss issues relevant to the filming of theatrical material; to Dr Susan Brock of the Shakespeare Institute Library, to Nicky Rathbone of the Shakespeare Section of the Birmingham City Library to whom I am grateful in particular for press notices and other printed material on Kurosawa's film, R AN, and Linda Briggs of the British Film Institute Library whose helpful concern and efficiency are deeply appreciated; to those who helped and gave advice on the organization of the material and the preparation of the manuscript, especially Dr Russell Jackson and Dr T.P. Matheson of the Shakespeare Institute. Finally, the help given me by the Library and Film Services Department of the University of Birmingham and by the Viewing service of the British Film Institute is gratefully acknowledged.

Plates 1–4, stills from the films H ENRY V and H AMLET by courtesy of the Rank Organization Plc, the diagram of the set for R ICHARD III by courtesy of the National Film Archive Stills Library. Plates 5–6 (London Films), 8–13, 14–15 (Columbia Pictures), and 16–17 (Toho International) supplied by courtesy of the National Film Archive Stills Department.

Introduction

The plays of Shakespeare have become undisputed literary classics. They have been encountered by vast numbers of students as words on the page, and only by a small fraction of that great number as staged performances. The texts have undergone exhaustive interpretative and bibliographic explication so that in addition to their own literary canonization, they have generated an immense volume of centrifugal literature.

Only since the beginning of this century has there been a move to apply an academic discipline to the study of Shakespeare in performance, and so to reaffirm the stature of the original corporate encounter of the plays as staged presentations. The thrust towards the study of the plays in performance has come about partly as a result of influential writing on this subject by authors of stature like John Russell Brown, J.L. Styan, Raymond Williams, Richard David and Stanley Wells. Between 1966 and 1981 John Russell Brown produced six books which stress the importance of the theatrical study of Shakespearean drama, the most controversial of which is his *Free Shakespeare* (1974). Stanley Well's *Literature and Drama* (1970), J.L. Styan's *The Shakespeare Revolution* (1977), Richard David's *Shakespeare in the Theatre* (1978) and the collection of essays, *Players of Shakespeare*, edited by Philip Brockbank (1985), have given wider dimensions to this consideration. On a more immediate level, the study of Shakespeare in performance has been promoted through the greater collaboration of the university and the theatre, both through their joint participation in projects and through the movement of university-trained actors and directors into the professional theatre.

One result of the awareness that textual study and theatrical presentation are parts of the same overall endeavour has been a return on the Shakespearean stage to the primacy of the dialogue. Scenic spectacle has been reduced and the central importance of the actor in the open space advanced. So powerful has this shift been, that in some recent productions at Stratford-upon-Avon the tendency has been to reinforce the self-consciousness of theatre by placing within the illuminated area of the stage distinctly theatrical objects which have no function as locational setting – a miscellaneous collection of properties, wigs and costumes standing in readiness, together with back-stage containers – and which give to rehearsed performance the calculated illusion of performed rehearsal.

The displacement of spectacle and the consequent investiture of the actor with the pre-eminent degree of dramatic responsibility from the start of the play has revealed anew the truism that the theatre is predominantly a medium of spoken language. What is equally true – as the years of silent cinema proved – is that the medium of film is *not* based on spoken language. The modern Shakespearean stage can justly claim the projection of the spoken word to be its essence, but the pith of cinematic expression even in Shakespearean adaptation is the moving image.

Yet theatre and cinema, like music, are temporal arts and they share with music a common means of generating dramatic energy. All three derive their dramatic capabilities primarily from the inherent opposition of arrested movement to the context of a dynamic structure; of still point within continuous movement. Within the dramatic structures of Shakespeare's dialogue, there emerge complex images which arrest the mind of the perceptive listener at points in the overall poetic and dramatic development, in the same way that intense moments in musical flow lay hold on involved response. So, too, the energy of the dramatic film arises from the suspension of the memorable visual image within a shifting but synthetic context of juxtaposed and discontinuous space.

The major difference between cinematic and theatrical presentation lies in the relationships of components rather than in essence: the relationship of action to time, and, more especially in the case of Shakespearean drama, the relation of the aural to the visual. While theatre can, and frequently does, incorporate spectacle of location as an organic dimension of its expression, so cinema has come to incorporate dialogue. Since the dramatic space of the theatre stage is relatively fixed and visually static, the dialogue can undergo subtle and complex manipulation. The opposite, however, holds true for the cinema. Its spatial disjunctions and the consequent demand for visual re-orientation necessarily inhibit sophisticated complexity of dialogue.

In adapting Shakespeare's dramatic material for the cinema screen, the film maker must, therefore, compensate for the changed relationship between what is spoken and what is shown, in accord with what is intrinsic to his medium. He must develop a cinematic language which is articulate on the visual level, a language which is essentially based on the manipulation of space – space between different entities in the rectangular frame which encloses the image, space between the camera and its subject, space which contracts or expands as the camera moves towards or away from, or around that subject. Will a particular dramatic situation be best served by sudden spatial disjunctions and discontinuities like those we find in Welles's OTHELLO? Or by a fluidity in space which the moving camera gives, for instance, to Olivier's HAMLET? What dramatic qualities will be given to a particular moment in the action by angle-shooting, the camera either being placed on a low level, 'looking up' at its subject, or being elevated above the action and so giving the viewer the sense of looking down upon it? What associations will the camera make, either simultaneously in the frame or in sequence? Photography will only capture the reflection of light from surfaces. In coming to terms with these questions, the film maker will not merely be affording the viewer different pictures of the action. He will be trying to penetrate dramatic substance. To focus the camera on what might be a fairly trivial family argument and then to punctuate this with a shot of gathering storm clouds, as Kurosawa does in RAN, is to present dramatic action and then to give that action a colouration and a magnitude not carried by the dialogue.

The cinematic resources used in a film should emerge as a coherent pattern which will give to the film an essential unity. Such a pattern can conveniently be thought of as a spatial strategy. By devising a spatial strategy which establishes and develops correspondences, oppositions and aesthetic progressions, the film maker must endeavour to invest his cinematic adaptation, on its predominant visual level, with a complexity and structural force which the medium of film does not naturally project in its dialogue.

Since the natural priorities of the cinema are not immediately compatible with the theatrical priorities of Shakespearean drama, the question that must arise is one of the legitimacy of the film maker's work. How far can the film maker be a creator? To what extent is he obliged to confine himself to being an interpreter? Lurking behind these questions is the assumption of some sort of authority bent upon ensuring that Shakespeare is not profaned, though such an authority almost certainly arises from the pre-eminent status which a literary study of Shakespeare's plays has asserted. Theatre is, by its nature, ephemeral and there would be something very wrong with it if productions of the same play over the years did not shift their emphasis in reflecting the hopes, fears, anger and current concerns of the societies from which these productions spring. The Royal Shakespeare Company's 1986 production of *Romeo and Juliet* was Shakespeare's play, but it deliberately set out to make its comment upon Mrs Thatcher's Britain of the 1980s and upon what was seen to be the displacement of philanthropic and humanitarian values by those associated with market forces and a monetarist morality. There is nothing essentially new in this. The play called 'The Murder of Gonzago' (which Hamlet later calls 'The Mousetrap') is not only staged with an emphasis designed to comment upon the current regime, but it incorporates specially added lines penned by its director, and a very effective dramatic piece it is.

But with regard to film, of course, the issue is different. This is partly because film is a fixture, establishing itself as another kind of text, and partly because, like theatre, it embodies impulses and emphases relevant to the time of its production; but unlike theatre, it cannot shed them. The film maker may be seen, therefore, as having a greater responsibility than the theatrical director. Not only will his work reach a wider audience, and probably an audience which is less able to set a particular presentation of a play in context, but the nature of the cinematic medium will give the presentation an authority which is alien to the theatre. Once again, however, the question of an assumed definitiveness arises, a supremely approved actualization of a Shakespeare text to which the film maker must strive to be faithful. It is clearly not helpful to suggest that the film maker has an obligation to be faithful to Shakespeare's intention. Who is to decide what that is, or was? It would therefore seem sensible to argue that a film maker will make the most effective film adaptation of a Shakespeare play if he is faithful to his own vision of what may be called the play's life force. It would seem more important to ensure that Shakespeare is not relegated to a museum for classic texts than to protect the plays from experimental presentation.

Charles Marowitz, whose productions of *Hamlet* and *The Taming of the Shrew* aroused such immense controversy, has maintained that the life force of a Shakespeare play is not embedded in the text, but results from an interaction between the imaginative mind and the text. The result will not be a presentation of the text as it stands, but will be irrefutable evidence that Shakespearean drama is vibrantly alive. 'You cannot make an omelette without breaking the eggs!'[1] Marowitz was, of course, talking essentially about theatre. But Frank Kermode has said much the same thing about the filming of Shakespeare's plays. In an article entitled 'Shakespeare in the Movies' he has this to say,

Certain plays . . . are commonly regarded as very great works. But common consent is not only not enough, it is in this situation a danger. The new maker has got to feel that the true nature of their greatness has eluded *him*, at any rate; that the testimony of others is mostly irrelevant; and that what he does with it must show what he found in it – not everything, but something – that confirmed his intuition that it was worth doing, and so at once justifies his authority and establishes that of the play . . . The point is simple; these texts, if we are to hold on to their greatness (and who says we can afford to lose it?), have to be reborn in the imagination of another.[2]

Kermode uses the word 'maker', and such an acknowledgement of the legitimacy of Shakespearean film as a creative endeavour is especially fitting, for scholars of Shakespeare as literature seem rarely to venture into the domain of Shakespearean film criticism. This is puzzling insofar as both the published text and the film exist – unlike the staged performance – as objects, and it is likely that over the years more people will form an idea of Shakespeare's *Romeo and Juliet* or *Hamlet* from the respective films of Zeffirelli and Olivier than will do so from any encounter with the printed text.

1 Cinematic and theatrical space

The temptation and the tendency to judge Shakespearean film in terms of some sort of theatrical achievement stems partly from that critical tendency to impose old criteria on new artistic fields, partly from the appearance on the screen of established stage actors in Shakespearean roles and partly from a persistent belief – which intelligent criticism has done little to shift – that cinema is really 'canned' and transportable theatre. The uncertainty about just what Shakespearean film ought to strive to accomplish will no doubt continue unless there is an attempt to discern clearly the subtle and significant differences which distinguish the two media in their presentation of dramatic material. They are differences which do not merely concern the mode of the work's presentation, but they crucially modify the relationship between the audience and the presented work. It is in the complex field of spatial relationships that the essential distinctions lie.

In his major essays on theatre and cinema, André Bazin writes helpfully and with profound insight on the complex relationship between these two arts, and points with precision to the distinguishing dramatic essence of film. The resonance of Bazin's observations continues to make them seminal in any discussion of the different kinds of space which the stage and screen constitute and his formulations will therefore play a major part in this chapter.

The nature of the audience relationship with stage space is both psychologically and architecturally determined. The action on the theatre stage is encapsulated within an 'aesthetic microcosm', the main purpose of which is to make a spatial distinction between art and nature.[1] We are conditioned to accept the staged dramatic activity in the same way that we accept the picture in its frame, the statue on its pedestal and characters who speak in verse so that they cannot possibly be connected with the intercourse of the day.[2] Even where the décor and the set aim to bring spatial illusions close to reality the stage can never strive for verisimilitude on its own because we, the theatre audience, know too much about it. We know that around the artificially illuminated space of the staged dramatic action there are actors waiting in the wings, there are battens of blazing lights and there are dusty men in paint-stained dungarees waiting to move the scenery.

The disparity between what the spectator in the theatre audience sees and what he knows is given particular emphasis on the conventional stage by theatrical frontality, and this disparity ensures that theatrical experience amounts to a reciprocal action between the presenters (not just the performers) of a dramatic work and the audience. The theatre audience is 'playing the game of theatre', which is in the first place a spatial game, for the spectator has to invest a specific and defined area with special significance. Bazin has written of the décor of the theatre as 'an area materially enclosed, limited, circumscribed, the only discoveries of which are those of our collusive imagination'.[3] Our entering into complicity with the stage director and the actors is a crucial element. Our willing suspension of disbelief has no threshold while it is skilfully manipulated by the presentation in all its aspects, yet it could nonetheless be said to be the framework within which dramatic action in the theatre remains authentic.

This element of collusion undergoes an important change in the response of the cinema audience. It does not cease to play its part but it is at once less conscious on the part of the spectator and less expected by the film director. Unlike the stage, the cinema frame does not encapsulate action within a microcosm. It isolates a central element in the action, but the full extent of that action – and of the spatial and social contexts of that action – must be credible beyond the constraints of the frame. The selected action we see must assume centrality for cinema's aesthetic purposes, but it must in no way (except for special effect) give the impression of being a staged composition. Bazin makes the distinction clear when he points out that 'the screen is not a frame like that of a picture, but a mask which allows only part of the action to be seen'. We accept that a character moving off screen is out of sight, but he 'continues to exist in his own capacity at some other place in the décor which is hidden from us'.[4]

The essential difference in the element of collusion in the cinema is that instead of actively 'playing the game', the cinema audience is conditioned to disregard technical anomalies. The collusion is with the cinematic medium, not with the director, the actors and stage designers who present the dramatic work. Rudolph Arnheim cites a telling example of this when he writes of film's monochromatic reduction of colour.

The reduction of all colors to black and white, which does not leave even their brightness values untouched . . . very considerably modifies the picture of the real world. Yet everyone who goes to see a film accepts the screen world as being true to nature . . . The spectator experiences no shock at finding a world in which the sky is the same color as the human face; he accepts shades of grey as the red, white and blue of the flag; black lips as red, white hair as blond. The leaves on a tree are as dark as a woman's mouth. In other words, not only has a multicolored world been transmuted into a black-and-white world, but in the process all color values have changed their relations to one another: similarities present themselves which do not exist in the natural world; things have the same color which in reality stand either in no direct color connection at all with each other or in quite a different one.[5]

A second example of unconscious collusion in the cinematic presentation of spatial realism arises in the transformation of the three-dimensional reality to the two-dimensional illusion. As Hugo Münsterberg observed in his perceptive study of the silent film written in 1916, our stereoscopic visual perception of the real world enables us to distinguish between a flat surface and a series of objects in depth. Yet the screen presents what we accept as depth on a flat surface. 'In motionless pictures', says Münsterberg, 'this is less disturbing; in moving pictures every new movement to or from the background must remind us of the apparent distortion.' Our psychological adjustment is in fact more complex, for not only does the lack of stereoscopic resolution register the flatness of the image, but there is a conflict of visual perception arising from the fact that the screen itself is 'an object of our perception and demands an adaptation of the eye and an independent localization'.[6]

The cinema aims at spatial realism. Nonetheless our collusion with the medium is such that we will tolerate – we shall even accept – photographic tricks so long as they are wholly convincing; so long as we are given at the visual level what appears to be spatially real, and so long as we can believe in a spatial reality beyond the boundaries of the frame.

Effective theatre design is essentially an architectural manifestation of the psychological dynamics which operate in the total experience of theatre. While different relationships between the staged action and the audience can be established in theatres built with thrust stages, open stages, arena stages or traverse stages, any theatre for dramatic presentation consists of three elements which are spatial; in John Russell Brown's words, 'a place for the audience, a place in which the actors perform and, optionally a setting for the dramatic action'.[7] The audience is generally seated so as to afford it maximum visual concentration upon the demarcated space within which the actors manipulate the pace, progress and impact of the dramatic work. The spatial separation of the actors from the audience which the architecture incorporates is the extension of those distinctions between art and nature and between the art-work and the percipient. Yet those distinctions become dependent upon their material and spatial manifestation. 'There can,' as Bazin insists, 'be no theatre without architecture ... Whether as a performance or a celebration, theatre of its very essence must not be confused with nature under the penalty of being absorbed by her and ceasing to be.'[8]

The architecture of the cinema is almost identical with that of nineteenth-century conventional theatre with its proscenium arch; and the indulgence in spectacle which typified the melodrama of the 1880s and the 1890s prepared the ground most appropriately for cinema. Eminently suited to the same kind of seating arrangements, cinema naturally appeared to be merely an extension of the theatre of spectacle. Nicholas Vardac, in his important and engaging book on the relationship between theatre and film, observes that 'when ... realism and romanticism had, toward the end of the century, attained real leaves, beeves and ships the stage could go no further. But the need for pictorial realism on an even greater scale remained. Only the motion picture with its reproduction of reality could carry on the cycle.'[9] However, the architectural similarity of the cinema with the theatre concealed the profound changes in the psychology of audience response. While the spatial divisions remain, the psychological effect of the modern camera's spatial versatility is to break down the constant of distance between the viewer and the detail in the framed image. Not only is the image itself in sustained movement, but so also is the view-point, for the camera's function is one of exploration rather than presentation; one of making the spectator conscious of the dynamics of space in breadth as well as depth. By zooming (adjusting the lens in a smooth movement to give the appearance of approaching or moving away from the subject), tracking (literally moving the whole camera unit along tracks to hold a moving object in the frame), tilting and being moved on a crane boom, the camera gives the spectator the illusion of horizontal and vertical mobility. In divorcing psychological space from architectural space, the camera can, and to some extent always does, induce a passivity in the spectator. This is part of what we have come to expect of the cinematic manipulation of space. We are no longer 'playing the game of theatre', and our involvement in the dramatic action of the film, our awareness of the rest of the audience and of ourselves as individuals are affected in ways which are distinct from theatrical experience.

When André Bazin describes the pleasure of the cinema experience as 'self-satisfaction, a concession to solitude, a sort of betrayal action by refusal of social responsibility', he is identifying with particular emphasis the spatial manipulation of the camera and its consequent authority over the audience.[10] Because the movement of the camera is an artistic dimension of the film's structure, and because the movement of the camera becomes in its psychological effects the movement of the spectator, the normal frontiers between the spectator and the work of art are broken down. The spectator is invaded by, and participates in the laws of the artistic structure.

This is of fundamental importance in distinguishing film art from theatre art. For just as frontiers are dissolved between the viewer and the art object in film, so too are frontiers dissolved within the viewer; the frontiers between the subjective participant and the objective critic. Béla Balázs, writing in the early 1950s, recognized both the dangers and the artistic potential of this shift of balance towards subjectivity.

The constantly changing set-ups give the spectator the feeling that he himself is moving, just as one has the illusion of moving when a train on the next platform starts to leave the station. The true task of film art is to deepen into artistic effects the new psychological effects made possible by the technique of cinematography.[11]

A further distinction – of which it is more difficult to be conscious – lies in the relationship between the actor and the spatial context in which he is seen to act. In the theatre, as a play proceeds, the focus of interest becomes increasingly vested in the actor. The play in fact becomes a process during which the stage décor becomes less important and the actor takes over, to an increasing extent, the dramatic responsibility. One very obvious reason for this is that structured change between and within characters on the stage takes place within a set representation of locality. It is as though theatre is reducing the variables to a minimum in order to insist that the human actor is the paramount focus for interest because he exercises choices and manipulates dramatic material amid the décor. 'In the theatre,' says Bazin, 'the drama proceeds from the actor; in the cinema it goes from the décor to the man. This reversal of dramatic flow is of decisive importance.'[12]

At one level this simply means that in watching a play in the theatre, we the audience are involved at one end of the circuit while the action on the cinema screen is a closed circuit independent of audience response. Béla Balázs captures more completely the nature of the dramatic flow between actor and décor in film, in a quotation from Goethe. 'The things surrounding men do not merely act upon them – men react on their surroundings too, and while they allow things to change them, they in return change things,' and he discerns the cause for the reduced status of the actor on the screen when he deals with what he terms the 'physiognomy of surroundings and backgrounds':

The eternal and insoluble contradiction between the living actor [on the stage] and the dead scenery, the flesh-and-blood figure and the painted perspective of the background anyway places the background outside the play; it relegates the background to the background as it were. Not so in the film. There man and background are of the same stuff, both are mere pictures and hence there is no difference in the reality of man and object.

Like painting, film can give the spatial detail which surrounds characters an anthropomorphic dimension and 'as in Van Gogh's late pictures, an even more intense physiognomy so that the violent expressive power of the objects makes that of the human characters pale into insignificance'.[13] The dramatic function of the natural environment, first considered and written about in relation to film by Urban Gad in 1918, has consistently been recognized as an important but sometimes intractable cinematic resource in the adaptation of stage plays. The characterization of nature became a major preoccupation for Kozintsev in making his KING LEAR film in 1971. 'I am trying to find a visual *Lear*. Nature in this context would have to become something like the chorus of Greek Tragedy.'[14]

The distinctions between film and theatre have so far been discussed very much from the point of view of the theorist. It would certainly be facile to suggest that certain rules for film adaptation are implicit within them. There remain, broadly speaking, two spatial strategies available to the film director who adapts a theatre play for the screen. He can decide to treat dramatic action with the object of preserving its theatrical essence as far as possible, by simply photographing the staged performance on stage space. Implicit in this strategy is the contention that a play produced on the theatre stage is artistically complete, and that cinema is simply a medium for its transmission and preservation. It implies, too, that the spatial properties of cinema can be disregarded in order to preserve theatrical frontality as well as the actor's centripetality. The second strategy is that in which the cinema brings its own spatial potential to bear on the material to effect an entire visual transformation by moving the action from the confines of the theatrical enclosure and creating new relationships between the actor and the décor, between space and time and between the dramatic presentation and the audience.

A classic example of the attempt to film a stage performance on stage space is Stuart Burge's OTHELLO (1965) which purports simply to shift the performance of the play (directed by John Dexter for the Old Vic in 1964, with Olivier in the title role) from the stage to the cinema screen. While Burge makes no pretence to be doing other than filming a stage presentation, the film is, in many ways, profoundly disappointing. A consideration of just why this is so will, I believe, throw interesting light upon the adaptation of Shakespeare for the screen.

The film is most robustly defended on the grounds of Olivier's characterization with its strong contemporary social relevance, and because of the value of the film as a record of Olivier's theatrical power in the role. Several critics draw attention to the contemporary relevance of a black man in a white society and the consequent precariousness of Othello's self-image. It is this which prompts James Fisher, in an article written in 1973, and Jack Jorgens in his well-known book to apply – in an unusual sense for film – the epithet 'realistic' to the Othello portrayed in this film.[15] Jorgens especially defends the film on the basis of this 'realism' which arises from 'the meticulous naturalistic details of the performance'.[16] There is an irony in justifying a film on its immediate contemporary relevance. The inherent ephemerality matches such an interpretation more appropriately with theatre than with film. At the same time, critics who champion the film on this basis do have time on their side, for they will be vindicated when the film ultimately achieves its stature as a historical document of dramatic interpretation.

The second line of defence, founded on the assertion that the film intends nothing more than to record a magnificent stage performance, is essentially unconvincing because it fails to take into account the inherent aesthetic clash between the very different dynamics of stage space on the one hand and screen space on the other. The actor on the stage is an autonomous manipulator of theatre space, but on the screen he is part of the manipulated space within the frame. Roger Manvell, in his very useful book, quotes Anthony Havelock-Allan as claiming the intention of the producers to be to 'preserve and enhance this OTHELLO and more or less present it as one might have seen it at the National Theatre . . . the whole object was to capture the absolute magic of the theatre'.[17] To assume that a stage performance would not be radically altered in its impact when transmitted through another medium appears to have been an error which blighted the film at its conception.

In the first place, the film fails to communicate an original theatricality because the camera focuses too often on only one character at moments when its exclusion of peripheral response leaves the central action bare. A clear example of this is Othello's relation of his winning of Desdemona's love to the senators. On the stage, the response of every person in the Senate chamber defines Othello's particular magic as a teller of tales and as a leader of men, yet the film merely presents in isolation the response of the Duke. The Senate chamber is ideally a theatre for both Othello and Brabantio. The entrance of each is internally dramatic in its own way. Yet in isolating individual characters from the theatrical totality, the camera destroys dramatic perspective so that the entrance of one character is very much like the entrance of another. There is no sense – as there surely should be – of Brabantio's coming into a new dramatic environment, with new and reciprocal expectations of behaviour. Both

Othello and Brabantio affect – and are affected by – the ambience of the Senate meeting with its atmospheric charge of urgency, yet the film fails to project collective atmosphere here as it does much later when Othello strikes Desdemona in front of Lodovico and the visiting emissaries from Venice. It fails to register in its frame compositions the presence of an audience within the play's action.

Equally frustrating is the film's incapacity to capture the important shift in the Senate's discussion *from* its momentary preoccupation with Brabantio's private concern as a father *to* its concentration once again on the threat of the Turkish fleet to the prosperity of the Venetian state. The inflexibility of the camera style with abrupt cuts from one close-up to another has the effect of reducing dramatic situations to a common low level of intensity.

A second important respect in which the film fails to achieve a theatrical impact is its discontinuity. The growing intensity of thought and emotion which proceeds in the theatre without constant interruption is not allowed to develop in the film because of the visual fragmentation of the editing. The constant cutting from shot to shot is especially deadening because no spatial richness is achieved by the montage. Because the camera is carried forward inside the proscenium, the variation of distance makes it impossible to hold a character in focus when he moves, so that the resultant abrupt cutting from one camera's perspective to another's is a technical rather than an artistic requirement.

The film is most successful in those moments when it works in line with the theatrical intention implicit in the original production. One such moment early in the film is when the camera selects the faces of Iago and Roderigo against a background of darkness as they prepare to rouse Brabantio. The shots establish character by relating individuals to shadowed darkness (their natural environment) and make the faces dramatic. The camera's isolation of the faces here actually extends theatrical concentration. Another instance is the camera's intense absorption with Iago at the end of Act I. The scale of Frank Finlay's performance is suitably matched to the camera's demands so that Iago's lines, 'Hell and night / Must bring this monstrous birth to the world's light' with a synchronized fading of light on the set to final blackness, bring the Venetian placing of the action to a delicately orchestrated close.[18] Cassio's drunken exit in Act II is also memorably effective, because once again the concentration of the theatre audience would naturally be upon Cassio. The camera's isolation of him, therefore, is a cinematic extension of theatrical intensity and suspense originally built into the production.

The pity is that these moments of effective cinematic intensification appear to be the result of good luck rather than good judgement, for their promise is annihilated by instances where the camera work runs deliberately counter to the theatrical intention with no cinematic compensation. One example is the sequence immediately following the successful shots of Iago and Roderigo preparing to wake Brabantio. As the play is staged, Brabantio appears on a level well above Roderigo and Iago. He peers out into the night, trying to locate and identify the voices which have woken him from below. The different levels clearly articulate a distinction between Brabantio and the other two which is no less valid for film than it is for theatre. Yet Burge uses a second camera to present Brabantio in isolation, reducing his dramatic eminence by denying him effective elevation and putting him visually on the same level as Iago and Roderigo. This spatial disorientation disrupts the development of the scene's tension in its refusal to establish the vertical distance between the motives of Iago on the one hand, and of Brabantio on the other. What is presented to the theatre audience is, for no good reason, denied the film viewer.

Together with the spatial dislocation and the lack of dramatic perspective which results from the frame's isolation of characters from their dramatic context, other clashes between cinematic and theatrical dynamics of space are compounded. Donald Skoller, in an unpublished thesis written in 1968, makes some penetrating observations about this film, and he draws attention to the effects of insistent close-up camera work under theatre lighting. The tendency is for surfaces to throw off 'too much sheen and glisten . . . for the tragic mood to be enforced'.[19] There is, too, a claustrophobic effect in the close-up shots in moments of fully projected rhetorical outburst from Olivier which gives the film an unintentional capacity for Brechtian alienation. Some of the spatial strategies which were planned for the three-dimensional stage lose their assertive power on the two-dimensional screen. The movement, for instance, whereby Brabantio seeks to divide the Duke and Othello by interposing himself, and the counter-move by Othello, does not constitute a strong statement on the screen.

The lack of exterior locales is very noticeable in the film. There is no relief from the interior of the stage set, and even within the conventions of the stage set there is little suggestion of exterior effect. The result is particularly enervating in the medium whose energy derives from the assertion of dramatic relationships wrought out of spatial diversity. Donald Skoller suggests that 'the powerful inner force of Shakespeare's tragedies requires ventilation when it is converted to two-dimensional cinematic shadow play'. While this is true, the sense of spatial paralysis probably has as much to do with frustrated cinematic expectations as it has to do with the substance of Shakespearean drama. The realism which the camera can so convincingly portray is deeply rooted in audience expectations, and for there to be the sound effects of a storm with no visual complement, no cloak stirring in the sound of a gale, heightens the sense of unacceptable artificiality.

Just as dramatic perspective of character is undermined by the camera's egalitarian concentration, so too the perspective of objects is distorted by cinematic magnification. Both the bracelet blade which Othello wears and the handkerchief are given a visual amplification by the camera, which throws awry their respective impacts. The bracelet blade becomes a clever gimmick, imparting to Othello's character a dimension totally alien to it, while the handkerchief loses the wisplike delicacy which contrasts so ironically with the terrible consequences it precipitates. There is, however, as Donald Skoller points out, a dramatic compensation in the camera's magnification of the cross and medallion which hang around Othello's neck. As a symbol of 'a cultural identity Othello has assumed, but cannot completely sustain' their natural prominence in the film close-ups is a reminder of Othello's self-conscious sense of social displacement.[20]

On a specifically technical level, the film's failure to achieve a satisfactory cinematic stature stems, above all from the insistent closeness of the camera. The result is that with Olivier's performance, the photographic scrutiny reveals details of technique as a distracting and unnecessary dimension of character projection. Constance Brown, in her review of the film for *Film Quarterly* written in 1966, is right in drawing attention to the 'severe myopia' of the camera as an indication of the film's having probably been 'tailored for TV'.[21] Certainly the film's impact is less oppressive on the small screen.

Aesthetically however, there remains the fact that the media of film and theatre work against each other for too much of the time. When Jorgens claims that the acceptability of this film awaits the capacity of audiences 'to accept the conventions of stage acting, to enter into the play-film world as they do in theatres, and to respond quite as fully as they do to behaving', he seems to ignore the fact that cinematic dramatization requires the relation of actor to décor.[22] The function of stage décor is to give theatrical resonance to dialogue, to facilitate the centripetal concentration of power in the actor. The screen, on the other hand, reflects a dramatic image which is centrifugal, but which retains its power through the dynamic reciprocity between actor and spatial detail. The aesthetic collision in Burge's OTHELLO results from a failure to reconcile these oppositions of spatial nature.

At the opposite extreme from the attempt to restrict cinema to the spatial dimensions of the stage lies an adaptive approach which insists on the paramouncy of the spatial potential of cinema. This is not simply a rejection of all things theatrical, for embedded within its aesthetic refinement the art of theatre contains a dynamic opposition.

Despite its centripetal concentration on the actor as the ultimate dramatic agent, the theatre stage does also suggest by implication a yearning for spatial expanse. It is as though the energy of the staged drama is deliberately pressurized in contained space, and the area into which it does finally expand gives the actor his pre-eminence. 'It is because that infinity which the theatre demands cannot be spatial that its area can be none other than the human soul . . . The dramatic infinities of the human heart moan and beat within the enclosing walls of the theatrical sphere. This is why this dramaturgy is in its essence human. Man is at once its cause and its subject.'[23] One preoccupation which the implicit yearning for spatial expanse invites in the cinematic adaptation of Shakespearean drama is geo-historical realism.

It is not difficult to understand the temptations which must have besieged the mind of an ambitious film maker at the time that liberation from the enclosed theatre space was thought to be the only important aim of cinematic adaptation. Financial resources and the mobility of equipment made it possible either to build massive and realistic reconstructions, or to film the action on authentic location. Both the names of places in the plays themselves and the apparent spatial frustration of the theatre stage seem, at first sight, to demand bold spatial experiment for the proper accommodation of Shakespeare's dramatic energy. The dangers of such purely spatial boldness were only to be discovered later.

As early evidence of the spatial enthusiasm which accompanied film adaptations of Shakespeare plays, one notes with interest that the credits for the 1913 silent film HAMLET proclaimed that the film's exteriors included a complete reconstruction of Elsinore Castle at Lulworth Cove.[24] However, the play which has attracted the most insistent locational treatment in film is *Romeo and Juliet*. George Cukor's film released in 1936 had a carefully researched studio set with much of the design and costuming based on Italian Renaissance paintings. Roger Manvell, whose survey of the field of Shakespearean film published in 1971 was the first broad coverage of sound adaptations, tells us that 'an area of one hundred acres was set aside to build the sets of Verona'.[25] Both Castellani's film of 1954 and Zeffirelli's very popular film of 1968 were shot in Verona. Castellani's film reveals most clearly the failure of a cinematic intention which aims primarily to give Shakespearean drama geo-historical authenticity and to deny theatricality in the interests of realism. Castellani's spatial obsession has the effect of reducing Shakespeare's dramatic power in three respects. It fails to relate spatial details in the frame to the play's dramatic meaning, and it refuses to give the architecture more than an ornamental significance. Secondly, Castellani seemed to believe that if real location and real history were implicit in the film's space, then Shakespearean dramatic characters had logically to become merely real, everyday people. Finally, Castellani clearly failed to understand that when theatrical dialogue is spoken on the cinema screen, its theatrical impact is not automatically preserved.

Perceptive critics were uncomfortably aware of the tendency for the visual splendour to overwhelm the poetic imagery of the play. Arthur Knight, conceding that Shakespeare's stage required the creation of visual detail through poetic imagery, and that insofar as Shakespeare succeeded in this poetic depiction, 'the need to reconstruct sets in solid, three-dimensional form disappears', nonetheless maintained that 'the motion-picture medium demands those shapes and forms. Its actors cannot exist in a void'. Caught in this ambivalent position, Knight makes a final statement which appears more committal than it is, asserting that in exploiting the space of Verona to the extent that he has, Castellani 'has recast a triumph of the poetic theatre for a form that is in many ways its very antithesis'. For Margaret Farrand Thorp, Castellani's spatial and cinematic exercises were at times unequivocally intrusive. Of Castellani's camera movement as Romeo runs to find refuge with the Friar she comments, 'He shows us every foot of that headlong, circuitous passage through Verona's streets, authentic, highly picturesque streets, but what have they to do with the story? And a chase with no one pursuing is not only bad Shakespeare but bad movie.'[26] Roger Manvell comments on the surprising enthusiasm with which Castellani's film was received at the Venice Film Festival of 1954, and suggests that those 'who rose to acclaim the first showing of Castellani's Italianate version of ROMEO AND JULIET were not applauding it because it was Shakespeare. They saw it as a splendidly colourful reincarnation of fifteenth-century Italy in Technicolour.'[27] Clearly, the film raised difficulties for the critics. Like Olivier's HENRY V it was a colourful historical reconstruction. Unlike Olivier's films, it sought to make geo-historical realism its justification. It seemed at the time of its critical reception to confirm the view of those who maintained – and still maintain – that it is impossible to have good film which is also good Shakespeare.

This last, and superficial, conclusion was in no small part the result of Castellani's all-pervading commitment to cinematic realism. The neo-realistic fallacy was one of complete consistency, which made it impossible to abandon realism on any level. Castellani's task, as he saw it, was to harmonize acting style and poetic dialogue with the spatial authenticity he had established, and he addressed himself to this by dismantling the theatricality of the play. Such a strategy is disastrous in the cinematic adaptation of a stage play. Its logical conclusion is rightly assessed by Peter Brook's observation that 'you can't just put a lot of people together who can't act, get them to walk around in real settings, and think it's neo-realistic'.[28] A remarkably wide range of acting styles can be accommodated within the composite artistic whole which constitutes enthralling cinema. To refuse to accept this is to deny the intrinsic distinction between the theatrical and the real event: between art and nature.

Finally there arises the question of reconciling the heightened utterance and increased density of poetic dialogue with the convincing realism of cinematic space. This is the most formidable challenge to the film maker who adapts Shakespeare for the screen, and it is in this respect that Castellani's film fails most lamentably. An increase in dramatic spectacle inevitably reduces the function of dialogue. Nicholas Vardac notes that 'dialogue in many climactic scenes of the melodrama [of the 1860s] was of secondary importance, and, as in the silent film, pictorial action, pantomime and business dominated. . . . Drama depended essentially upon the sensational action, the spectacular scenic conceptions, and the cleverness of the overall episodic pattern.' The *New York Times* critic, reviewing the New Haven production of *The Auctioneer* in 1901, alluded to 'the makers of this play – it would not be fair to say authors', and continued, 'Large sections of the play were made up of stage business. For instance, the second act, which occupies the better part of an hour, probably has less than 400 lines of dialogue.'[29] The emasculation of the dialogue in this film is the result of Castellani's failure to compensate for the particular dynamics of cinematic space.

However exclusively the cinema frame may select, it does not, as we have shown, enclose. In dispensing with theatrical encapsulation, the concentration of action within space is dissipated. The selected image, as we have seen, becomes part of, and determines, what we believe to exist outside the frame, making 'the space of the screen . . . centrifugal'. This quality of centrifugality, which Burge's film of OTHELLO unnaturally curtailed, determines both the specific illusion of cinema and the nature of the actor's location on the screen where he is 'no longer the focus of the drama, but will become eventually the centre of the universe'. Unless the film director manipulates his resources in the specific interests of sustaining the dialogue's resonance, cinematic centrifugality will dissipate its impact so that 'the dramatic force of the text, instead of being gathered up in the actor, dissolves without echo into the cinematic ether'.[30]

There is no easy resolution of the contrary dynamics of theatrical and cinematic space. The richness of locational detail in Castellani's film is not dramatically well used, but it is too simplistic to assert, as John Fuegi does, writing in 1972 that 'it is obvious that the doctrine of *things* dominates and ruins this film'.[31] The dramatic stagnancy of the film arises from the expansion of spatial coverage together with a deliberate reduction of dramatic character. That a Shakespearean film can incorporate spatial realism and still retain its dramatic impact is manifestly illustrated by Zeffirelli's ROMEO AND JULIET (1968). Zeffirelli's camera work is much more searchingly aggressive than Castellani's, but the distinctive feature of Zeffirelli's film is its retention of theatrical focus. The spatial strategy is a triumph of convincing realistic indulgence which never vitiates either clarity and complexity of dramatic moment, or delineation of character.

The secret of Zeffirelli's success is his use of Verona's central piazza as the central area of the film's dramatic action. Whatever action explodes in the square sends out ripples to the rest of the city, to involve in greater numbers the family forces of the Montagues and the Capulets. In this way Zeffirelli ensures that the centrifugal spread of the film's action is consistent with the natural centrifugality of the cinematic image. A second potential which Zeffirelli exploited was the natural theatricality of the city square's space. Zeffirelli's square encloses realistic activities of everyday life, but its enclosed atmosphere is charged with expectancy so that every entrance and exit is theatrically heightened, every character is theatrically acknowledged within the film's action and every moment in the fights is seen to affect those who are spectators. Zeffirelli characterizes Mercutio in the film by making him wholly dependent upon his theatrical value for recognition among the adolescents of Verona. It is his neurotic compulsion to attract and play to an audience, as his instinct for exploiting levels and focal positions in the square makes clear. Ironically, both Mercutio and Tybalt are trapped in an ultimate theatrical situation whose attraction is irresistible, and which moves through vicious derision to tense comedy and finally to death, with Tybalt carrying the locus of action out of the square and Mercutio isolated in the reality of his dying while his audience in the square continue to applaud the convincing realism of what appears to be continuing theatre.

The success of Zeffirelli's strategy lies in his recognition that Shakespeare's own dramatic strategy of incorporating theatre within the presentation of a play could with equally positive impact be applied to film. Where Castellani paralysed theatrical expression in the interests of realism, Zeffirelli incorporated it to elevate the significance of incident and so to retain the dramatic resonance of character and utterance in realistic space.

Not every Shakespearean play can be so readily adapted to a city environment which allows the centrifugal development of action to spread as it does in Zeffirelli's Verona. *Macbeth* and *King Lear*, for instance, are plays of isolation where action is driven psychologically inwards. These plays will call for a spatial strategy which must reconcile the theatricality of dialogue and character with a different type of spatial realism. A way has to be found of integrating the cinematic space with the subtextual and thematic substance of a particular Shakespeare play, for as John Reddington writing in 1973 for *Literature Film Quarterly* makes clear, it is insufficient simply to give Shakespeare's dramatic action a meticulously realistic setting. Writing of Polanski's MACBETH, Reddington faults the director on 'introducing a reality so detailed that the eye and mind are satisfied, while the spectator's intuition, constructive imagination, and dreaming soul are simply not involved in the relationship at all'. Given the nature of cinema's spatial potential, it is impossible not to confront the question of just what the function of spatial realism in the presentation of Shakespearean drama might be. Clearly it is fallacious to argue that Shakespeare's drama is independent of spatial articulation, for as Reddington rightly argues, space and place are elements of the 'world which comes into existence between the speeches and acts of [Shakespeare's] characters, upheld by them, ever secreted by them'. The spatial demands which a Shakespeare play makes of the medium of cinema is not the presentation of a geo-historical setting for action and dialogue, but rather an articulation which projects aspects of the play's dramatic substance. Brook's choice of a cold northern location for his KING LEAR attempts to meet this organic demand of the play. The wintry bleakness of North Jutland becomes, as Reddington maintains, 'a landscape of the mind, a place dreamed by its inhabitants, one whose temperatures, textures and lights alter with moods, acts, speeches of the characters'. While both Brook and Polanski incorporate spatial realism in an attempt to advance beyond the mere establishment of an authentic geo-historical location, it is Brook whose spatial strategy is consistently penetrating in a way which engages with Shakespeare's complexity. Where Polanski 'films a castle, not Macbeth's castle', and witches 'anyone might have seen', Brook's cinematic effectiveness arises from his capacity for 'filming places which have absorbed some of the life of the character in them'. The spatial contexts are organically associated with the characters, so that the film's universe 'is particularly theirs as it is Hamlet's prerogative alone to meet the joking philosopher in the grave digging [scene]'.[32]

It would indeed be an odd outcome to our discussion if it transpired that Shakespeare's plays stand the best chance of a wholly satisfying transfer to the screen in those countries which are farthest removed from his overwhelming verbal influence.[33]

It is not all that 'odd', for the translator, in reducing the complexity of the poetic imagery, establishes for the film from the start a new and potentially more harmonious balance between what is shown and what is said. The film maker in this situation is free to initiate his concept of the presentation in terms of the artistic potentials and the artistic disciplines of the medium of cinema. The process of translation, in short, does not stop with the language of the dialogue. It becomes, for great directors like Kurosawa and Kozintsev, a process whereby the dramatic work is spatially translated from the language of the theatre to the language of the cinema. Where Brook's film KING LEAR tended to make its aesthetic compromises by restricting camera movement and by rigidly controlling its spatial effects, the films of Kurosawa and Kozintsev clearly establish 'the conquest of the realism of space' as an uncompromised priority.[34]

It would be wrong to assume that either Kurosawa or Kozintsev were involved in a deliberate and vigorous cinematic reaction against the theatre. The work of both is in line with Vardac's argument that cinema is part of an evolutionary dynamic which began with trends within the development of theatre itself. One must look, therefore, with circumspection at Manvell's assertion that Kurosawa's film THRONE OF BLOOD (based on Shakespeare's *Macbeth*) is 'the work of a man who is a film-maker first and last', for the spatial strategy of Kurosawa's film is strongly influenced by the traditions of Japanese painting and by the conventions of the Noh theatre. Kurosawa has acknowledged that his style of composition within the cinema frame has been influenced both by his early training as a painter and by spatial characteristics which are 'peculiar to Japanese art'.[35]

The spatial strategy of THRONE OF BLOOD will be discussed in detail in a later chapter. Here it is only necessary to draw attention to the extent to which Kurosawa's spatial strategy is philosophically and psychologically integrated with the dramatic substance of the plot, theme and character.

While the interior scenes are essentially theatrical, the exterior form of the castle, its position on the landscape, its particular architecture and its symbolic power are all cinematically invested with a significance which belongs wholly to the dramatic development of this particular film. If the castle constitutes 'a world within that of the all-encompassing forest' which man makes 'to seal himself off from an amoral nature', the forest which surrounds it becomes a multi-layered embodiment of the film's thematic substance as well as being an objectification of the psychological complexity of the central character. 'The reality of the forest is overwhelming,' observes Blumenthal, whose essay written in 1965 is the most illuminating single piece of analysis on the film. 'It breathes, and sweats, and twitches, and speaks in the unknown tongue. It is easily as powerful a presence as Washizu [the Macbeth figure] himself; and this is exactly as it must be, since for Washizu this first encounter with the forest is nothing less than a headlong plunge into the self.'[36] Kurosawa's film is a supreme example of what Bazin meant when he wrote of 'the conquest of the realism of space' as being that which distinguishes cinema from moving pictures; not simply a technical conquest, but an artistic one.[37]

Grigori Kozintsev has made two Shakespearean films, HAMLET (1964) and KING LEAR (1971). His diary notes on the making of these films are invaluable in revealing the creative process and the adaptive priorities which make the films so powerful. Whereas the theatrical influences upon Kurosawa's cinematic sense were traditional ones, Kozintsev was attracted by new frontiers of theatrical endeavour. Three innovators who influenced him most profoundly were Meyerhold, Stanislavsky and Gordon Craig. Kozintsev seized hold of Craig's declaration that it was 'impossible to produce the theatrical play *Hamlet* on the stage' because the 'massive essence of the tragedy' had exhausted theatrical resources for a modern audience. This is a clear indication that for Kozintsev the problem in his performed presentation of Shakespeare is one of dramatic accommodation, and it is a dynamic rather than a static challenge. The Elizabethan stage was no more a final answer for the staging of Shakespeare than the eighteenth-century orchestra was the final answer for the performance of a Bach *Brandenburg* concerto.

In his conviction that artistic presentation and aesthetic response are not protected by canonization Kozintsev allied himself with the evolutionary movement within theatre, and his response to Craig's *Towards a New Theatre* reveals in embryonic form Kozintsev's cinematic spatial orientation. Simplicity and economy were the key concepts in Craig's vision of theatrical space and its thematic articulation. The conventional stage set was transformed into a powerful elemental statement which operated through the interaction of matter. Kozintsev observed closely Craig's visualization of *Macbeth* in which the interaction of rock and mist articulate the conflict in the play. 'The mist was an accumulation of moisture; the moisture undermined the rock, the vapours ate away the stone. The rock collapsed.' The economy lay in understanding the nature of material interaction. The simplicity lay in the two 'shades . . . brown (rock) and grey (mist). You don't need anything else.'[38]

The principle of Kozintsev's cinematic articulation lies in the complexity of thematic levels at which his spatial detail operates. The influence of Craig's theatrical thinking is most clearly discernible in Kozintsev's deployment of stone, iron, fire, earth and sea. It is the nature of elemental texture and substance that relates to the thematic fabric of the plays and it is these elements which in his view 'should oust period stylization'. The system of equivalents which he records in his notes on the making of HAMLET gives an inevitable impression of naïveté, but it reveals an approach which results in profound cinematic expression.

Stone: the walls of Elsinore, the firmly built government prison, on which armorial bearings and sinister bas-reliefs had been carved centuries ago.

Iron: weapons, the inhuman forces of oppression, the ugly steel faces of war.

Fire: anxiety, revolt, movement, the trembling flame of the candles at Claudius' celebrations; raging fiery tongues (Horatio's narrative about the ghostly apparition); the wind-blown lamps on the stage erected for 'The Mousetrap'.

Sea: waves, crashing against the bastions, ceaseless movement, the change of the tides, the boiling of chaos, and again the silent, endless surface of glass.

Earth: the world beyond Elsinore, amid stones – a bit of field tilled by a ploughman, the sand pouring out of Yorick's skull, and the handful of dust in the palm of the wanderer – heir to the throne of Denmark.[39]

It is an approach which culminates in a spatial strategy which prompts Peter Brook to identify Kozintsev's HAMLET as a film in which 'everything . . . is related to the director's search for the sense of the play – his structure is inseparable from his meaning . . . He knows what bars and wood and stone and fire mean to him.'[40]

There is an important respect in which *Hamlet* is a theatrical paradox. The nature of Hamlet's isolation is made manifest in the theatre by the fact that it is directly shared through the actor with the audience. Kozintsev recognized that this predicament cannot be shared in the same way in the cinema because the relationship between the actor and the audience is indirect and because the impact of dialogue in film is reduced. In order to exploit the paradoxical form of Hamlet's isolation Kozintsev approached the problem by juxtaposing the spatial detail in the visual image with the mood, tone and sense of Hamlet's deeply felt observations.

In the theatre they usually pronounce the words, 'Denmark is a prison' against a background conducive to thoughts about imprisonment. I am beating my brains out to find a set that is delightful to look at . . . a park – a fountain glistens in the sun, children play on a path, a girl passes on her pony. It is in these surroundings that one must talk about Denmark the prison.

The most immediate challenge to any film maker who approaches *Hamlet* is the treatment of Elsinore. The castle offers the major spatial opportunities of the play and the film director has to decide whether Elsinore is essentially a place or a concept, and the extent to which it is subjectively or objectively seen. Kozintsev is quite clear about his priorities. 'Elsinore is a speculative concept in Shakespeare. It is impossible to translate it directly and completely into plastic form.' Furthermore, the presence and effect of Elsinore in the film must be implicit rather than explicit. 'The screen must show separate parts; the general plan can only be imagined. Otherwise, everything seems small, reduced.' Three important developments follow from Kozintsev's clear commitment to project Elsinore as a concept rather than a place. First, he exploits the centrifugal properties of cinematic space, which promote an imaginative continuity of space beyond the frame. By insisting that the walls 'must have a continuation in height and length beyond the frame of the sequence' Kozintsev promotes an artistic tension between that which is seen within the frame, and that which is believed to be its continuation outside the cinematic rectangle. For the continuation is not merely spatial extension. The credible but unshown continuation takes on philosophic and thematic dimensions. Kozintsev's insistence that the castle of Elsinore refuse visual encapsulation, that 'the boundaries should not be distinct, nor forms complete', gives Elsinore the implicit and unseen presence of 'the state, not only a palace or a fortress', and makes it a manifestation of 'life itself, and not only the way of life at some given time'. The function of Elsinore is like that of the forest in Kurosawa's THRONE OF BLOOD, though Kozintsev's Elsinore is by its very nature an embodiment of a political abstraction, 'the state with its armies, police and holidays'.

Secondly, Kozintsev's treatment of Elsinore involves the viewer in a distinctly active spatial participation. While Castellani and Zeffirelli use cinema in the service of geographical and historical realism, they are, to some extent, still proclaiming 'place' to be a unity as it is on the stage, but without theatrical boundaries. Kozintsev approaches Shakespearean space from another angle completely. He understands that one of the spatial properties of the medium of cinema is global mobility. The distinction he makes is that between unity of place and unity of aesthetic synthesis, in which the spectator is responsible for assembling not merely a spatial whole, but a metaphysical whole which relates to the significance of the action. 'I will state it again: The general view of the castle must not be filmed. The image will appear only in the unity of sensations of Elsinore's various aspects. And its external appearance [will appear only] in the montage of the sequences filmed in a variety of places.'[41] The realism of Castellani and Zeffirelli gives us an authentic and detailed picture, while Kozintsev's realism gives us the rough-hewn timelessness of a mosaic.

I have never been convinced by the idea of filming Shakespeare in the actual settings of the plays . . . I could not have filmed H A M L E T in the real castle at Elsinore: it bears no resemblance at all to Claudius' kingdom. It is no accident that the playwright never visited these places: he had only the most approximate conception of them . . . And so one should have as few 'details' as possible and no 'style'; it should be the world of history without external historical characteristics; a world which is absolutely real (filmed on location), without existing in nature, constructed out of a montage which will last for two hours.[42]

Thirdly, while Kozintsev eschews any suggestion of style which relates action to a context of geo-historical realism, he nevertheless accepts history as an element in the organic structure of his Shakespeare films. H A M L E T is spatially conceived and visualized as a layered structure in which time and value systems can be exposed in cross-section. The medium of cinema has the capacity to relate spatial distinctiveness to time-strata and to reveal them almost in the manner of an archaeological documentary:

The time strata must seem to be laid bare in the visual development of Elsinore. The layers of the centuries become evident, like the rings of a huge cross section of a tree . . . The scene with the ghost is an ancient medieval layer, a stratum of romance: the stone faces on bas-reliefs, coats-of-arms, ancient masonry, the battlements of fortresses. Later, another formation: the frescoes and Gobelin tapestries of the Renaissance – the world of the youth of the Wittenberg student (the rooms of the Prince). And, finally, the last ring: the affectation of gala halls, remodelled by order of the King.[43]

It is as though the pattern of a formulative equation were at work here: time (historical period) = value system = spatial features. Where ideas can be related to space, the abstractions of philosophy can be related to the concrete images of cinematic realism.

This relationship of time to spatial detail is evident, too, in Kozintsev's thinking during the making of his 1971 film K I N G L E A R. But here the relationship takes on a more sophisticated flexibility. Kozintsev is clearly keen to avoid the naïveté which would anticipate a rigid set of parallels linking established philosophical systems with particular visual metaphors or set spatial motifs. He writes of the need to reveal 'not carefully worked out philosophical systems, but layers of poetry' which assume a geological unity of time-space like deposits on the bottom of the ocean, where oceanologists find 'not only material in the form of organic and mineral substances, but also time – whole epochs . . . It is this that I want to show in the poetic texture; a chronicle of thought on an enormous scale – deposits of beliefs, errors, prophecies, denials – strata of centuries.'[44]

If *Hamlet* and *Macbeth* are plays which afford a cinematic articulation through the relation of thematic substance to architectural structure and enclosed isolation, *King Lear* demands a spatial strategy which is emphatically contrary, for the major spatial statements made in *King Lear* are about the world which lies outside the walled shelters, the warmth and community which constitute the fragile but particular assertion of man. In devising a spatial strategy whose primary intention is to dramatize nature, Kozintsev gave practical extension to the implications of Béla Balázs's observations on the capacity of cinema to invest scenic elements with a 'physiognomy'. Balázs wrote that while the photographic art was concerned with the physical reality of the world, it nevertheless depended no less than does any art medium on the investment of an artistic perception, both on the part of the creator and on the part of the percipient.

Everything that men see has a familiar visage – this is an inevitable form of our perception. Our anthropomorphous world vision makes us see a human physiognomy in every phenomenon . . . This anthropomorphous world is the only possible subject of all art and the poet's word or the painter's brush can bring life into none but a humanized reality.

The key to the dramatization of real spatial expanse is the transformation of natural topography into articulate 'landscape'.

How is the countryside turned into landscape? Not every bit of nature is a landscape in itself. The countryside has only a topography, which is a thing which can be exactly produced on a military map. But the landscape expresses a mood, which is not merely objectively given; it needs the co-operation of subjective factors before it can come into existence. The phrase is 'the mood of the landscape', but there is no mood save that of some human being.[45]

The selection of topography and the 'sculpting' of that topography is central to Kozintsev's spatial strategy in his film KING LEAR. He is not merely concerned that landscape should *say* certain things within the context of the drama but that it should actually *be* the natural world in which man must assert himself and find his definition. For Kozintsev, it is necessary to avoid the danger of sentimentalizing the great spatial statements to be made about the world of Lear, and it is not wholly a matter of imposing a subjectivity of mood upon an available topography, but more urgently a sense of the right topographical potential. 'A film landscape is concealed, hidden under another sort of covering. At first you do not so much see it as feel it, guess the possibility of its existence.'[46]

Kozintsev's sense of a hidden landscape which has to be uncovered and revealed as an artistic presence is a good example of the valid application of Michelangelo's theory of artistic creation to the medium of film. Walter Pater maintains that 'Art does but consist in the removal of surplusage . . . The finished work lies somewhere, according to Michelangelo's fancy, hidden in the rough-hewn block of stone.'[47] The 'sculpting' process emerges as an almost literal process in Kozintsev's descriptions. Of the explored locations in the Kazantip peninsula, he writes:

The outlines of Lear's country began to stand out, to shine through the surrounding scene of collective fish-farms . . . If one were to remove from this stretch of land the few rocks which were of a different shape from the others, the rhythm would become evident, one would see the succession of identical vertical outcrops. They became fragments of gravestones, an abandoned cemetery.

The making of a film, then, was a continual dialectic between idea and physical reality; giving the idea substantial form in terms of topographical potential and its anthropomorphous association.

I felt that this shape of the landscape had not been created by the forces of nature . . . the architects of hate had amassed fragments of altars, ruins of libraries, slabs from defiled cemeteries, the ancient rocks of Europe with sledge-hammers, axes and crowbars.

For the storm scene Kozintsev was able to use a landscape with particularly appropriate suggestions of bleakness. Again the discovered physical reality was a partner with – rather than a fulfilment of – the creative imagination. On climbing to the top of a desolate ridge near a shale-burning electric power station, the camera team suddenly came upon this prospect:

A quite unbelievable meadow stretched out before us. It was covered as far as the horizon with uniform light grey, almost white layers, curving a little at the edges, and the rhythm of this endless repetition of curving lines was so clear that it was as if molten lava had suddenly been frozen and the waves of ash had turned to stone . . . Nothing like it existed upon earth and yet there it was in front of us, an irrefutable reality. This scenery had been prepared for us over the decades by the outpouring of the ashes from the burnt shale . . . Now it was no longer only the wind machines and sheets of water which defined the image, but the very rhythm of this dead earth, in whose folds the tiny fingers of people were lost, pawns in the encroaching terror of emptiness.[48]

Clearly Kurosawa and Kozintsev were able to use cinematic space with a special licence which was the result of their apprehension of Shakespeare's plays as source material for organic cinema. As translators they were not burdened with any sense that in making films they were reducing the impact of Shakespeare's dialogue and theatricality in its original language. For a film director who works with and wishes to project the dramas through their original dialogue, the development of an effective cinematic spatial strategy is much more difficult. Because the plays are written for theatrical expression, the intrinsic nature of their texts will exert strong pressure on the film director to follow the course of Burge and Dexter in their filming of OTHELLO. On the other hand, a director whose allegiance is primarily to the cinema and its particular spatial potential will be strongly motivated to transform the plays into dramas acted out in the openness of cinematic space, and consequently to lose the theatrical resonance of the dialogue.

A successful cinematic adaptation of a Shakespeare play must clearly treat the material in the dramatic terms of the cinema itself, but that should never be taken to imply the elimination of that theatricality which is inevitably embedded in the text. 'To adapt' as Bazin rightly asserts, 'is no longer to betray, but to respect.'[49] Bazin is quite clear on the nature of the spatial conquest which the film director has to achieve. He must capture the 'interior dimension' implicit in the play's theatricality, but at the same time he must avoid any sense of spatial containment.

[He has] to give his décor a dramatic opaqueness while at the same time reflecting its natural realism. Once this paradox of space has been dealt with, the director, so far from hesitating to bring theatrical conventions and faithfulness to the text to the screen will find himself now, on the contrary, completely free to rely on them. From that point on it is no longer a matter of running away from those things which make theatre, but in the long run to acknowledge their existence by rejecting the resources of the cinema.

One means of solving the spatial paradox for cinematic adaptations of Shakespearean drama is through the introduction of relatively short sequences of spatial realism with skilfully managed transitions. This can be managed so that there is no obstruction on the consciousness of what is, for the rest, in itself theatrical and stylized décor. Bazin calls such brief intervening elements of realism 'aesthetic catalysts':

The cinema being of its essence a dramaturgy of Nature, there can be no cinema without the setting up of an open space in place of the universe rather than as part of it. The screen cannot give us the illusion of this feeling of space without calling on certain natural guarantees. But it is less a question of set construction or of architecture or of immensity than of isolating the aesthetic catalyst, which it is sufficient to introduce in an infinitesimal dose, to have it immediately take on the reality of nature.[50]

This principle of isolating and introducing an 'aesthetic catalyst' is partly what lies behind the transformation from theatre to cinema, in Laurence Olivier's films particularly. One thinks, for instance, of the small wake of dust left by the departing English ambassadors in HENRY V as Katherine watches them in the distance. It gives to the painted *Book of Hours* landscape a sudden startling realism, as does the plucking of one rose in the theatrically stylized garden of the French Palace. Welles's MACBETH employs a similarly minute yet deft touch. The cheap cardboard décor suddenly takes on an arresting and thematically integrated realism when water is not only seen, but heard to drip from the walls. Papier-mâché immediately becomes rock.

The history plays provide Olivier with clear spatial opportunities. The points at which he moves from theatrical derivative to unrestricted cinematic realism are not difficult to anticipate in HENRY V and RICHARD III. The battle scenes provide the realist pole in both films, employing as they do great numbers of extras together with the timeless authenticity of horses moving over real earth under a real sky. The theatrical pole in each film derives credibility, in cinematic terms, from the historical context of the plays. As histories, they are dramatic reconstructions in time and therefore also in space. The nature of the realism required of the theatrical setting for the interior scenes is clearly removed from the nature of reality as we encounter it.

The suspension of disbelief is consequently less conscious. To some extent this is also true of HAMLET with its complex setting of earth, sea, sky and the Elsinore architecture. In Orson Welles's films, the clear divide between theatrical and realistic polarities is far less evident. Only in MACBETH is there a clear move, at moments in the action, from the papier-mâché set to exterior locations. Both OTHELLO and CHIMES AT MIDNIGHT reveal a spatial strategy which exploits, for dramatic effects, the photographic potential of real locations. The Shakespearean trilogies of both Welles and Olivier, however, assert a stature which depends ultimately on the extent to which their spatial strategies accommodate essential theatricality within a dramatic framework which is filmic.

2 Laurence Olivier's HENRY V

In addition to being an adaptation of Shakespeare's play, a morale-boosting film for the Britain of 1944 and a fusion of historical event and myth and legend, Olivier's HENRY V is also a cinematic treatise on the difference between cinema and theatre as media for the expression of drama. This last dimension of the film's complex stature is coming increasingly to be acknowledged as this adaptation's claim to enduring significance. More important than any scenic amplification which cinema is able to afford the original theatrical concept is the organic structure within which the elements of space and time are cinematically organized. This relation of space to time can be usefully examined on two levels: the external level (the reciprocity between the work of art and the historical moment of its creation) and the internal level (the way that spatial details within the film's visualization signal time strata as artistic substance).

In two respects the immediate political and historical circumstances surrounding the film's creation give its spatial strategy a dynamic relevance. Firstly, the film clearly derives certain spatial manipulations from stage productions which preceded it and which established the play's particular theatrical tradition. Tableaux, trumpets, moving dioramas, rich medieval costuming, a prominent musical dimension, an elaborate coronation scene – and even a white horse for Henry – can all be traced back to productions of the eighteenth and nineteenth centuries, when the spectacular elaborations of McCready, Kean and Charles Calvert marked the play with a particular stamp of epic pageantry in performance.[1]

It was only to be expected that the film would in turn influence theatrical stagings which came after it. The productions of Joseph Papp and Terry Hands in the mid-1970s bear particular witness to the fact. Papp produced the play in New York's Central Park in 1975, and strove specifically to capture the exterior, realistic dimensions of the film by moving the action of the play from an austere stage to 'a naturalistic setting with realistic props; four cannons, pikes, poles, arrows, a promontory up which Henry [could] rush before Harfleur'. There were actual camp-fires lit in the darkness before the day of battle, and arrows were shot 'flying into the lake'.[2] Terry Hands's production for the Royal Shakespeare Company at Stratford in 1976 aimed to achieve spatial effects of the film in a different way. Hands followed the film's shift from theatrical performance to cinematic presentation by suggesting a movement from one level of reality to another within the theatre. The movement of the plane of action was implied by use of a great canopy which opened out, and by the costuming of the actors, who changed their dress from rehearsal track-suits (at the start of the play) to period costumes which were donned as the action developed. Only the Chorus retained his rehearsal clothing throughout, as he held the connection between the levels of action.

More recently, the staging of the play at Stratford, Connecticut, in 1981 made explicit its spatial derivations by effecting 'a playful crossing between the world of theatre and the world of illusion within the play'. In this production, Christopher Plummer played the parts of both Henry and the Chorus 'much as Olivier takes on the roles of the actor playing Henry (back-stage) and of Henry himself (on stage)'. The set too was adapted to incorporate a reminiscence of the Globe structure, and there was much deliberately similar detail in the staging of Henry's reaction to the Dauphin's gift. The cask and the arrangement of the tennis balls within it looked identical with those revealed in the film, and like Olivier, Plummer tossed his crown to hang on the back of the throne.[3]

The second respect in which external time affected the spatial strategy of the film lies in the film's special relevance to the wartime circumstances of Britain in 1943–4. Like the films of Eisenstein, Olivier's HENRY V was directed partially towards social control. In its endeavour to project a romantic illusion, the film incorporates colour-plate illustrations from the original manuscript of *Les Très Riches Heures*. The text in that manuscript is accompanied by calendar pictures painted by Pol de Limbourg and Jean Colombe. The use of these pictures as a basis of set design gives the film a spatial delicacy and visual charm which justifies their own artistic validity. Yet, at the same time, the pictorial stylization moves the film close to the realm of the fairytale, whose brightly coloured glamour and spectacle was highly appropriate for the aesthetic appetite of the time. Equally well suited to the susceptibilities of a war-time audience was the comic reduction of the scene in which the Archbishop of Canterbury and the Bishop of Ely explore the legal justification of Henry's claim to the French throne. The latter effect is especially important, for it raises weighty questions about artistic integrity in the interpretation of Shakespeare's play.

The most unyielding criticism on this score comes from Gorman Beauchamp who, in a powerfully argued essay written more than thirty years after the film's release, considers the entire issue of Olivier's studied distortion of the play. He points out that the intricate issues of legitimate succession are deliberately obscured by the presentation of the scene as 'farce . . . which is fundamentally dishonest in that it directs attention away from, rather than toward, the central problem of war's justification'.[4] In a slim volume devoted wholly to a discussion of this film, Harry Geduld with more deference to Olivier's intention suggests that this scene is debased essentially by the fact that its 'buffoonery over the documents' is also designed to make an implicit statement about theatre. The strained artificiality of the theatrical conventions and the derisive interruptions of the groundlings, maintains Geduld, are designed to emphasize at the start of the play 'the shortcomings of theatre as a medium for presenting a dramatic epic like *Henry V*'.[5]

More subtle in its effect upon the dialogue's direct impact is Olivier's use of camera movement. In discussing the technique of filming moments of strong Shakespearean rhetoric, Olivier has pointed out that to accommodate the gestural and vocal expansiveness of 'Shakespearean climax', the camera must be pulled back to a distance from the actor.[6] This makes very good sense, and as a means of reconciling theatrical style with cinematic mobility it is employed to good effect in Henry V. Nevertheless, while it affords the actor's rhetorical projection its natural dramatic shape, the camera's withdrawal inevitably makes its own statement. One instance of this is the framing of Olivier in the stirring speech before the conquest of Harfleur. As Henry's rhetoric gathers force, the camera moves back and upwards so that at the speech's climax, Henry is framed among his soldiers from a high-angled distant camera position in the upper rigging of a ship. In moving to this position, the camera's implicit statement is to stress Henry's relative smallness, 'that despite his obvious valour, he has begun his campaign as the underdog'.[7] The reduction of Henry's dominance in the frame and of his vertical advantage in relation to the camera conceals the savage explicitness of his war-like exhortation. The camera movement here gives the speech a 'colouration' of romantic and plucky resolution, an effect achieved through 'visual image working against verbal image [which] draws our attention and their context . . . toward . . . a romanticized, non-contextual image of the hero-king'.[8]

A second instance of the camera's making a high-angled reduction of Henry at a moment of triumph is the moment of his entrance through the gates of Harfleur. This shot further increases an audience sympathy for Henry, for it frames him as he gives instructions for the merciful treatment of the city's captive inhabitants. An expressive variation occurs at the climax of the St Crispin's Day speech immediately before the Battle of Agincourt. Here, the camera pulls directly back, keeping a horizontal level with Henry. In eschewing the high subtended angle, the movement of the camera no longer gives Henry a sympathetic diminution, for his cause is now fully established, and he can proclaim his intentions as an equal.

The inclusion of the Battle of Agincourt in Olivier's film has raised less critical comment than the textual cuts or the simplification of Henry's character. Yet it is, for modern sensibilities, a highly controversial addition of spectacle to Shakespeare's play, and before considering its value as cinema it is necessary to accept the different perspective which it gives the dramatic impact of the film. While it has been suggested that Shakespeare was prevented from developing spectacular realism as an extension of his dramatic material by the confining limits of the theatre, and that he would have welcomed the visual potential of cinema, a more perceptive view holds that Shakespeare's overtly theatrical presentation of battles is in itself a very pointed statement about war. As Beauchamp observes, the only encounter which is directly staged in the play Henry V is that between Pistol and M. le Fer, and by promoting Pistol's 'ridiculous exploit' to a position where it becomes 'the sole synecdoche for, the single dramatized episode in, this capstone of Henry's French Campaign', any military magnificence and heroism with which the romantic imagination might have invested Henry's victory is diminished by satire.[9]

Where Shakespeare's play presents military glamour and conquest as absurd by revealing the instincts which operate beneath its rationale, the promotional power behind the making of the film in 1943–4 would clearly have been more sympathetic with a depiction of Agincourt as a glorious legend, a romanticized presentation of a bloodless, chivalrous encounter in which brutality was made an abstraction and arrogant disdain, luxurious self-indulgence and aristocratic pride were made the casualties.

The relation of visual signals within the film's spatial manipulation to an internal stratification of time is at once more complex and more significant, for it reveals a dynamic interplay of levels of action within an apparently simple structure. Spatial signals in the film indicate three layers of time: Renaissance time, medieval time and what one might call 'universal time'. The first of these is signalled by the model of London and the occasion of performance filmed in the Globe Playhouse. The second covers the action related specifically to the estrangement, and reconciliation through marriage, of the realms of France and England, together with the campaign, major battle and the personal affinities and differences which give it particular dimensions – that is, the time of the central historical event. The third layer, universal time, is less easy to relate to specific aspects of the film, or indeed to define, for it is not historically objective. Universal time is a convenient term here for that imaginative reconstruction of time stimulated and reinforced by myth – in this case, the Agincourt myth. It is in essence romanticized, fluid and peopled with archetypes, for it is a removed epoch conceived of as unambiguous by the contemporary imagination. For all its elusiveness of definition, this level of universal time is artistically crucial, for the power of myth on the imagination makes possible the liberation of time from history (a phenomenon which surfaces, too, as a political manifestation in the emergence of nationalism).

The liberation of time from history is the primary dissociation on which that important genre the fairy tale is based, and, as suggested earlier, the fairy tale embodies a special relationship of nature to art which modifies our logic of space. Just as characters become archetypal, so space becomes ideal. Therein lies the major artistic achievement of Olivier's film, whereby the artistic representation of the French landscape styled on the plates from *Les Très Riches Heures* becomes aesthetically satisfying as cinematic space.

The interplay of the three layers of time so far considered is not only wrought in Olivier's film. The three layers are very much evident in a theatrical experience of the play in performance. It is the particular nature of their inter-relation and visual treatment which is intrinsic to the film. This is equally true of space. The play itself incorporates areas of action which can be isolated and identified. It is the special property of the film to bring its own dynamic to bear on these discrete elements – which the theatre accommodates on one stage – and so to create a unique cinematic structure within which entities of space sometimes coalesce, sometimes are sundered to make clear where one entry ends and another begins.

Like any play, Shakespeare's *Henry V* concerns itself initially with two areas of action: the microcosmic space of theatre, and the amorphous space of the imagination. Both of these spatial realms become constructs of the real space of events in history. Olivier exploits the cinematic potential of a Chorus whose monologues consciously explore the relationship between the spaces of history, theatre and imagination. But to these three areas of action, Olivier adds a fourth, the historical occasion of the play's own performance. Out of these four spatial entities is woven the structure which makes the film an organic whole.

There are two aspects to notice about the camera's treatment of its material. Firstly, there is a sustained ambivalence whereby the spatial detail in the frame seems to hover between theatrical stylization and cinematic realism. Secondly, there is no simple progress, as the film proceeds, from theatrical fragmentation to cinematic flow. Rather there is a complex and subtle manipulation of the spatial elements, so that the visuals take on the credibility of cinema without losing the consciousness of theatre. The model of sixteenth-century London with which the opening shots of the film engage us does not pretend to be other than a model. Yet the camera's operation upon it, making it so clearly a photographic subject in a style we are accustomed to having cinema treat the real city, confers upon it an additional realistic dimension.

This is especially so when one considers that by 1944 newsreels had established, as regular fare on cinema screens, the aerial photography of cities as evidence of allied or enemy bombardment. What would seem to be an aerial approach over a London out of another age, with the Thames surface glassy and blue, constitutes a masterly and complex combination of convention with illusion. This suspended ambivalence of perspective prepares us for the idiom of the film's language and flow, for it is immediately followed by what is theatrical reconstruction of the whole social bustle of actors preparing to become the play's characters, and of the audience preparing to participate in the experience of theatre. However, this is constructed so that it can be filmed in minute realistic detail. Once again, there is the ambivalence of what we know to be artifice given realistic camera treatment, with actors acting as actors who are not yet characters.

The next major development in the spatial fabric of the film is its visual isolation of the staged play in the Globe theatre as filmed theatre presentation. The bumbling and protracted debate in which the bishops attempt to justify Henry's claim is deliberately made ridiculous, received as it is with jeers and derision by members of the theatre audience. Apart from the interpretative reasons for presenting this scene as burlesqued comedy – which are rightly questionable – there are more acceptable justifications in terms of the requirements of media transposition which the film is, in this early stage, exploring. The comedy of incompetence being acted out on the stage carries with it Olivier's assertion that the film will not concern itself with the mere presentation of a photographed theatre performance. The brief moments of this scene, during which the camera is wholly focused on the stage action, are interspersed with sound-track signals which keep alive our consciousness of a dual role. We are members of both the Globe theatre audience and the cinema audience. We lose our awareness of our double-audience situation only when Henry is presented by the French ambassador with the Dauphin's gift of tennis balls.

We become wholly involved in the theatrical nature of this scene because the theatricality itself is operating on two levels. Firstly, it is a staged scene with the character of Henry established as believable. Secondly, the king's situation among the subjects in his immediate presence is necessarily theatrical. In an absorbing article for the Royal Shakespeare Company's production of *Richard II* in 1973, Anne Barton has pointed out that

Only Shakespeare . . . seems to have seized upon and explored the latent parallel between the king and that other twin-natured human-being, the Actor. Like kings, they are accustomed to perform before an audience. Like kings, they are required to submerge their own individuality within a role, and for both the incarnation is temporary and perilous.[10]

Political theatre is encapsulated within scripted and staged theatre, and these in turn are both treated as cinematic presentation. Three audiences watch the king respond to the French jibe. It is as though the whole weight of the theatre's potential is consolidated at this point, and we are poised for cinema's move out of the Globe theatre and into the unconstrained areas of cinematic realism.

Our expectations are only partly met, for the move from the Globe coincides with the play's move to Southampton with preparation for Henry's embarkation for France. Even so, the move has about it unexpected intricacies, for it is no mere direct cut. It is a transition made and subtly integrated with the fabric of the play. The move from the Globe is made, but the theatrical presence of the Chorus is still with us. What does emerge is a significant shift in the relationship between the camera and the Chorus. In an unpublished thesis on Olivier's Shakespeare films submitted in 1978, Sandra Sugarman Singer has made some most helpfully detailed observations of the transitions in the film. She observes that the unity of 'physical Chorus and vocal Chorus [which] existed together and were seen as synchronic' dissolves at this point. The camera no longer shows a 'story of the Chorus telling a story' but, instead, it directly reveals 'a different story about which [the Chorus] speaks'.[11] The shift from narrative congruency to narrative co-operation between Chorus and camera indi-cates a major movement of the film's spatial concentration. The move in time and space is from the occasion of performance in the Globe playhouse in Shakespeare's London to the historical action and story of King Henry's campaign in medieval France.

The transition from Southampton, across the Channel to France, is made with a further development of the camera/Chorus relationship. With the lines

> Thus with imagin'd wing our swift scene flies
> In motion of no less celerity
> Than that of thought[12]

there is the start of accompanying music. The Chorus, filmed in close-up, is faded in against a black background, and then the camera tracks slowly back to leave the

Chorus in the distance, in an extreme long-shot. The screen grows brighter and the Chorus appears to float in space as swirling mists begin to envelop him. He extends his arms, and then with the lines

> Oh, do but think
> You stand upon the shore and thence behold
> A city on th' inconstant billows dancing[13]

he turns his back on the camera and is 'completely blotted out by the mist', while the camera tracks forward over the ships crossing the Channel. In turning his face away from the camera, the Chorus becomes 'a part of the audience, for he looks as we do, towards what the camera will show'. The camera's image dissolves to a long-shot, high-angle view of the French palace, and the Chorus, now no longer visible, remains with us only in voice. He will reappear only when the film returns ultimately to the space and time of the filmed performance in the Globe. For the intervening duration he has, in Singer's words, 'gained the physical freedom of the camera [and] lost his physical being'.[14]

The Chorus has kept alive the consciousness of theatre. With his departure, another figure takes on that role with a less obvious theatrical effect. Apart from the Chorus, only Pistol in this film makes direct eye-contact through the camera as he speaks to the cinema audience – anticipating in this a major aspect of Olivier's strategy in RICHARD III. Pistol is clearly the most prominent and important of the comedy players and in his special relationship with the cinema audience he carries forward the emphatic theatricality which has distinguished the film's treatment of the comic scenes on the Globe stage. Despite suggestions of realism achieved through the camera's selection of expressive detail and the off-frame sound-track laughter which presented cinematically a wider social situation than merely that which is projected from the stage, Geduld is right in seeing the performances of the comedians as 'more self-conscious, more in the nature of theatrical "turns"'. In the same way that Robert Newton (who plays the part of Pistol in the film) commanded affectionate attention from cinema audiences, so Pistol appears to elicit a show of accustomed pleasure from the groundlings who 'seem to be responding to a star comedian rather than to the role he is playing'.[15]

On the stage, furthermore, Pistol wears what looks like a leek with the feathers in his hat. In his later appearances, after the film's move out of the Globe, he continues to display this leek as a visual reminder of the theatrical dimension of the film. The leek is a specific illustration of the subtle complexity of Olivier's spatial strategy. It affords the action a multiplicity of occasions in time and space, and in so doing it introduces to the mind of the spectator an awareness of the film's narrative complexity. While for the other characters make-up and costuming has lost its theatrical emphasis, and while the major thrust of the film's spatial and temporal concern has clearly left the Globe occasion of performance, Pistol's leek achieves what Peter Brook believed (more than twenty years later) to be unattainable on film – simultaneous and multi-layered dramatic relevance.[16] The cinema audience is asked not to suspend disbelief, but rather to engage with the dramatic action in a new way.

The space of the Globe theatre and the space of the central historical action in medieval France are linked by two other significant strands: that of water imagery, and much more significantly that of music. The musical connection is especially complex, because while music accompanies both the action within the Globe theatre and the action in time and space outside it, its distinctive orchestral and choral textures make clear the division between *theatrical* and *cinematic* music.

Cinematic music is used to give atmosphere to dialogue or action and is an overlay to the structured action of the scene. Theatrical music, on the other hand, is part of the scene's intrinsic structure and reality. Its source is naturally accommodated within the locality of action photographed by the camera. Theatrical music is produced (and seen to be produced) by the theatre musicians who are part of the Globe theatre company. Some instances of cinematic music are the choral effects which accompany the camera's ranging over the model City of London and the *sforzando* which accompanies the Chorus' initial invocation of the audience's imagination, 'Suppose within these walls. . . .'.[17] This last instance displays a complexity which is almost of the order of Pistol's leek, for like the leek, the music transcends one single level of action and space. It is cinematic music, yet the camera and Chorus are still very much 'within these walls'. Clearly the texture and tone-colour of the music remove it from the music produced by the theatre musicians, and so its function must therefore be to establish a tension between an aural awareness of film while the eye is still engaged with the immediacies of the theatre.

Cinematic music achieves its most memorable stature in two sequences. One is the musical accompaniment to the Duke of Burgundy's speech of reconciliation where the Auvergne folk-theme gives the spoken verse an elegiac suggestion of song as the camera follows the gaze of the Duke to move outside the confines of the French palace. The other is the musical accompaniment to the action of the Battle of Agincourt. Certainly Walton's battle music in this film is among the finest cinematic music written in its sustained power of movement and the versatility of its comment on details of the preparatory action. The range of the music's function is impressive as it captures the English resolve and the French complacency, pointing with sparkling humour the cumbersome descent of the heavily armed French knights on to the saddles of their chargers, accompanying the reflections of the French horses as they step through puddles with a jagged tremolo on the strings, and giving a dramatic rhythmic development to the gathering pace of the French cavalry charge photographed with the camera moving forward in a sustained tracking shot from abreast of the formation.

Whatever criticism the inclusion of the battle provokes about the distortion of Shakespeare's play, there is no doubt that it is an outstanding piece of cinema. The sustained integration of musical and visual development is wrought through montage which juxtaposes the gathering momentum of the French charge with the poised stand of the English army as it waits for the French to come within the range of its archers. The dramatic visual emphasis arises from the opposite natures of the two armies: the movement of men, horses, flying pennants and the colour of the French battle-dress set against the tense stillness and functional austerity of the English; the vast line of French horsemèn set against the mere handful of English; the sweeping speed of the cavalry and the tracking camera set against Henry's raised sword held against the sky and the line of English archers drawing back the arrows on their bows.

In his *Lectures on Dramatic Art and Literature* published in 1809, Schlegel observed that the staging of Shakespeare's battles raises an inevitable problem of dramatic perspective. On the one hand, there is an element of the absurd in the suggestion that 'the fate of mighty kingdoms' is decided, even on the theatre stage, by token warriors 'in mock armour'. On the other hand, realistic battle effects too readily displace 'that attention which a poetical work of art demands'.[18] It is an aesthetic problem for which the resources of cinema do manifestly offer a solution because cinema is capable of orchestrating a very wide spectrum of spatial suggestions and giving unity to diversity through music. Contrapuntal and convergent spatial strategies such as detail selection, montage, camera movement, variety of colour and movement in the frame can be given an overall aesthetic shape by an accompanying orchestral versatility of colour and rhythm. Cinema can then produce a fusion of visual and aural energy which sustains the engagement of the ear by balancing the spectacle with intelligent musical articulation.

The water imagery in the film is less complex. It provides a direct linking device for the various spatial levels of the action. The glassy Thames in the model of London, the thunderstorm which breaks over the Globe theatre, the ships crossing the Channel to France and the pools of water which reflect the French cavalry preparing to charge at Agincourt, constitute a unifying structural element in the spatial composition of the film. More particularly, the violent downpour which suddenly drenches both the players and the audience in the Globe switches concentration from theatrical involvement into the area of cinematic realism, both in its immediate visual effects and in subjecting the actors and the audience of the Globe to the same ordeal suffered by Henry's army, whose 'gayness' and whose 'gilt are all besmirch'd / With rainy marching in the painful field'.[19] It also subtly qualifies the unclouded view of the past that might otherwise predominate, and so makes this an unromantic, recognizably English, wet day.

The return of the dramatic action to the Globe in the closing moments of the film is achieved once again through a series of transitions through non-defined distinctions between medieval France and Elizabethan England on the one hand, and between theatre and cinema on the other. The film's achievement in these shifts has gone largely unnoticed by critics who have written generally about the narrative potential of cinema. Jean-Luc Godard is more often credited with being the pioneer in the manipulation of diegetic space in the cinema. In an article written in 1972, Peter Wollen supported this latter claim:

In Hollywood films, everything shown belongs to the same world and complex articulations within that world – such as flashbacks – are carefully signalled and located . . . Traditionally, only one form of multiple diegesis is allowed – the play within the play – whereby the second, discontinuous diegetic space is embedded or bracketed within the first . . . Godard uses film-within-a-film devices in a number of early films . . . The first radical break with single diegesis, however, comes from WEEKEND, when characters from different epochs and from fiction are interpolated into the main narrative.[20]

The film WEEKEND was released in 1967. Olivier, with HENRY V, had broken away from single diegesis more than twenty years before.

Two final points to be made by the spatial fabric of Olivier's HENRY V are its pictorialism – a cinematic tendency that will surface again in our discussion of HAMLET – and its dominant colour motifs. The use of the *Book of Hours* plates as scenic design for many of the film sets establishes a profound relationship between painting, photography and poetry, which Singer identifies as 'a prevailing visual attitude' in Olivier's Shakespeare films.[21] Jack Jorgens points to the particularly static depiction of the French in the film, noting that 'save for the battle, there is very little movement in the French sequences', and he quotes part of Geduld's observation about the intention behind the film's pictorialism in the interior scenes of the French palace.[22]

Geduld maintains that the intentions behind Olivier's strategy are 'to reduce the incongruities between the stylized, two-dimensional set and his three-dimensional actors', and to ensure through reducing all movement to a minimum 'that the actors always seem to belong to the pictorial composition'.[23] While the pictorial function of the French court scenes is clear enough, Geduld's deduction of Olivier's motive is questionable. There is enough evidence elsewhere in the film to suggest (as has been shown above) that Olivier's intention is not simply 'to reduce incongruities' of dimension. Wherever possible, the directorial intention has been to allow the image to function on more than one level in order to keep alive the film's tension between what is spatially theatrical and spatially pictorial. The incongruities constitute a necessary ingredient. The film's respect for aesthetic ambiguity is corroborated by Jorgens when he notes the reminiscence of the Globe flag and trumpeter on the battle-field, and the elevation of Henry exhorting his troops as a reminder of Burbage on the Globe stage. He suggests, too, that 'the arch into which the banquet is crushed at the French court' recalls the arch over the inner stage of the Globe.[24]

The most noticeable of the colour motifs is the constantly recurring juxtaposition of blue and red. It is established in the opening shot of the film with the combination of sky and red roofs of Shakespeare's London carrying through to assume the final heraldic importance in the joining of the French and English kingdoms. The white horse (which, as noted earlier, had become traditional) gives the filmed Henry his allegorical stature.

While Olivier's HENRY V is in many respects an innovatory film, it does also draw on other established genres. One of these is the Western genre. Geduld draws attention to the dimension of Olivier's characterization of Henry, his 'likeable displays of casualness and sportsmanship' which give his dramatic destiny a special aura of inevitable success and which associate him peripherally with the image of heroic nonchalance cultivated by the RAF. The glimpses of his physical nimbleness (for instance, his athletic vault into the saddle in contrast to the French being lowered on derricks) also recall 'traditional heroes of Westerns whose rugged individualism and inevitable triumph over their adversaries have become clichés'.[25]

The affinity of Olivier's HENRY V with the Western film genre is not, however, confined to Henry's 'particular quality of lyric and exuberant inevitability'.[26] In his essay on the Western film André Bazin points out that while the Western exists as literature, it has a very limited appeal as literary material. It is as film that the Western achieves its immense popular success, sustaining its power of attraction across a wide range of cultural diversity. The challenge that arises, then, is one of attempting to define the specific essence which ensures that this particular kind of fiction so clearly finds its expressive culmination as cinema. He identifies a number of narrative elements in the classic Western story which make it especially appropriate material for the screen:

1. The relation of action, conflict and spatial context to the formative process of romanticized history;
2. The epic nature of the genre arising out of simplicity of narrative concentration on archetypes rather than on complexity of character, and the consequent closeness to the establishment of myth;
3. A spatial strategy which relates man to close detail on the one hand and to natural terrain on the other;
4. The separate roles of men and women in society;
5. The relation of action to morality on the one hand, and to law on the other;
6. The early and unambiguous polarization of moral categories;
7. The particular significance of the horse as a visual proclamation of man's alliance with nature.[27]

Though muted in expression, all these ingredients can be discerned in Olivier's film, contributing to its popularity as a romance of heroic spectacle. Of particular relevance to this discussion are those elements of the Western film which concern the treatment of space. Two sequences in HENRY V justify examination in this light. The most obvious of these is the build-up to the battle climax at Agincourt, with its relation of men and horses to open space. 'The Western', writes Bazin, 'has virtually no use for close-up, even for the medium shot, preferring by contrast the travelling shot and the pan which refuse to be limited by the frameline and which restore to space its fullness.'[28] Henry's parleys with Montjoy and the gathering momentum of the cavalry charge are reminiscent of shots and sequences in battle scenes from John Ford Westerns.

The second sequence is very different and the parallel is less direct. Henry's ultimate conquest of Katherine, with its clear suggestions that rugged success on the field of battle does not in itself endear man to woman has a strong affinity with the classic Western resolution. Like the hero of the Western, Henry is faced with obstacles in his approach to Katherine, which are very different in nature from those he has overcome on the battle-field. He has finally to grope his awkward way through the unfamiliar territory of French courtly elegance, its manners of amorous propriety and the cultivated refinements of the French language as used by the women of the court. There is a subtle spatial suggestion of Henry's ordeal in the love scene with the Princess. After the realistic heroism of the battle with its spatial elements of earth, sky, pools of water and galloping horses, Henry has suddenly to contend with the ornamental pictorialism of the French palace interior, so that his approaches to Katherine take the visual form of intrusions into posed compositions framed by arches. The new territory of 'manners' which Henry has to conquer is thus spatially articulated in the shift from the realism of the battle ground to the composed balance of the French court with its pictorial groupings.

This is not to suggest that Olivier has made HENRY V structurally congruent with the Western. Clearly there are complexities of dramatic development such as the traditional national rivalries among Henry's soldiers, the comic interplay of Pistol, Bardolph and Nym, and the relation of period costume to realistic space which the Western genre does not accommodate. The important point to emerge from the generic affinity is that both Olivier's HENRY V and the classic Western find a focal register of origin in the medieval romance. The cowboy is, as Bazin observes, a reincarnation in the New World of 'a knight-at-arms'. His ordeal in winning the affections of the woman of his choice 'comes close to reminding us of the medieval courtly romances by virtue of the pre-eminence given to the woman and the trials that the finest of heroes must undergo in order to qualify for her love'.[29]

Olivier's HENRY V is a remarkable Shakespearean adaptation, for despite the diversity of its constituent elements, the spatial strategy of the film engages both an emotional identification and an intellectual alertness without the imposition of an ostentatious intrusion of style. There is wrought a unique congruency of the film's movement with that of the imagination, a congruency which is prompted in the first place by the structure of the play. The film will stand against any criticism because of its organic structuring of space and time. Stephenson and Debrix consider the evolution of a 'time-space' entity to be a resource of cinema which is of major importance in investing film with its artistic distinction. Their comment on time and space in cinema, and the relation of the 'time-space' entity to the imagination might refer wholly to this film:

While the spatialization of time and the temporalization of space are useful concepts, the two are finally inseparable. One of the achievements of cinema is that it can effect an ideal synthesis. It divests time and space of their everyday, commonsense (but not scientific) characteristics and, investing them conjointly with the immateriality of thought, associates them together in a new whole – cinematographic space-time. Despite appearances, this is a mental rather than a physical entity . . . It is this which makes cinema truly an art and one of the richest and most developed of them all.[30]

1. HENRY V (Olivier). Characters related with spatial realism: the night before the Battle.
Laurence Olivier (Henry) and Morland Graham (Sir Thomas Erpingham)

2. HENRY V (Olivier). Henry woos Kate: the angular lines of Henry's body suggest the
awkwardness of his invasion of the pictorial composition which typifies the spatial
dispositions in the French palace. Laurence Olivier (Henry), Renee Asherson (Princess
Katherine) and Ivy St Helier (Alice)

3   Laurence Olivier's HAMLET

Hamlet poses for the film maker a problem very different from – and much more difficult than – the histories of *Henry V* and *Richard III*. The structures of history – even the dramatic structuring of history – can be articulated to varying degrees through the relationship of men to things, of ideas to the concrete world and of motives to actions, without conscious distortion. But of all the plays of Shakespeare, *Hamlet* is least of all a play which readily enlists spatial detail and the world of objects for its major thematic developments.

There is a castle, there are swords, there is a crown and there is poison. But much of the thematic centre of *Hamlet* is removed from the means of life and death into the area of their respective values and significance. With the abstract kernel of the play so concentrated in the symbolic value of the objects recounted, the film director has very little spatial material to work with. Robert Duffy, who has written a perceptive and intelligently favourable account of the film in placing it against other *Hamlet* films, notes the claustrophobic nature of the play and the lack of spatial variety which the action of the play affords as a major adaptive problem for film:

Hamlet is a play which admits no easy translation into film. Much discussed 'epic' qualities, particularly the emphatic and rapid shifting of locale and time frame – so often cited as one of the most 'cinematic' of Shakespeare's techniques – simply do not operate to any great extent in the play. In fact, the emphasis on locale remains considerably less important here than in most other Shakespearean plays. The play exudes an aura of claustrophobia, as recent film directors have well noted. The convention of unlocalized stage, which in the Roman plays, the histories, and the other tragedies seems to underline a sense of human action played against a macrocosmic backdrop, here seems to invert itself, to stress the essential sameness of all locality where the philosophical underpinnings of human action, not its Protean texture, are given form. Most of the action in *Hamlet* takes place within doors. Whether at the home of Polonius or somewhere in the palace, the locales seem largely undistinguishable. On the stage, we *see* Hamlet freed of this physical prison only in the encounter with Fortinbras' army, and perhaps in the graveyard scene.[1]

A second, though hardly less intractable problem for the film maker is the fact that many of the crucial moments of action in the play's development are deliberately structured to take place outside the staged action of the play, while others, with equal deliberateness, are presented to the eye. The play, in this sense, is a delicately poised balance between apparent stasis within Elsinore and the sudden intrusion of items of startling news from outside its confines.

The frequency in the play of such scenes reported rather than represented adds to the atmosphere of enclosure characteristic of Hamlet . . . the Ghost narrates of his murder (I.v), a Messenger describes Laertes' arousal of the people (IV.v), Gertrude tells of Ophelia's death (IV.vii). That scenes of narration occur so frequently in the play makes for an interesting problem for film adaptation. Since Shakespeare seems to have intended many of these scenes narrated after the fact to counterpoint the action seen on stage, their visualization in a filmed *Hamlet* may run counter to the purpose of their composition, thereby compromising in some measure the film's fidelity to its source . . . Certainly a fully cinematic *Hamlet* must come to terms with these and other un-filmic tendencies, and somehow accommodate them to the demands of effective film-making.[2]

However, when we consider only those moments which Duffy lists, it becomes apparent that they constitute superbly exploitable cinematic material, liberated as they are in description from any stylized stage synchronization with dialogue. One of Olivier's preoccupations must surely have been to avoid the temptation to make great cinema of the off-stage material in this play, as he so effectively had managed in the battle scenes of HENRY V.

Much critical comment is condescendingly disparaging about the film, claiming that Olivier's sense of cinema – so successfully evident in HENRY V – is unsuited to the demands of *Hamlet,* and that it is a fumbling attempt to apply a cinematic strategy with few new ideas to material which remains unyieldingly theatrical. One comes away from reading this response with the sense that one is witnessing a critical reaction to the general acclaim which greeted the epic flamboyance of Olivier's earlier film. There is more than just a suggestion of anticipated and complacent disappointment, for instance, in Robert Herring's editorial article for *Life and Letters* published in 1948.

I could forgive him almost all the tricks he has played if it were not for the death-leap at the final killing of the king. This is showy, vulgar, and entirely unnecessary, nor does it atone for the elimination of Fortinbras, of which I strongly disapprove, to introduce, as it were, Fairbanks.

Herring continues to denounce Olivier's cinematic endeavour and to dismiss especially the camera's photographic selection with unmistakable contempt.

However, he has chosen to cast his film in the form of a play, rather than to explore the true possibilities of cinema, and so we must consider whether he has made the best use of his material. I do not think he has . . . Mobile camera-work is not the same thing as movement, and in the opening scene, the plot remains static, while the camera reels around, rather drunkenly, showing us nothing that we could not guess; except that Denmark is a mountainous country . . . A lot of time is taken up with camera-work that could be spared. I suppose it is inevitable that we should be shown Ophelia's death, and also have a glimpse of the pirate ship; but surely there is no need to follow Ophelia along those miles of corridors to see Hamlet visiting her, to have such long processions or to have the camera swivelling with such banality round the empty chair after the duel-scene.[3]

Such trenchant criticism of the camera movement written in the year of the film's release has left its mark on reactions to the film – so that even Roger Manvell's standard work, published twenty-three years later, gives a muted impulse to its echo. 'Of the three Shakespearean films directed by Laurence Olivier, HAMLET is possibly the one which most repays detailed examination. It may have certain faults, and even "longueurs" – camera movement is sometimes inexplicably overdone, becoming technically self-conscious and destroying the atmosphere.'[4] Underlying this adverse criticism is the suggestion that HAMLET's artistic merit is questionable because of the tenuous relationship between camera movement and thematic development. However, as we noted in the chapter on HENRY V, Olivier is not concerned with the question of medial commitment, but rather with a manipulation of spatial elements, which generates a tension and an oscillation between the theatrical and the cinematic.

To assert as Manvell does, that 'the film treatment of HAMLET is very different from that of HENRY V' reveals a somewhat superficial appraisal of the latter film. It is not essentially the treatment, but the intrinsic substance of the play which is so different. There are some remarkable similarities in the film treatment which to some extent establish Olivier's claim to auteurship, and there is no doubt that a constant cinematic intelligence informs and shapes the direction of both films.

Within the first two minutes after the start of the film, Olivier introduces spatial features which are clearly reminiscent of HENRY V. The film starts with a darkened screen which brightens slowly to show a visual composition of theatrical properties: a mask, a crown, standards, foils and spears, a goblet, a dagger, a horn and a drum, accompanied by the sound of an orchestra tuning up. Just as Olivier gives us theatrical preparation in the opening moments of HENRY V, so here, too, he opens the film with a clear signal that *Hamlet* is essentially a theatrical construct to be played before an audience. The initial disposition of theatrical equipment foreshadows, too, the important part which theatre will play within the greater action of the whole *Hamlet* play – not just the inner play enacted before the court, but also the many theatrical moments at which events, either formal or informal, are watched and listened to by 'audiences' seen and unseen.

The company of travelling players itself appears three times in the film. Their second appearance is the one in which they rehearse and are given technical directions by Hamlet. Just before they come on to their stage for this rehearsal, there is a very clear recollection of the start of the film itself. The camera focuses on the static composition of theatrical props, and again there is the accompanying sound of an orchestra tuning up. Clearly, together with all the statements which are being made within the film, there is also one here about the nature of film and theatre, and about this film within the wide context of *Hamlet*'s history of performance.

Even more powerfully reminiscent of HENRY V is the fade-in that follows the initial visual composition, of swirling mist which clears to reveal, from a long-distance, high-angle shot, a model of Elsinore. The mist closes over the dimly glimpsed outlines of the castle battlements and towers, and there then appear on the screen the lines of Olivier's prologue. The sound-track accompanies the visual with the lines spoken by Olivier unseen. The use of the model castle and the insertion of a prologue both recall devices employed in the first thirty minutes of HENRY V, and here there emerges an interesting narrative dimension to the film HAMLET. The Chorus in HENRY V is a compelling narrator-figure, but his function does not remain constant. It is conceded in clear defined stages, to the camera. In HAMLET, the narrator-figure who speaks the prologue and offers the interpretive key to this dramatic presentation is never visualized at all. The narrative persona becomes the camera almost at once. Singer's observations of the film suggest that Olivier signals very clearly the important part which a narrative line will play in his cinematic presentation. There is, within the first seventy seconds of the film, a noticeable swing away from, and back to the modelled figures on the castle battlement. With fades and dissolves, the image changes from the close freeze-frame of the six figures on the highest tower (which is held while Olivier's voice speaks 'This is the tragedy of a man who could not make up his mind') to an identical replication of the composition photographed from a distance in long shot of 'figures that appear to be crude little dolls. The "real" people on the "real" tower have been replaced by small wooden figures which, in the next moment fade from the scene, leaving only the empty toy tower.' It constitutes, in Singer's view, a visual signal 'that the scenes which unfold before us do so under the control of an all-powerful story-teller, who manipulates his figures to suit his narrative'.[5]

Another feature which links this film's spatial strategy with that of HENRY V is the cyclic visual structure. In both films, we are returned at the end to the dramatic locality of the start. Just as in HENRY V the cuts make transitions in time and place so that we are moved rapidly from medieval France to Renaissance England and to the Globe theatre where the action began, so in HAMLET we are eventually brought back with Hamlet's funeral procession to those opening shots of the Elsinore battlements. Olivier's structuring is conscious, but it is not a device imposed upon HAMLET from the earlier film. Rather it was a generative idea from which the film evolved. Olivier, in an introductory essay on the film, has written 'Quite suddenly, one day, I visualized the final shot . . . And from this glimpse, I saw how the whole conception of the film could be built up.'[6]

In both films, moreover, the cyclical spatial structure makes of the presentation a journey. In HENRY V it is a journey through time and space, whose movement, though subtle, is not unduly complicated. The HAMLET journey is more difficult to trace, and its details will be examined later in this chapter; it is a complex journey with moral, psychological and philosophical dimensions. It is important to note, though, at this point, that while the spatial journeys are cyclic, returning us to the starting points of the films' action, we are not returned to the same aesthetic starting point. Unlike Polanski's MACBETH, whose conclusion suggests that human beings are trapped in a cyclical historical process which operates inexorably and independently of the moral perceptions and the moral courage of the individual, Olivier's HAMLET returns us with a sense of our having undergone a valid experience. We are left with the assurance that human worth and dignity have been sacrificed in order to allow for the possibility of a better world.

To sum up, Olivier employs a spatial strategy in HAMLET which derives very clearly from that used in HENRY V. This is effective primarily because Olivier recognizes the distinctively narrative nature of cinema as a significant potential which differentiates the aesthetic experience of film from that of the theatre. In each of the two films the camera, together with the Chorus – or its vestige in the latter case – shows from a flexible point of view the story of the play. In each case the narrative function devolves upon the camera so that the method of dramatic presentation becomes one of visual narration. This process of narrative devolution completes itself, as we have noted in the initial minutes of Olivier's HAMLET. The camera becomes, as Singer suggests, 'the independent, restless, omniscient, sometimes voyeuristic eye of a strong, distinct personality'.[7]

Herring's self-assured assertion that Olivier 'has chosen to cast his film in the form of a play, rather than to explore the true possibilities of cinema' invites detailed response, and since Herring's verdict on the film's failure as a cinematic achievement, there has emerged a considerable amount of intelligent comment which refutes it.[8] Duffy, writing twenty-eight years after the film's release, claims that *Hamlet* demands 'a more subtle, more poetic treatment than *Henry V*'. He notes, too, that the critics of Olivier's HAMLET have tended to neglect the play's resistance to cinematic treatment, and have over-emphasized 'the picture's flaws, citing its elimination of characters and scenes, its transitions and frequent blindness to elements crucial to a "full" reading of the text'. As he points out:

What is of real importance to students of Shakespearean film should be as much the cinematic means he employs as the thematic coherence he expounds. In this area, despite occasional lapses and more frequent excesses, he distinguishes himself. His HAMLET stands as a pivotal work in Shakespearean film, perhaps more important than HENRY V, because the actual demands of adaptation were immensely greater.[9]

The pivotal nature of Olivier's adaptation of *Hamlet* is achieved both by Olivier's refusal to abandon the aesthetic oscillation between theatre and cinema, and with specific filmic qualities which remove it from theatrical constraint.

In an article published in 1977, Bernice Kliman calls Olivier's HAMLET a 'film-infused play', and she sets out 'to show how thoroughly and consciously in every detail Olivier applies his first purpose: to use film both to suggest and transcend the modern stage through settings, acting and lighting'. She maintains that Olivier had perfectly sound reasons for not simply filming a play; that he wanted to 'free himself from two restrictions of the stage; space and perspective' and she sees behind Olivier's work a vision of film which Shaw had – a means of expanding the spatial and aesthetic boundaries of theatre. She observes, too, a connection with the work of Eisenstein whose last theatrical productions were staged in immense settings within which the audiences were moved about 'to avoid the static perspective of a fixed seat', so that the final result of Olivier's HAMLET is a presentation which 'works against the inherent naturalism of film with film's own techniques. Thus he has overcome two limits of theatre – the limits of space and of the fixed point of view – without sacrificing the feeling of the theatre.'[10]

The particular spatial dimension which the camera brings to this film is flow. It is not typical of the general tendency in cinematic development which has, since Eisenstein, exploited what Susan Sontag has called 'a logical or discontinuous use of space'.[11] Cinematic narrative has always rejoiced in its ability to cut in fragments of action separated by vast geographical distances, in a matter of seconds, and to effect this spatial truncation of reality so skilfully that a modern cinema audience accepts with uninterrupted concentration massive momentary spatial disjunctions. Yet, in HAMLET, Olivier resists the temptation to cut constantly from one shot to another. The film interiors are set in a vast, uncluttered, studio-built castle. Of the two-and-a-half hours of action very little takes place outside this set. The long, uninterrupted takes, the insistent movement of the camera and the use of deep-focus photography, bringing both foreground and background in focus, never give us the claustrophobic sense of a confined space which Tony Richardson's film of the same play tends to impose. Claustrophobia might well be one of the thematic elements in a film of *Hamlet*, but it must be achieved as an artistic effect and not as a result of the fear that the camera might, if it is allowed freedom, reveal irrelevant detail. Kliman is right in stressing the fluid connection of spaces in Olivier's film:

Even when he cross-cuts for example from Polonius, Claudius and Gertrude plotting the 'unloosing' [of Ophelia], to Hamlet overhearing; or from Claudius plotting with Laertes, to the very different communication of Hamlet and Horatio, Olivier is careful to keep the spaces between cross-cuts unified. He connects the spaces with his moving camera and through deep-focus photography.[12]

Where Kliman seeks to show in her reference to Olivier's construction of Elsinore that the film remains anchored to a theatrical concept, Duffy stresses the essentially cinematic conception which the castle's architectural presence affords.

He preserves much of the vague and unlocalized universality of setting that seems close to Shakespeare's intention, but injects enough of the tangible to provide the cinematically necessary solidity and form. Camera movement . . . serves to establish a spatial continuity which solidifies the presence of Elsinore as something more than a mere setting. His textual elimination of the political dimension of the play removes Olivier's Elsinore from the storm and stress of everyday physical reality, and places it midway between heaven and earth. His Elsinore partakes jointly of the symbolic and the real. Like the bondage they embody, the walls and columns transcend the physical reality their solidity implies.[13]

One of the more subtle achievements of the film is the association of particular spatial detail with character. While it is arguably true that the visualization of Ophelia's drowning is a spatial intrusion replicating the Millais painting and that it consequently reduces Gertrude's poetic description of the scene to a restricted and stale image, Duffy rightly points out that there is a significant thematic relevance in the image, consonant with an established spatial development through the whole film.

Throughout the film Ophelia is visually associated with the outdoors. Olivier often composes her scenes to include a glimpse of the countryside, visible in deep field. A floral pattern decorates her walls. Only she seems to have direct access to the daylight world of generation.

Part of her mad scene occurs in exterior shot. No dialogue intrudes: we see her run barefoot across a log bridge and dash into the palace. The drowning sequence then, functions as a natural culmination of this pattern skilfully established by Olivier. He errs only in holding the pictorial insert too long in view. It necessarily suffers in direct juxtaposition with the language.[14]

Only the resources of cinema can link a character so subtly with natural elements, and establish such a flowing associative pattern.

Another associative pattern to emerge is that of *shape* and *form* in those compositions which connect Gertrude with her environment. Duffy draws attention to the 'repetition of round shapes' in the décor of the Queen's apartment. 'A huge circular pattern adorns the marble floor of the Queen's room, and finds a visual echo in the round canopy of the bed, the concave tapestry that follows the line of the wall, and the great circular reach of her dress as she sits on the bed.' While admitting that these are small elements in the spatial strategy of the film Duffy correctly regards them as evidence of 'the subtle visual detail of which the camera is capable in interpreting Shakespeare'.[15] While the association of specific spatial detail with character is more open to the charge of psycho-analytical naïveté, it is a cinematic device more ambitious in projecting specific character significance than Kozintsev's association of interior décor with 'types' (the student, the medieval king, the 'modern', opportunistic, usurper king) already noted above. Olivier strives to illuminate character rather than type.

The pattern which links Ophelia with the images of nature and of plant growth gives rise to another spatially expressed thematic line in the film: the juxtaposition of open, natural light with the cavernous, enclosed gloom of the castle interior. Ophelia's apartment is the only one with real windows and seemingly the only one accessible to sunlight. The contrast between light and darkness is given added weight by Olivier's sequential shifting of the entrance of Horatio and the sentries so that after Hamlet's first soliloquy, the camera shifts away from the shadowed gloom of Hamlet's position and moves on a long slow track to Ophelia's windowed room for Laertes' farewell to her. Polonius' interest in Hamlet's attentions to her concludes the scene. The sequence that follows is especially revealing of Olivier's manipulation of the light and darkness, and its associative implications for the characterization of Hamlet and Ophelia. Ophelia watches Hamlet seated in his chair at the far end of the hall. Admonished by her father, she does not approach. She keeps her distance, and Olivier cuts to a reverse shot from Hamlet's position. We watch her as Hamlet must, with hesitant hope, and we see her turn aside, leaving in the frame only the bright distance of the open countryside in the depth of the picture, through the inner frame of the archway. With a small camera movement Olivier then focuses our attention closer on the brooding figure of Hamlet in the frame as he sits immersed in the gloom, unmoving as he was at the end of the soliloquy. The dark inertia of his presence frames the whole sequence of shots from the triumphal exit of Claudius and Gertrude from the council chamber, to Ophelia's withdrawal. Thus two strong juxtapositions emerge in the long-distance scene between Hamlet and Ophelia. Firstly there is that of light and darkness, and secondly there is that of movement with stasis. Ophelia's liveliness is projected in her affectionate gestures, the 'glad animal movements of her by-play with Laertes', while Hamlet's 'static brooding in the darkness is used to frame Ophelia's "bright" scene, thereby making the contrast all the more evident'.[16]

Another manipulation of the opposition of light and darkness is apparent in the use made of shadow. Hamlet's introspective and unhappy preoccupation is intruded upon at first by the encroachment of shadows which herald the approach of Horatio and the sentries, Bernardo and Marcellus. It is as though Hamlet has to return to the world of physical substance through an intermediary encounter with incorporeal images. This is a deft cinematic touch in view of the fact that the sentries have come to tell Hamlet of the Ghost seen on the castle battlements. A more important and distinct filmic statement is the falling of Hamlet's own head-shadow over Yorick's skull in the grave-yard scene. As Hamlet approaches the grave-side, his shadow moves into the frame from the lower left sector, and advances over the earth until the shadow of his head coincides exactly with the round shape of the skull lying where it has been thrown by the grave-digger. The shot is held long enough to make a clear and unequivocal statement. Hamlet remains off-screen, only his shadow giving the visual signal of his arrival, until after his first line, 'Whose grave is this?' The reciprocal idea is less emphatically suggested when Hamlet holds the skull against his own cheek and the shadow from the skull darkens the side of his face, giving it a hollowed-out appearance on the line, 'Make her laugh at that!'[17] It is as though for a moment Hamlet's presence fleshes out the dead bone, and as though, too, there is a reciprocal movement in which the skull gives physical form to Hamlet's own preoccupation with the tantalizing alternative to life and its obligation. The skull's symbolic stature is, of course, discernible in any competent stage production. But the cinema, with the selective resources of the frame and with the photographic potential of composition through camera angle and lighting angle, can make an especially memorable statement which governs the response in a way which is clearly filmic rather than theatrical.

Two other important shadow effects in the film are developments of this major statement made by shadow in the first grave-yard scene. The first occurs at the point of Osric's presentation of Laertes' challenge where Hamlet understands that he is faced with a 'king's wager' of far greater significance than Osric suggests. At this point, Hamlet turns and walks away from the camera so that his head goes into shadow. The shadow also comes down to hide the upper part of the decorative mural behind him. The shadow only allows a pair of ankles and feet, apparently hanging in vacant space, to be seen. Secondly, there is the great shadow effect of the final funeral procession, with a low sun setting behind the silhouette of the Elsinore tower and battlements.

Olivier's decision to exploit the possibilities of deep focus in HAMLET was to have profound effects upon the nature of the film as a whole. For one thing, it made possible the relation of characters to spatial expanse, and to specific architectural features. In so doing, it made necessary the vast size of the interior floors and the high reach of vertical elements like pillars, walls and stairs, and so freed the camera from spatial constraint in its flow and movement. For another, it made necessary the use of monochromatic film instead of colour, for monochrome film afforded a clarity of definition in long-distance photography which the relatively new colour emulsions of 1948 did not. Monochromatic film, too, was more versatile in accommodating interior lighting conditions through small-aperture exposure which is necessary for deep-focus clarity.[18]

Deep focus involves the viewer in a surprising aesthetic paradox, for while on the one hand it is a photographic device which strives to assert visual control over distance in depth, in so doing it moves the photographic image away from reality towards the two-dimensional completeness of painting. The image retains its normally acceptable perspective, but, like the painting, everything – background and close foreground – is simultaneously in focus. The eye, in viewing the image, does not have to make the focal adjustments which it must make in reality. Moreover, deep focus brings the cinema frame, in a most important respect, closer to the theatrical image.

In an invaluable essay published in 1978, J. L. Styan draws some essential distinctions between theatrical and traditional cinematic presentation:

Only the spectator is in a position [in the theatre] to connect the characters or the groups, by making simultaneous perceptions. These perceptions are the basis for interpretation by an audience, and to relate and synthesise what is perceived from moment to moment is to make drama meaningful . . . The camera can select . . . but in so doing, the director does our perceiving and so our thinking for us, and simultaneity may be lost, the very basis of tension felt in the [theatre] audience.[19]

In bringing a greater field of image depth in focus, deep-focus photography uses space to connect rather than to isolate the separate compositional elements, and it allows for a degree of visual selection within the frame, on the part of the viewer. The closing of the gap between the theatrical and cinematic image is incidentally in line with the complex balance between film and theatre which we have noted consistently in Olivier's work thus far.

The effectiveness with which deep-focus photography does solve problems in cinematic adaptation is supremely well illustrated in Olivier's HAMLET. Styan identifies two spatial problems which obstruct the successful transfer of Shakespearean material to the screen: the separation of characters in depth, and their separation in lateral distance.

The presence on stage of the characters positioned in depth can exercise a powerful control over an audience's disposition toward them . . . On the three-dimensional open stage, this upstage-downstage, north-to-south differentiation of characters comes easily. The camera, on the other hand, has a problem; to gain focus on one character, it may easily lose it on the other if there is blocking in depth.[20]

3. HAMLET (Olivier). The horizontal dimension: deep focus as an expression of the relationship between Hamlet and Ophelia. Laurence Olivier (Hamlet) and Jean Simmons (Ophelia)

The long-distance love scene between Hamlet and Ophelia is a highly pertinent instance of the camera's ability to *connect* characters in depth, and the use of deep focus makes this connection poignant in a way that the stage could not achieve.

The problem of lateral separation would appear at first sight to be more difficult to solve, and in fact to invite a sequential treatment in which the camera cuts from one dramatic element to another. Styan seems to presuppose that cinema must resort to this when he considers Shakespeare's stage-craft: 'Shakespeare divides a scene by taking a character or characters aside from the main group, especially if the image of the main group and what it represents remains important as we focus on those who are separated. The requirement is that of split vision.'[21] Strangely, Styan fails to take account of the fact that the need for lateral distance between characters is in most cases a result of the physical dimensions of the stage and of the fixed frontal point of view which the theatre architecture imposes on the audience.

In his biography of Laurence Olivier, published in 1979, Foster Hirsch observes how deep focus is used in HAMLET to accommodate dramatic distance, and he cites one instance where Olivier solves the very problem mentioned by Styan. 'There is,' he writes, 'an especially inventive use of deep focus early in the film, as Hamlet, on the ramparts, oversees the revelry of the court in the castle below. Seeing Hamlet and the revellers at Claudius' party in the same shot offers a powerful image of Hamlet's isolation from the social world of the court.' One should take the matter further than Hirsch does, and suggest that deep focus in this shot does not merely suggest separation, but that it has a more ambivalent strength of expression. For it shows both Hamlet's wished-for isolation, and the indissoluble involvement which he has to endure as Denmark's prince. There is always something of this ambivalence in a deep-focus shot. However, Hirsch is ultimately right in his perception of Olivier's use of deep focus to relate spatial distance to theme in HAMLET:

Mise-en-scène in HAMLET in fact, becomes an integral expression of theme. Within the same shot characters are often separated from each other by vast spaces; the use of deep focus allows us to see characters in the rear of the frame, at the end of long corridors or across large rooms, and the physical separation, realistically rendered, is emblematic of the emotional distance or the distrust between characters.[22]

The spatial distance between Hamlet and the court revels is interesting in a further important respect. Not only does it remove Hamlet from the court gathering, but it also elevates him above it. In the exploitation of spatial distance which deep focus affords him, Olivier concerns himself with different levels in the film. This shot, combining high-angle shooting together with deep focus is a crucial one in establishing two of the elements at once, of the filmic language of the HAMLET film. The elevation and distancing of Hamlet from the court gathering is reiterated in the closing moments of the film, as Hamlet looks down on the dying Laertes and hears him expose Claudius' guilt. The shot taken from behind Hamlet's right shoulder in deep focus prepares us now for Hamlet's leap down to Claudius. Angle shots and levels are used to give maximum photographic impact to the dramatic material. The film's initial visualization of Elsinore, with the high-angle shot of men on the castle battlements, announces the distinctly filmic departure from the confines of the theatrical proscenium. The sequence in which Polonius questions Hamlet about his reading is visually composed, with Hamlet and Polonius on different levels so that the camera angles used can stress the dominance of Hamlet in the game of psychological manipulation which each is playing. It also suggests, in a subtle way, the conflict between physical closeness on the one hand and emotional and intellectual inaccessibility on the other, which constitutes much of the painful confusion of Hamlet's dilemma. If Hamlet's intention to return to Wittenberg is 'most retrograde to our desire', then the only way out of an incompatible milieu is upwards.[23] Another dimension implied by the different levels in the scene with Polonius and Hamlet is that of theatre, of an actor–audience relationship. Hirsch suggests that:

This positioning of the actors nicely underscores Hamlet's play-acting; he is literally on a stage 'playing' to the gullible Polonius beneath him. Hamlet's raised position emphasises his self-appointed role as mocking lord of the revels, as skillful actor weaving webs in which to ensnare not only the foolish prating Polonius but the cunning Claudius as well.[24]

An especially significant use of the high-angle shot is to be found in the sequence during which Claudius and Laertes plot the destruction of Hamlet in the forthcoming duel scene. The camera moves up and away from the two at the table in the hall as they plot their deception: firstly on a right diagonal line when Claudius suggests the use of an unbated foil, and secondly on the left diagonal when Laertes mentions the poison in his possession. Finally, on Claudius' 'I have it', the camera draws directly away, framing them in long shot as puny figures seen from the great height of the upper reaches of the great columns and pillars.[25] While Hamlet is not visually present in this complex shot, there is a suggestion at this advanced point in the action that the camera–narrator is showing us a conspiracy and giving us the point of view in height and distance which would be closest to Hamlet's own. We are shown what we would like Hamlet to know, and from the elevated and distanced position from which we believe that Hamlet would view it. One reason for the tendency to associate this point of view with Hamlet's own is that the composition and camera movement is almost identical with the earlier one in which Polonius, Claudius and Gertrude agree to hide and overhear what Hamlet and Ophelia say to one another. On this earlier occasion, the camera moves up and back on a long diagonal, and at the end of its distanced elevation, with the conspirators held in long shot, it includes Hamlet overhearing and watching from behind a pillar in the left foreground of the frame. In the later shot, the movement, and particularly the high angle of the camera, make a moral judgement upon its own picture. This idea is given force by the fact that after leaving Claudius and Laertes, the camera shifts transitionally to glimpse the sky before tracking along to meet Hamlet and Horatio descending the stairs.[26]

In each of these cases where Hamlet – or the camera–narrator with its implicit sympathy with Hamlet – is placed to look down upon the court and the instruments of its manipulative deception, it may be argued that the elevation of the point of observation manifests the moral consciousness of the film. It also suggests that people are only accessible to each other when they are placed on the same level. In this latter respect the pattern affords substantial confirmatory evidence. Hamlet must climb to the uppermost heights of the castle battlements to make contact with the Ghost. Marcellus, Bernardo and Horatio come down to make contact with the brooding Prince. There are two points at which Claudius controls the immediate plans for Hamlet: once in the initial council chamber scene where all are gathered together to hear Claudius' opening proclamation and once when, after the killing of Polonius, he and Hamlet confront each other for Hamlet to learn that he is to be sent to England. The two points at which Hamlet is in a position to control Claudius are in the play-within-the-play scene, when Claudius apparently falls into the trap by betraying the hidden truth, and when Hamlet comes upon him praying. The final

death blow to Claudius is delivered when Hamlet leaps down upon him from the
upper level of the castle hall. Hamlet makes crucial contact with his mother only after
he has climbed, deliberately and slowly, to her chamber. Hamlet and Polonius make
final and deadly contact in that chamber, when the agent from the court-world
'below' has breached the rules too blatantly and intruded upon the upper level, a level
of contact to which only Hamlet, his mother, the soldiers and the Ghost of his dead
father – those whose moral potential is related to the past reign in Denmark – may
legitimately have some claim. For the duel, Osric comes *up* to deliver the message of
Laertes' challenge, and both Hamlet and Horatio acknowledge the significance of the
challenge before starting their journey *downwards*.

The entry and movement of ceremonial processions also reinforces the significance of vertical movement in the frame. On two occasions, the royal procession
makes its way down to witness a theatrical event, and on both occasions it moves
along the broad, descending curve of the staircase from the top-right sector of the
frame. The first occasion is their arrival for the play. The second is for the fatal duel
between Hamlet and Laertes. Each of these emphatic downward processions is
counter-balanced by two upward movements by Hamlet; one a relatively small
movement, and one a major vertical climb. After the king has disrupted the
enactment of the play, Hamlet leaps up on to a chair, singing out his new-found
certainty of Claudius' guilt. Then follows the long, slow climb up the stairs to his
mother's bed-chamber.

The court's descent to witness the duel between Hamlet and Laertes is the most
dramatic downward movement in the film. The long, ceremonial procession establishing its strong diagonal from top-right to lower-left corners of the frame is
counterbalanced by the foreground movement of Hamlet and Horatio who move
down slowly on their own diagonal from top-left to lower-right. This final major
descent is thus given heavy spatial emphasis with the double diagonal cutting of the
frame. The earlier diagonal procession down the same stairs to the play-within-the-
play is now emphasized as merely a double diagonal along the same top-right to
lower-left line. There is an initial procession of ceremonial torch-bearers who come
down and then hold their positions on the stairs. They are then followed by the
second procession of the royal couple and their train, who move down the stairs
between the lines of stationary torches. Walton's processional music adds emphasis
to this spatial articulation, accompanying it with a heavy, repeated rhythmic motif in
which the brass and percussion sustain a solid *ostinato*, making the woodwinds force
their more melodic decoration.

This whole effect finds its antithesis in Hamlet's agile run up the stairs with his
shout of 'Treachery, seek it out. Let the doors be locked!'[27] Hamlet's discovery of the
treachery takes him up to the balcony above Claudius, from which point he plunges
down to kill the King. The final major upward movement in the film is Hamlet's
funeral procession, which rises from the castle's hall where Claudius' influence has
been most resonant, up through the other dramatically significant areas of the castle,
to the highest tower, where Hamlet's encounter with the Ghost reached its climax.

The vertical flow of the film, then, can be charted as five inverted parabolas:

1. From the high shots of the castle ramparts and the sentries' dialogue in the opening scene, we descend to the castle interior to hear Claudius' first public speech. We are taken up again after Horatio and the sentries tell Hamlet of the Ghost's appearance.

2. After the encounter with the Ghost, the action descends again to the castle lobby where Ophelia and Hamlet are secretly watched by Polonius and Claudius. The scene ends with Hamlet's upward rush to the openness of the upper ramparts of the castle for the 'To be or not to be' soliloquy.[28]

3. From this precipitous height, the action descends again for the enactment of the play, after which we follow Hamlet on his long climb up to his mother's bed-chamber.

4. From Gertrude's apartment, the action again descends and splays out on the one hand to the grave-yard scene and Ophelia's burial; on the other, to the conspiracy of Claudius and Laertes. From the floor of the castle chamber where Claudius and Laertes plan the killing of Hamlet, the camera makes its long diagonal ascent holding the conspirators in its angle of subtention until it swings around to meet Hamlet and Horatio coming through an arched opening.

5. They are then met by the panting Osric on whom the long climb has taken its toll. From that point on, all through the dialogue of Osric's presentation of the challenge, Hamlet and Horatio are descending the castle stairs. From the ending of the duel, the movement is a rising one, to culminate with Hamlet's body being borne aloft to the tower top.

There has been considerable consensus of adverse criticism of the placing of the well-known 'To be or not to be' soliloquy on a high point of the castle ramparts. It has been seen as gimmicky, and even Foster Hirsch whose biography of Olivier is generally acclamatory, regards the soliloquy as being especially mishandled in the film. 'The placement of the soliloquy looks less like a means of thematic enhancement ... than a half-hearted way of opening up the drama by giving it variety of setting and texture.'[29] Yet there is sufficient evidence to offset this argument. Firstly, as we have shown, the vertical dimensions of the film's movement constitute a spatial articulation of both the moral and the psychological structure of Olivier's adaptation. Jorgens corroborates this view. 'The heights in the film are not meaningless exercises in vertigo. They are linked to Hamlet's sense of disorientation, to the ghost, and to god-like knowledge, and to freedom and aspiration as opposed to the world of compromise, deception and imprisonment below.'[30]

Secondly within the framework of Olivier's interpretation, it is fitting that Hamlet should address the question to himself in a place where his isolation and privacy are guaranteed, a place to which even his trusted friends did not follow him before. For this soliloquy reveals an imaginative involvement with issues beyond the immediate domestic or political preoccupations, and it is an imaginative encounter with ultimate choice, of which no one else in the play is capable. It is Hamlet's imaginative power which sets him apart. Had he spoken these lines at any lower position in the castle's enclosure, one might indeed have wondered who was overhearing them, and what Polonius would make of them. In fact the symbolic importance of the castle's architecture would have given that soliloquy dimensions considerably smaller than those it gains with the spatial suggestions of openness, isolation and vertical consciousness with which this film invests it.

Thirdly, it can be cogently argued that the placing of the soliloquy is part of a three-point pattern in the film's spatial structure. The initial preoccupation with the topmost towers of the castle culminated in Hamlet's meeting with the Ghost, who is in one sense a representative of death, but who also gives Hamlet a purpose in living. The final return to the topmost tower (and to the establishing location shot with which the film began) is the culmination of Hamlet's funeral procession. The philosophical midpoint between these two associative visualizations of height with the preoccupations of life on the one hand, and death on the other, is Hamlet's contemplation of the possibility of choice between them. If Olivier's HAMLET is indeed 'the tragedy of a man who could not make up his mind', then this moment of isolated discourse played against the sustained spatial suggestion of precariousness does make cinematic sense.

This matter of cinematic sense arises, too, as a justification in its own right. Roger Furse, the film set designer, defends the funeral procession's climb to the topmost tower of the castle battlements in the film. 'I doubt', he writes, 'whether it could be defended logically; but logic and dramatic fitness are not the same thing.'[31] There is an aesthetic and dramatic fitness about the spatial implications of the situating of the soliloquy, too. It is a fitness which Don Cook selects for mention in his review of the film:

The handling of the great soliloquy is an example of the . . . imaginative motion-picture direction which Olivier has put into the production . . . The restless camera follows him up the stairs, and wanders through dark, dank corridors of Elsinore Castle, and finally seeks him out sitting alone on a high embattlement overlooking the sea breaking on the rocks far below. From above and behind him it moves down and finally comes to rest on Olivier's blond head, and from within Hamlet's mind come the words, 'To be or not to be; that is the question.' The camera swings around, catching Hamlet against a background of fog-like cloud, and he takes up the soliloquy, 'Whether 'tis nobler in the mind to suffer . . .'[32]

Finally, the sequential shift of the soliloquy in the film placing it after Hamlet's overheard encounter with Ophelia gives added point to the high position from which Hamlet delivers it. Hamlet's long and rapid climb up the steps establishes an emphatic vertical distance between him and Ophelia after his discovery of her naïve complicity in her father's conspiracy with Claudius.

As far as it is possible to discern a separate function for the film's exploitation of horizontal space, that function seems to relate most clearly to character confrontation, juxtaposition of mood and tone, and to the shifting narrative point of view. The long-distance, deep-focus scene between Hamlet and Ophelia, as has been

4. HAMLET (Olivier). The vertical dimension: the heights of Elsinore. Laurence Olivier (Hamlet)

shown, juxtaposes the airy brightness of the world of nature with the sombre gloom of the castle interior in a way which reflects dimensions of their respective characterizations. Also, as already noted, it is on horizontal levels that important direct confrontations between Hamlet and Claudius, Hamlet and Gertrude and Hamlet and Laertes occur. Most important is the conscious juxtaposition of activity with stasis in the horizontal spatial line. Roger Furse, writing of his own intentions in the set design, makes this point. In commenting on his plan for the entry of the travelling players, he notes:

We prepared for this entrance by having no set at all save the floor, which was bounded by black velvet, so that Hamlet was alone in the dark, undefined background. When the players come tumbling in, the space is suddenly alive with movement and the brightness of torches. The static design provided, as it were, a target for all the activity.

The opposite dramatic effect is achieved at the end of the scene in which Polonius questions Hamlet on his reading. This scene, as we have already noted, takes place on two separate levels. But there is horizontal movement along the two levels at its close.

At a point in the dialogue, Hamlet moves off on his level, followed by Polonius on his. They pass a succession of repeating features — alternate pillasters and heraldic paintings. When Shakespeare comes to Hamlet's final, rather cruel snub to Polonius' courtly leave-taking and the mysteriously effective repetition of 'Except my life, except my life, except my life,' I tried to design a fitting static composition made of two sharply pointed arches, underlining the repetition and giving a hint of an unseen sunlit courtyard outside.[33]

In both these moments, there is not only the abrupt change in dynamics, but, as in the long-distance, deep-focus scene between Hamlet and Ophelia, there is the juxtaposition of light and darkness punctuating and transforming the mood and tone of the scene.

The subtlest moments in the spatial movement in the frame are, as we have seen, where there is the complex deployment of more than one spatial resource at one time; deep focus together with angle-shooting (as we noted in the shot of Hamlet looking down on the court revels) and in panning or tracking shots — or still camera shots — where there is a combination of vertical and horizontal movement along diagonals in the frame. Staircases, for instance, are used with considerable effect in the film. The long, curved sweep of the royal procession down the stairs into the castle hall culminates on each occasion in a 'theatrical event' whose apparent innocence cloaks a hidden crucial element of guilt and deception. The impressive downward processional sweep becomes then an effective prelude to a pivotal revelation. Another interesting shot is that of the movement out of the hall of Claudius and Gertrude after the receipt of Hamlet's letters. They move off up separate diverging staircases, making clear in spatial terms Hamlet's success in driving a wedge between them.

A splendidly memorable use of diagonal movement within the frame is Hamlet's slow climb up the stairs to his mother's apartment after the disruption of the play-within-the-play. His ascent is photographed with the camera angled up so that Hamlet moves behind the dark serrations of the shadowed edge of the steps, which appear to cut into his body as it moves heavily up towards the crucial confrontation with his mother. It is a superbly eloquent visualization of pain.

Jorgens is broadly right when, applying A.C. Bradley's dictum about the Shakespearean tragic hero as a man who suffers both internal and external conflicts, he suggests that 'the difficulty in "imaging" *Hamlet* on the screen is that there are two Hamlets . . . A director must reckon both with the conflicts within Hamlet, and with his outer clashes with other characters.'[34] If it is to find a spatial articulation not only for the outer Hamlet in a narrative structure but also and perhaps predominantly for the Hamlet who searches for psychological and philosophical resolutions, the camera must explore and establish a spatial manipulation which is in essence expressionist.

Justified as it may be, the line of criticism which tends to dismiss Olivier's film on the grounds of its Freudian interpretation of Hamlet's paralysis of resolution seldom takes account of the organic integration of the spatial world of the film with the characterization of Hamlet. Where Ophelia is related to images, and Gertrude to shape and form, Hamlet's sombre brooding and his search for some understanding of his own confusion is externalized in the construction and the photographic treatment of the Elsinore world. Roger Furse has written that 'Almost all of the action was to happen in the castle at Elsinore. Olivier wanted a dream-like cavernous place as the setting for the drama which is centred in the shadowy regions of the hero's mind.'[35] Jorgens, too, stresses the relation of the HAMLET space to the Hamlet psychology:

> Roger Furse's 'mise-en-scène' for the film liberates the play's language and actions from deadening literalness and reinforces the psychological nature of the drama. The vague Kafkaesque castle, with its large rooms, pillars, corridors, and archways, its misty ramparts and tortuously winding staircases, its bleak stone walls and ominous areas of impenetrable shadow, is as suggestive of the mind's labyrinths as Welles's sweating caves in MACBETH.

While Olivier's statements about the film tend to avoid a clear commitment to the Freudian symbolism, the evidence within the work is irrefutable. The interpretative pattern constituted by the visual emphasis is clear.

> Olivier's camera lingers often over Gertrude's large, suggestively shaped bed. Hamlet's impotence is indicated by symbolic castration as he drops his dagger into the sea in the 'To be or not to be . . .' soliloquy, his inability to strike home with his sword until the end, and his simultaneous fear of and longing for death, 'a consummation devoutly to be wished'. From the beginning, when Claudius must break up a passionate kiss between mother and son ('Gertrude! Come away'), Hamlet's scenes with the Queen in her low-cut gowns are virtually love scenes. A setting dominated by archways, corridors, phallic pillars, cannon, and towers echoes the theme further, so the film becomes in a sense, an Oedipal cinepoem.[36]

There is a large sense in which the spatial structure of the film is related to the characterization of Olivier's Hamlet. Mary McCarthy, in an essay first published in 1956, has written of Olivier's characterization that there is a discernible 'unsteadiness' both in the character of Hamlet and in the play as a whole, and she claims that 'Sir Laurence Olivier's is the only HAMLET which seizes this inconsecutiveness and makes of it an image of suffering, of the failure to feel steadily, to be able to compose a continuous pattern, which is the most harassing experience of man.'[37]

The film cannot be considered consistently expressionist because the narrative point of view of the camera is consistently restricted to Hamlet's view of the world. Only those moments in which Hamlet encounters the Ghost, where the camera's focus pulsates in time with the stressed heart-beats on the castle battlements and in Gertrude's chamber, or when the eyes of the Ghost appear briefly in the waves below Hamlet at the start of the 'To be or not to be' soliloquy, are moments of classic expressionism. However, it can be argued, on the basis of the evidence so far shown, that the spatial exploration of horizontal and vertical dimensions represents in a major structural sense the painful search which Hamlet has to undergo and the final resolution to which he journeys; for there is no doubt that Olivier's film does conclude on the emphatic note of resolution. The movement along horizontal lines does not constitute an obvious pattern. It is rather interrupted and punctuated by juxtapositions of mood, meetings, confrontations, and moments of privacy turned to sourness through an insistent voyeurism on the part of those who report to the King. It is on the horizontal levels in the castle that intimacy is turned to theatre; theatre to intimacy. It is in the manipulation of vertical space that the pattern emerges clearly. The film completes, as we have seen, a cyclical journey in its rise-and-fall distribution. The completion of this vertical spatial pattern is in fact a visualization of Hamlet's own psychological fulfilment, and it is the integration of this cinematic structural element which gives the film its totality of aesthetic experience: what Jorgens calls 'an unequivocal sense of fulfilment'.

Hamlet occupies for a brief time his rightful place on the throne of Denmark as his subjects bow before him; then 'the rest is silence'. After this saint-like death, a ritual procession takes him heavenward and grants him both mythical status and redemption . . . Olivier's HAMLET concludes with a crescendo of regeneration.³⁸

If there is one over-riding aspect of spatial manipulation which draws a clear line of distinction between theatre and cinema, it is the mobility of the camera. What the camera does with different lenses, mechanical attachments, and the mechanical means of its mobility as a whole unit, is to affect the spatial relationship between the spectator and the action. It does so by changing the angle of vision, following important movement, exploring the natural or architectural environment of action, magnifying detail or widening the angle of vision to relate action to its spatial context.

Adverse critical response to Olivier's HAMLET is, as we have seen, practically unanimous in considering it flawed by meaningless and excessive camera movement. In a book on film aesthetics published as late as 1965, Kenneth MacGowan writes, 'By and large, the moving camera is a dangerous weapon. It can so easily destroy illusion. The lens is, after all, the eye of the spectator. It must follow the action. If it seems to be wandering off for no obvious reason, the spectator will be puzzled, he will lose his bearings.'³⁹ This general statement is supported by George Barbarow, writing specifically on Olivier's film in 1949. 'The camera begins to move at the very start, and seems to be moving almost all the time . . . the movement and multiplicity of viewpoints insidiously conspire to destroy one of the most important powers of a stage performance, the fixed viewpoint.' The suggestion here seems to be that the relatively new variable had better be reduced to a bare minimum if not avoided entirely, in the interests of both the spectator and the dramatic work. Barbarow even maintains that in the filming of theatrical material, the camera 'should be fixed at one point and remain in this position without moving, while each scene is played out before it' thus becoming 'a non-participant observer of the play'.⁴⁰

'The history of film', writes F.E. Sparshott, 'is the history of the invention of its means', and the mobility of the cinema camera comes second only to editing as a major achievement in the continuing technological advance which has opened up the artistic potential of film.⁴¹ Camera movement is a legitimate resource in the language of cinema, and that criticism which tries to assert that it has no place in theatrical film does not convincingly justify its stance. Furthermore, as a cinematic dimension of Olivier's H A M L E T, the movement of the camera is both thematically and structurally integrated. The narrative structure of the film, as we have already shown, depends upon it, for it assumes the identity of an omniscient persona and so gives to the film a dimension which is not part of the play as written or theatrically performed. Secondly, it is related, as is the spatial context of the action, to Hamlet's own slow and sombre search for resolution in his own mind. The movement of the camera imparts a special articulation to this. Thirdly, the nature of its movement enhances the mood and tone of the whole film, giving its melancholy a flow and tenderness. Its passing, transient exploration of the architecture and the pictorial suggestions in the castle suggest a reflective yearning for the reign of the old King Hamlet – an era that is past – enlarging the sense of loss beyond the apprehension of one character. The travelling, fluid transitions which the set design and the camera movement afford allow also for a continuity of action and obviate the breaks between scenes which are customary in the theatrical segmentation of time and space. Finally, the camera's movement links ideas associatively through space without the isolating dislocation of abrupt cutting. This fluid linkage is particularly effective in the final journey of the camera in Hamlet's funeral procession, the camera moving slowly past the various rooms of the castle while the ignition of the cannon charges illuminates them briefly – a counterpoint of continuous movement with flash effects.

An instance of camera movement which functions on all the levels so far mentioned is the movement of the camera from Hamlet (sitting alone after his first long soliloquy) across the hall and through a series of arches towards Ophelia's circular and windowed room. The camera seems to carry something of Hamlet's own desired movement, and just as it emerges from the dark of the castle interior to turn right to Ophelia's door, Laertes walks into the frame from the left and stands in the doorway, blocking the camera's view of Ophelia. The visual and aural concentration is from that moment wholly on Laertes' farewell to Ophelia.

Apart from its functional value in effecting the scene transition and in juxtaposing Ophelia's world with that of Hamlet, the long travel through the series of arches suggests the tenderness of Hamlet's unfulfilled sexual desire – a suggestion which is heightened by the fact that in blocking the camera's view of Ophelia and in standing guard at the entrance to her chamber, Laertes' visual intrusion corresponds with his dramatic function. He has not only come to bid farewell to his sister, but also to warn her not to become involved with Hamlet's hitherto observed manifestations of affection. The gradual brightening of the frame together with the high string modulations in Walton's music give a tonal impact to the slow deliberateness of the camera's movement.

It is certainly facile to imply, as some critics have, that the camera movement in the film is an attempt to add a filmic veneer to what is substantially theatre. The camera movement was part of the organic conception at the start. Roger Furse has written of the close relation in the film's conception of 'the invention of the background to the details of dialogue and the actor's movements', and he has noted that the 'essence of the film is that it is *not* still. It is in motion, and in my opinion the designer's business is to do everything he can to assist that mobility and flow; not to freeze it into a series of orderly compositions which can only impede the action.' The lack of furniture on the set was deliberately planned in order to avoid the creation of static and 'theatrical' photographic localities, but also to increase 'the sense of space we were aiming at, and [to provide] above all, for the speed and free movement demanded alike by Shakespeare and the cinema'.[42]

Camera movement is sustained and insistent at three points in the film: the establishing movement from the battlements down, passing and glimpsing the various dramatically significant parts of the castle's interior; the long procession with Hamlet's body borne to the topmost tower; and the play-within-the-play scene.

After Marcellus' line, 'Something is rotten in the state of Denmark', the eyes of all the soldiers look down right.[43] The camera takes this as a starting point and, following the soldiers' line of vision, it separates from them and begins its slow, searching journey. It passes the limits of the soldiers' vision and begins its descent of the spiralling staircase of the tower until it reaches the Council Chamber. The camera travels through a dissolve, to focus momentarily on Hamlet's chair. From there it moves to the right in a slow panoramic sweep, to pass over the wall and its fresco of the old King Hamlet. It gives us a brief and distant view of Ophelia's arched corridor with its distant windows on to the open light, and with an upward tilt, the camera holds its focus on the great sumptuous bed in the Queen's apartment, moving slowly towards it.

This movement is the establishing of the great 'journeying' structure of the film and, at the end after Hamlet's death, the camera retraces its steps with only a slight alteration of its route. The mood, tone and aesthetic effect of the return are, as we would expect, very different, for the places we are shown in the final moments of the film reveal a spatial pattern of tragic experience. Sandra Sugarman Singer notes the tone of the final moments of the film when she describes 'the eye through which we see the last moments of the film' as belonging to 'a solemn spectator', who is not necessarily identified with us. There remains the invitation for us to participate in this 'solemn' point of view from which the final upward journey is visualized. (Despite its length, Singer's description is worth quoting in full because it captures not only the visual details of the journey but also its tonal nuances.)

From its position to the Right of the throne [the camera] watches motionless, as Horatio kisses the brow of the dead Hamlet. It then tracks Left, moving behind the throne and leaving the screen black for a full five seconds. In the dark there is the report of the first cannon.

The camera emerges, continues to track Left, passing a pillar and some arches, and then pausing in sight of an open doorway through which we see the cemetery in bright sunlight. A cannon fires just outside the doorway as the soldiers bearing Hamlet enter from Frame Right. They pass the fresco of the late King [Hamlet], the camera tracking with them as far as Hamlet's chair, where it stops. For the last time its deep-focus lens affords us the view from Hamlet's chair down the length of Ophelia's corridor, to the sunlight at the end, where now a third cannon fires. While the camera has been still, the soldiers have rounded the corner of the archway, once more moving out of frame to the Right. The camera then makes as if to follow them, but makes its tracking backwards, so as to keep Hamlet's chair in view, finally pulling away to blackness. No longer a frenzied presence, it is rather, a subdued escort, now preceding, now following the small group [of funeral bearers].

The camera holds its next shot, of a dark interior stairway and the bearers enter the frame Down Left, and continue along the spiralling path to the tower. The camera tracks back momentarily, allowing them to pass giving a close-up of Hamlet's dead head, before continuing to follow the progress. There is the sound of a cannon and a flash through the window of the Queen's chamber. The soldiers continue up the steps (which Hamlet climbed to confront his mother), and after they are past, the camera tilts slightly to track in toward the bed. Its three pillows are no longer visible.

The procession climbs to the highest tower above us, and from below, we only see the shadows of the figures on the stone wall. At the top they assume their opening-shot positions, the camera tilting up to hold them in a low-angle shot, in the distance.[44]

The most controversial scene is the play-within-the-play scene. The camera does not take up a fixed position once it has shown the long, curving descent of the royal procession. The camera moves in a broad and smooth semi-circular sweep around the mimed action of the players, keeping that action always at the radial point of its movement. The camera passes behind the chairs of Gertrude and Claudius four times, its deep-focus lens capturing a composite image of the action in long shot, framed by the heads of the King and Queen viewed in close-up, from behind. The momentary composition at this point is reminiscent of an earlier deep-focus shot when the Ghost of the old King appears framed by the heads, shoulders and spears of Marcellus and Bernardo, again seen in the foreground from behind. It is a significant reminder which indicates, in its contained way, the technique of the journey structure in the film. We have been taken to a visual composition which we have encountered before, but our knowledge gained in the interim transforms the visual experience to one of sharp expectancy. Framed by the two heads, there now appears not the Ghost, but the re-enactment of what the Ghost related. The details of the re-enactment are visually identical with the visualized tableau which Hamlet pictured as the Ghost related the manner of his death. Hamlet's visual construction of the event is presented without alteration to the eyes of the guilty couple.

In its last semi-circular sweep, the camera's interest is wholly focused on the King and Queen, especially Claudius. As it passes the royal couple, the camera now removes its attention from the play to hold them in the frame. The camera continues on its arc so that the angle on the royal couple changes, giving us Claudius' profile and then an oblique left-frontal shot of him as he rises with his knuckles in his eyes to cry, 'Give me some light!'[45]

Now it is true that the mobile and apparently detached point of view is, if we are to lay down rules and demand consistency, at odds with the expressionist endeavour of other parts of the film, those spatial suggestions which make Elsinore the visual expression of Hamlet's psychological architecture. Yet in another sense there is a valid consistency of a different type. As we have seen in both this film, and in HENRY V, Olivier's aim is not to set up cinematic rules and conform doggedly to them but rather to set up tensions and oscillations between cinema and theatre and so to exploit the expressive potential which cinema affords him. The narrative point of view *can* be made flexible through the visualization of a moving camera. The detachment of the visualization does not fail on the aesthetic level in the play-within-the-play scene. It is arguable that in refusing to anchor itself to Hamlet's visual point of view, it is moving as Hamlet's imagination might, to see the enactment of the murder as Claudius and Gertrude must see it, for Hamlet would have stage-managed the action in accordance (as we have realized through its close resemblance of detail) with his earlier vision of it.

Jorgens defends the insistent camera movement as reflecting 'the impossibility of fixity in a world of flux'.

Olivier's play-within-the-play scene is an epiphany affirming that significance shifts with the perceiver; it is a graphic illustration of the subjective nature of reality ... The camera travels in a large semi-circle behind the spectators allowing us to see the play from the points of view of Ophelia, the courtiers, Hamlet, Claudius, Gertrude, Polonius and Horatio. The pantomime becomes in turn a mystery, an exciting fiction, a boring puppet show, an open threat by Hamlet against the King, and a nightmarish revelation of a real murder.[46]

Certainly the 'inquisitive roving camera' is more than merely 'an extension of the audience's curiosity', for it shapes our perception and colours the tone of our experience.[47] It has not only a narrative, but a revelatory power. Those critics who isolate camera movement in Olivier's HAMLET and condemn it as unnecessary seem to suggest that it should have a meaning which is translatable into a verbal equivalent. Yet this is as unrealistic a demand as requiring that the rise and fall of a melodic line in music should be verbally explicable. Camera movement in HAMLET is part of an organic orchestration, and Skoller is right when he regards camera movement as 'an effective counterpoint to the narrative elements of the scene that can perhaps be alluded to through words like "melancholy", "tentative", or "anguished", but can only be fully realized and experienced through direct perception of the movement itself'.[48]

There remain three aspects of the HAMLET spatial strategy to consider. The first is a group of narrative visuals which constitute 'tableaux' or internal visualizations. Just as Olivier used the imagination of the theatre audience in HENRY V as one area of action in the presentation of the material, here, too, he employs the same device. The only difference is that the 'imaginative area of action' is in the mind of a character in the drama. The moments of action concerned are those which reach the centre of the staged action as reported items of news. The first three of these are: Hamlet's visual imaging of his father's murder as the Ghost recounts it, Ophelia's memory of Hamlet's visit to her in her closet as she recounts it to Polonius, and Horatio's mental picture of the sea encounter between the ships as he reads Hamlet's letter. Each of these is framed by a blurred iris-type edging within the normal cinema frame, and they are accompanied only by the narration of the events visualized. The fourth tableau is different. It is not framed as the others are, and in addition to its being accompanied by Gertrude's narration, there are also Laertes' interjections and response, and there is the voice of Ophelia singing. It is the only tableau with a sound intrinsic to it, and although it is narrated by the Queen, it is clearly not from her point of view that we see Ophelia floating down the river. The visualization, in re-creating Millais's famous picture, becomes the only moment in the film which uses an existing work of art to set up the ambivalence of presentation which Olivier managed with such skill in HENRY V. (Singer points to an interesting deviation from the Millais painting. The movement in the painting, she notes, is from left to right, whereas in the film it is reversed.)

Secondly, there is a tightening of the film's structure which is afforded by occasional, momentary visual reminiscences. One of these is the re-enactment of the old King Hamlet's murder, whose details, as we have noted, replicate those of the original visualization. Another is the telling piece of ironic wit combined with pathos, when Hamlet suddenly puts the blond wig on the head of the boy-actor, thereby recreating Ophelia's presence. It suddenly makes us aware of the multiple levels of our engagement with the action in the film, and it uses Elizabethan stage convention to heighten our awareness of the dialogue between film and theatre which is intrinsic to HAMLET. The placing of the wig has the unusual effect of bringing Ophelia cinematically closer, and of distancing her theatrically. At the same time, it suggests the complexity of Hamlet's own feelings about her.

Finally, there is the relationship between space and time in the film. The spatial detail in the film does not give many hints of the time-scale of the events of the drama. The flowing continuity imparted to the action by the movement of the camera tends to make the time-span seem relatively short with no significant time gaps. There is one rapid transition in both locale and mood, however, which seems awkwardly abrupt. One feels that intervening time should have elapsed. This is the transition from Ophelia's grave-side (with Laertes grieving over his sister's death) to the castle interior (where Claudius and Laertes plot the destruction of Hamlet). The exterior scene ends with Laertes in the upper foreground, watching the distant filling of his sister's grave. He turns at the door and suddenly the camera is framing a strong, slow tracking shot of Claudius and Laertes walking together with the castle wall behind them. Inelegant though the abruptness of this transition seems, it does enforce the gathering speed with which final events are accumulating and point to the narrow divide which now separates life and death in the climactic movements of the politics of Elsinore. Perhaps, too, it underlines a most important quality in Laertes' character − his emotional volatility.

The shortness and scarcity of outdoor shots, too, makes it difficult to fix the time of day at any point. One spatial detail which does raise the possibility of a clear time signal is the sprig of rosemary which Ophelia places on Hamlet's chair. This small item is still there when the camera passes Hamlet's chair for the last time. There is then a suggestion, which Singer also notes, that the time duration from Ophelia's revealed madness to the end of the film is 'a matter of hours'.[49] Singer notes, too, that if one couples that information with the low sun in the final sequence in which Hamlet's body is borne to the topmost tower, it is possible to argue that the final action from the revelation of Ophelia's madness to the close of the film happens within a single day.

There is no doubt that the spatial strategy of Olivier's HAMLET is at once more organically integrated as a sustained articulation, and more subtly eloquent than is the versatility of the spatial resources deployed in HENRY V. Single ideas are more thoroughly exploited in the later film. While there are aspects of the sets and much about the acting which tempts one to see the film as a theatrical concept overlaid with a cinematic treatment, there is overwhelming evidence, as we have shown, to argue powerfully the contrary case: that the film is radiant with its essential cinematic conception, and that it constitutes an orchestrated whole whose spatial structure is irrefutably filmic. If theatrical elements do shine through the orchestration of the final work, it is not an artistic lapse but a triumph. As Bazin points out:

Previously the first concern of the film-maker was to disguise the theatrical origins of his model, to adapt it and to dissolve it in cinema. Not only does he seem to have abandoned this attitude, he makes a point of emphasising its theatrical character. It could not be otherwise from the moment we preserve the essentials of the text.[50]

4 Laurence Olivier's RICHARD III

What makes Olivier so remarkable and significant a director of Shakespearean film is the sense in which his approach to the aesthetics of filming theatrical material is paradoxical. His concept of the nature of dramatic action is, as we have seen, essentially and unwaveringly theatrical. Yet his films abound with those moments which bring theatricality to the film and then advance its impact in a way which only cinema can. The relationship between film and theatre – in which cinema would seem to be subservient – is suddenly and unexpectedly subverted so that the entire medium of expression is ultimately cinematic.

It is possible to postulate the general features of Olivier's approach to the filming of Shakespearean material by pointing to conceptual similarities in his three Shakespeare films. Yet it becomes clear that within this broad framework he relates his cinematic strategy to the specific potential which each individual play offers.

Two instances of his overall approach come readily to mind: his perception that cinema is essentially narrative, and his visualization of a cyclical journey structure in each of his three films. Within these two broad strategies, the differences are, however, very clear. In HENRY V the narrative function which the Chorus performs for the play is gradually conceded to the camera. In HAMLET the narrative dimension is launched with the inserted and vocalized 'prologue' which Olivier speaks – and which also appears printed on the screen – and is then immediately conceded to the selective visual strategy of the camera-persona. In RICHARD III, the narrative dimension has its own subtle and distinct properties, for it is, as we shall see, much more within the control of Richard than it ever was in the control of the central characters in HENRY V or HAMLET. The cyclical journey structure manifests itself in RICHARD III too, but here it has less impact as a device than it does in either HENRY V or HAMLET.

In order to show that the distinctions in both the narrative presentation and the cyclic structure of the films are not merely superficial distinctions in the application of a tried technique, it is necessary to consider in general terms those aspects of the plays which link them on the one hand, and which separate them on the other.

Since both *Henry V* and *Richard III* are histories, one might expect them to have more in common as regards their adaptive strategies than *Richard III* and *Hamlet*. Yet these latter plays are linked by their concern with a central character who is at odds with the society he is in. Olivier's film RICHARD III, then, becomes, like HAMLET, a psychological study developed along the lines of attitudes to and conceptions of power, morality and love. Olivier explores and visualizes the nature of the disharmony which separates the principal character from the world in which he functions. What distances R I C H A R D III from H E N R Y V is the treatment of character and the relation of the respective principal characters to the context of social values in which each acts. Henry's action, and his acquisition of power over the French, is shown to be wholly in harmony with that framework of spiritual expectation consonant with medieval kingship. In short, Henry is heroic, successful and virtuous. Richard, on the other hand, transgresses without moral scruple every medieval stricture on the acquisition of power. He is villainous in motivation and in act, both in the eyes of his own society and in ours.

The differences in the relationships of Henry and Richard to their respective worlds of action are made very plain in the spatial strategies of the films. Henry's world is an historically remote world, one in which the stylized depictions of the Middle Ages become real. The world of Richard is one of interiors, of closets, doors and windows, where the ebullience of colour is vitiated by ironic visual comment: the cynical comment of Richard's dark mind. H E N R Y V presents a vindication and a culmination of medieval values. R I C H A R D III presents a break-down of medieval order, with Richard as a rampant Machiavellist taking every advantage of a decadent court clinging to a delusion of spiritual and moral order. Jorgens, writing of R I C H A R D III, maintains that 'If Olivier has made an historical film, it is in the sense that out of respect both for Shakespeare's thematic interest in ritual and for his sure instinct for theatrically explosive scenes, Olivier showed how rituals faced with Richardism can no longer make the world cohere and have meaning.'[1]

So, while both plays are histories, and this common category might lead one to expect the later film to be an expansion and a consolidation of the cinematic strategies of H E N R Y V, we shall find that Richard's relation to his world of action invokes a narrative tone and a narrative point of view which require a more claustrophobic and more economic spatial treatment. We are led to consider in more depth the spatial derivation of R I C H A R D III from H A M L E T. Yet at the outset the spatial autonomy of R I C H A R D III becomes clear, for while the deployment of action in expansive interiors and the movement of the action from one interior location to another in R I C H A R D III recalls the interiors of Elsinore, the expressionist use of architectural dimensions is never used in R I C H A R D III to externalize the psychological isolation of the principal character as is the case in H A M L E T

Although the spatial strategy employed in R I C H A R D III is determined by the requirements of the play and is not merely a structural imposition, there is no doubt that R I C H A R D III is clearly a product of the same cinematic intelligence which created H E N R Y V and, more particularly, H A M L E T.

Just as H E N R Y V opens with its fluttering parchment bill announcing the performance of the play and H A M L E T opens with an assortment of theatrical properties, so too R I C H A R D III has its own recurrent visual motif or logo which opens the film and gives it a thematic line of development. Pictured on the screen is a two-dimensional drawing of a crown. Beneath this appears the announcement of the film's intention, to portray a 'legend'. This 'dialogue between word and picture' develops so that the 'picture' crown becomes a 'real' one suspended over the coronation ritual at Westminster for the crowning of Edward IV.[2] The action of the film effectively starts with the lowering of the crown on to the head of the new King Edward, but there follows through the film a recurrent suspended placing of the crown. After Edward's death, it is held aloft over Richard's head, and finally it is placed above the head of Richmond – though it does not descend to crown him. The film ends with the archbishop's hands dissolving from the frame, the 'real' crown reverting to its earlier graphic depiction and then moving up and out of the frame, thus balancing the opening descent of the pictured crown in the frame.

The metamorphosis and movement of the crown at the start and ending of the film constitute Olivier's framing device for the historical legend. Sandra Sugarman Singer writes of this movement of the film's logo:

Olivier's circle is complete. The expected link between history and story, the act of story-telling as a function of word and picture, the activity of the imagination which can turn a two-dimensional drawing into the crown of England – all are issues raised in the first moments of the film and symbolized in the return to the graphic image of the crown.[3]

The broad cyclical movement evident here is reminiscent of similar structural treatment in both HENRY V, with its ultimate return to the occasion of performance, its model London and its fluttering parchment bill carried by the wind, and in HAMLET, with Hamlet's ultimate funereal return to the topmost tower of the castle with the final positioning of the figures on the battlements.

Foster Hirsch maintains that of his three Shakespearean films, 'Olivier's RICHARD has the loosest integration between form and content', by which he seems to mean an incongruity between the colourful film décor and the mood of the play.[4] The mood of the film is in fact lightened by Olivier's inclusion of the coronation of Edward IV which also ensures that the film's structure is both unified and aesthetically sound, as Constance Brown, in an article written in 1967, convincingly argues:

Olivier added the coronation partly to elucidate for modern audiences Shakespeare's version of the political situation existing in England before Richard achieved the crown, but its formal function is also evident. The first coronation is that of Edward, certainly not an outstanding king but more or less a legitimate one. The coronation of Edward is followed by the coronation of Richard, the 'Red King', the tyrant, the king of misrule. The third coronation is that of Richmond, representing the restoration of order and the return of authority to its proper place.

The parabolic curve from legitimate king to tyrant to legitimate king is clearly defined through the use of crown images.

The 'parabolic curve' and the spatial manipulation of the crown through these three coronations gives the film a breadth of meaning which the play does not project.

Had Olivier tried to adapt RICHARD III simply by snipping out some of its less inspired passages, he would have accomplished little. Instead, by giving predominance to a theme obscured in the play, he has given his film a significance that the play does not have. Olivier's film, like the play, is a portrait of an individual tyrant. Unlike the play, Olivier's film surpasses melodrama to become a portrait of tyranny.[5]

The second aspect of Olivier's cinematic approach which broadly governs the treatment of all three films is the narrative authority of the camera. We have seen that the narrative authority in HAMLET is an infusion created by Olivier. The narrative dimension of RICHARD III, like that of HENRY V, is implicit in the play. Richard himself has some eighteen opportunities of direct address to the theatre audience, so it is natural that Olivier weaves other narrative possibilities into the voyeuristic predilections of Richard's personality. The camera, for most of the first half of the film, is hinged to Richard's own cynically amusing point of view, and often we discover only after a particular event has been shown, that we have witnessed it as Richard's close confidants.

One example of this subtle sharing of Richard's view is the scene in which Clarence recounts his dream to Brackenbury. The camera moves to the dialogue of Clarence's relation of the dream through six shots:

1. Richard takes Clarence's death warrant from the King.
2. The King and Jane Shore leave the room.
3. The chanting monks cease their incantation and close the missal.
4. There is a cut to the interior of the Tower.
5. There is a second cut to the barred window of Clarence's cell.
6. A third cut takes us to Brackenbury and Clarence for Clarence's speech.

After the recounting of the details of the dream has ended with Brackenbury's words of reassurance, there is a cut back to the barred window and the camera pulls back through the window to reveal the sinister hat on the head of Richard. As Singer suggests, 'We can only assume that he has been a silent, unseen observer to the whole scene [inside Clarence's cell] which we have *unknowingly* witnessed through his eyes. Like the characters he manipulates, we the audience find ourselves controlled and directed by him.'[6]

There are other moments in which Richard's entrance 'on cue' suggests that he has been a hidden witness. One is the King's deathbed scene in which Edward attempts to reconcile the estranged relations of the family. On his line 'There wanteth now our brother Gloucester here / To make the perfect period of this peace', Richard enters.[7] Another instance is the scene in which, after King Edward's death, there is a council meeting to appoint a regent for the young Prince. As Hastings offers to speak in Richard's favour, Richard again enters.[8] Finally there is Richard's opportune meeting with the escorted Clarence on his way to imprisonment in the Tower. All these reinforce the suggestion of our having been drawn into voyeuristic complicity with Richard.

More interesting, and of greater significance to the wider field of aesthetics of filmed plays, are those speeches which Richard addresses directly to the camera. Olivier has noted the difference in nature of the soliloquies in *Richard III* from those in *Hamlet*.

Hamlet contains a great deal of spoken thought, but it is contemplative. On the other hand, Richard talks to the audience all the time like Iago does, and says, 'What a good boy am I. Aren't I clever?' This is absolute audience approach, not meditation. When I do it in the film, I talk to the camera, and take the camera into my confidence. I take it by the arm and walk it about with me as if I'd just come to town with it . . . I treated the camera as a person . . . It's nothing new really; people are seeing it on television all the time.[9]

In order to establish and exploit the conspiratorial nature of Richard's relationship with the audience, the spatial relationship between Richard and the cinema audience is treated as it might be in a theatre, with an aesthetic impact which we have not encountered in either H AMLET or HENRY V. Yet this manipulation of audio-visual space does significantly more than simply turn a cinematic moment into a theatrical one. For just as we are attracted to Richard by his cynical humour and self-assurance, and simultaneously distanced from him by his Machiavellian shamelessness, so the camera frame in these direct-address shots becomes at once a distancing artistic device (making of reality a pictorial image) and a means of seducing us as Richard's intimate confidants.

Richard's seduction of our moral sensibilities is achieved largely through the sheer daring of his approach, on both the technical and dramatic levels:

'We'll do it together, you and I', he seems to suggest, making sleepy eyes at the camera, looking it up and down as some men contemplate a prospective lover. It was the first time a cinematic character addressed himself to the audience so directly and personally, much less invited them to participate in a conspiracy. It is a delightfully brazen sort of behaviour, characteristic of the audacity people admire in powerful men.[10]

Olivier's use of the direct address to the camera, which defies the naturally assumed aesthetic laws of the medium, is another of those brilliant strokes whereby he brings a distinctly theatrical action to film and then gives it an impact which only cinema can. The success of its effect depends upon the fact that it amplifies elements which are implicit in the play in the character of Richard. The boldness with which he affronts the aesthetic laws of the medium is consonant with the assuredness with which Richard challenges the accepted procedures of royal succession and affronts the apparent spiritual order of the realm. Secondly, the natural tendency of cinema towards voyeurism corresponds with the voyeuristic trait in Richard's personality structure, and because they hold this in common, Richard and the camera become easy accomplices. The fact that any camera makes the viewer an automatic visual confidant ensures that the triangle of complicity between Richard, the camera and the cinema audience is complete.

A most important dramatic tension emerges from this, for while Richard is persuasively engaging, the cinema audience has constantly to distinguish its enjoyment at being taken into Richard's confidence on the one hand, from its moral revulsion at his actions on the other. But the cinema audience's ambivalence is essentially different from the corporateness of the theatre audience's experience. In writing of the difficulty with which the cinema handles the soliloquy, Henry Hart in a review of the film written in 1958 draws special attention to Olivier's direct-address device in RICHARD III, and makes an incisive observation about the response of the cinema audience to the pictorial image. 'When an actor looks directly into the camera, the optics are such that his on-screen image appears to be looking directly into the eyes of each and every person in the audience.'[11] A further reason for the effectiveness of the direct-address shots, then, lies in those special dimensions of response which Bazin noted as being peculiar to the cinema audience's passivity, 'a self-satisfaction, a concession to solitude, a sort of betrayal of action by a refusal of social responsibility'.[12] It is this 'concession to solitude' in particular which is exploited in the darkness of the auditorium by the intimacy, size and inviolability of the projected image.

The point at which we become most poignantly uneasy about our amused complicity with Richard corresponds, as Constance Brown rightly observes, with Olivier's characterization of him.

After accepting kingship, Richard holds out his black-gloved hand for Buckingham to kiss. He thrusts it forcibly toward the camera, and holds it extended in the air like a huge black claw. The hand is extended toward the audience as much as toward Buckingham. For the first time the audience is advised that what it has approved by laughter and condoned in the earlier part of the film is its own destruction. From this point on, Richard's tyranny is no longer so purely amusing.[13]

The force of the irony at this moment resides in the fact that the apparent extension of the hand towards the audience is, in purely spatial terms, a silent development of the direct address to the camera with which Richard achieved, in part, our moral capitulation.

Our complicity in Richard's voyeurism which is so compellingly managed in the first half of the film is more consciously consolidated through two other spatial strategies. Firstly, there is the insistent viewing of action through doors and windows which are opened for us by Richard. Secondly, there is a subtle use of deep-focus lenses, enabling us to view an action in the distance and yet to be conscious of Richard himself in the foreground – and so of his manipulative power over events. Richard's long opening soliloquy begins with him throwing open the throne-room doors. Later he opens doors again, to view the lugubrious funeral procession with Lady Anne mourning the death of her husband. During Richard's long walk along the gallery, some twelve minutes into the film, we are directed by him to watch the results of his setting the King against Clarence. There is a succession of windows through which we see King Edward accusing Clarence. Richard pauses by each window in turn, and finally opens one just long enough for us to see what he judges fit. There is a deliberately tantalizing element in his manipulation of our view.

The integration of the deep-focus compositions, while they keep us mindful of Richard's power over the development of the action, also shape our perception of the action in accordance with Richard's priorities, for always his presence in the foreground, however subtly suggested, is large in relation to the smaller figures in the depth of the picture. This particular idiom of size-related expression is established early in the film when the screen is seemingly filled with the pomp and ceremony of Edward's coronation. Our attention is hardly focused on the details of the ceremony, when the dark shine of Richard's hair asserts its visual prominence in the lower-right corner of the frame as he slowly turns to the left, invading and dwarfing the significance of the ceremony with his sharp-nosed profile in close-shot.

Hirsch is right, on a purely technical level, in seeing the deep-focus shots as a derivation from HAMLET. 'Olivier continues here his employment of realist film techniques such as the depth of focus and the long take first fully articulated in HAMLET . . . Richard often spies on his intended victims from windows or raised galleries.'[14] But it is important to note that the tone of relationships established in spatial depth in RICHARD III is markedly different from those in HAMLET. It is invariably Richard's victims who are consigned to the depth of the frame. Constance Brown, particularly, has illustrated this in drawing attention to the scene in which the young Prince Edward sits on the throne while Richard and Buckingham plot his death. She maintains that Olivier 'visualizes the inadequacy of the child, Prince Edward', when Richard and Buckingham take him into the throne room. The Prince runs in and stands momentarily with his back to the camera, looking up at the empty throne. The camera tracks away from him, and upwards so that he is left, 'a small, solitary, red smear against soft grey and is dwarfed by the room'.[15] The relation of size and distance then undergoes a further development, for while the Prince is left, small and puny in the background, Richard and Buckingham in their foreground conspiracy frame him, forming an ironic triptych. As we have noted in our discussion of HAMLET, Olivier made use of more than one spatial articulation simultaneously for particularly forceful effects, and here he incorporates a window frame together with deep focus, with especial significance. For as they conspire in the foreground, Richard and Buckingham are themselves separated by a window bar. It is, as Hirsch notes, 'a touch of ironic foreshadowing', since the fate of the young Princes is the issue which later divides the conspirators.[16]

The symmetrical placing of Buckingham and Richard in the foreground of the composition, with the two young Princes distanced in the centre, is reminiscent of two shots we have noted in HAMLET: the two sentries, Marcellus and Bernardo, framing the appearance of the Ghost, and the heads of Claudius and Gertrude framing the action, as they watch it, of the play-within-the-play. Also reminiscent of HAMLET is the use of that most symmetrical of structures, the arch. Yet in this, too, there is a development especially advanced for this later film. Unlike the open interior spaces of HAMLET, which afforded the camera unrestricted movement and flow, the arch motif in RICHARD III is constantly used to frame action. This not only imposes

upon the camera a more disciplined compositional intent, but it also provides a transitional flow of a particular kind, from one shot to the next.

An example of this is the reinforcement of the film's ironic comment in the transition from Clarence's cell in the Tower, after his murder, to King Edward's bedchamber. The last glimpse we have of the process of Clarence's murder is the overflowing spillage of wine flowing from the tub, along the stone floor, through the barred and arched drainage outlet to the river. From there the camera takes us through the arch of the stained-glass window of the King's chamber. We see Jane Shore carry a pitcher of wine to place it in a wall-niche which is scalloped out to give the gothic arch points in its design, and she then passes a screen with a double-arch motif as its embroidered pattern.

Other symmetrical elements in the frame's composition reinforce both the visual unity of the film and that dramatic dissonance between the apparent values of the polity on the one hand, and Richard's view of them on the other. The alliance between Richard and Buckingham achieves a symmetrical culmination both in words and visualization. Richard's acknowledgement of Buckingham as 'my other self' is given visual expression in their stance at the end of the king's deathbed and in later moments until the point of their dramatic estrangement.[17] When Hastings is accused of treason by Richard, the members of the council withdraw from him and leave Hastings at the end of a long table. He is shown sitting alone, hovered over by two angels painted on the fresco behind him. It is a finely ironic use of the film's development of symmetrical composition, as is the reiterative framing of the two monks who chant the missal in Edward's throne-room. They perform their office with a bored mechanical detachment, and again their function is both visually and thematically integrated, for the dual nature of their empty, droning vocalizations becomes a telling pictorial expression of the vacuous ritual to which Edward clings as a basis of power. In the scene where Buckingham calls on the citizens to plead with Richard to take the crown, Richard appears above them flanked by two monks – possibly the same two who chanted the missal to Edward – 'Two props of virtue for a Christian Prince / To stay him from the fall of vanity'.[18] The frame composition also includes two blinkered horses in the foreground as the citizens give their desultory acclaim to Richard's apparent consent. One further development of the irony achieved through symmetrical suggestion is the visual 'echo' which Constance Brown observes in Clarence's cell. In telling Brackenbury of his nightmare of drowning, Clarence moves towards the barred window of his cell. Beside the window a small crucifix hangs on the wall. At the end of his narration to Brackenbury, Clarence reaches the climactic, fear-ridden line, 'Seize on him, Furies, take him to your torments!', and as he delivers this, he flings himself back against the wall, throwing his

5. RICHARD III (Olivier). Richard's direct address to the camera makes the cinema audience a collective accomplice. Laurence Olivier (Richard)

6. RICHARD III (Olivier). Richard and Buckingham stand at Edward IV's deathbed. The vertical feature on the wall behind them ironically foreshadows their later estrangement. Laurence Olivier and Ralph Richardson (Buckingham)

arms back above him.[19] 'The parallel of Clarence's position to that of the crucified Christ on the opposite wall is unmistakable.'[20]

The recurrence of a symmetrical composition, then, is not simply an ornamental gimmick to give the film a pictorial discipline. Rather, it is there to reflect the ornamental nature of the social order which Richard will shatter, and to expand – because the artificiality of that order deserves to be shattered – the complexity of our ambivalent response to Richard as a character. While in HAMLET the camera's movement constituted an exhausting, but thematically valid search for pattern and order, here, in RICHARD III, the camera finds both pattern and order, but a pattern and order which have no sustaining substance, and so have no claim to our sympathy. Indeed, the film achieves its culminating irony when Richard himself tries to impose a pattern of symmetrical order on a reality of a different kind which cannot sustain it: the Battle of Bosworth.

The Battle of Bosworth is the section of the film which most obviously recalls, in its realism, the battle scene of HENRY V. Filmed on outdoor location in Spain, the battlefield is a clear spatial juxtaposition of an open, natural landscape with the closed, fashioned interiors of the earlier parts of the film: a juxtaposition of the world of nature with the man-made world of power-symbolism and political machination. However, Richard's preparations for the battle are depicted by a visual device which recalls that latter interior world; a device which prompts Cottrell to suggest that it attempts to 'achieve the stylised look of tapestry'. Cottrell's remark is oddly cryptic, for he does not enlarge on the comparison he draws. He does, however, note the juxtaposition of the 'tapestry' idea on the one hand, with the 'savage realism of the hand-to-hand fighting' on the other.[21]

The suggestion of tapestry, as Singer has rightly assumed, fits that part of the battle preparations in which Richard plots out the deployment of his army. After his quiet self-acknowledgment, 'Richard's himself again', he rides his mount around to face his men.[22] The camera then cuts to show a high-angled view of a sandy surface. Richard speaks his lines of exhortation and announces his strategy, and as he speaks the line 'My foreward shall be drawn out all in length' the tip of a sword moves across the surface in the frame from right to left.[23] As he continues, the formation lines of the army take shape and darken in colour across the lower framed area, until the neat pattern of regimented lines is completed. The sword tip functions as a drawing or weaving instrument, creating a colourful depiction of symmetrical order.

Not only is this symmetry a culmination of the theme of deceptive order masking the reality of structural disintegration (for most of Richard's army will, in the reality of battle, desert him) but it is a culmination in a wider sense, for it brings together other lines along which the structure of the film has been built.

The creation of the army on Bosworth Field is the moment in which the theatre-making elements, the pictorial and the narrative, meld. Richard is the artist, both story-teller and painter, who, like the Chorus in H E N R Y V, creates his setting. He will then step into the setting he has created to play his role in it.[24]

While it can be argued that the three major elements in the film's structure do manifest themselves simultaneously in the tapestry effect of the army's planned formation, it is nonetheless important to point out that in this film the theatrical, pictorial and narrative dimensions are tightly woven throughout. At the start of R I C H A R D III we are made aware of theatricality on the occasion of King Edward's coronation, and the theatrical mode is then taken up in the long opening monologue by Richard as he takes us and the camera with him. We are committed to a much more sustained awareness of theatre than is the case in either H E N R Y V or H A M L E T, for unlike the establishment of a dichotomy between 'theatrical' and 'real' space which the two earlier films effect through the use of models and aerial shots, R I C H A R D III affords us no overall view of the social or architectural world outside the court. The only memorable exception is the brief scene in which the small and unwilling crowd of London citizens is persuaded to approve Richard's claim to the throne. Even that is spatially a very enclosed scene, and the only hint of a wider context for Richard's machinations comes in the occasional distant glimpse of the masts and superstructures of ships on the River Thames. The commitment of action to interiors (apart from the battle) is essentially theatrical, as is Richard's visualized awareness of the cinema audience.

In our discussion of Olivier's HAMLET, we drew attention to Jorgens's argument that the theatricality of that film actually reinforced its thematic substance. There is an interesting element common to both HAMLET and RICHARD III which binds theatricality of occasion within the film to the predominant theatrical mode of the film itself. In both HAMLET and RICHARD III there is a theatrical exploitation of what might be called 'disruption of spectacle'. In both these films a violent disruption is wrought upon the ceremonial proceeding of a funeral. In HAMLET there are two other disruptions: the theatrical presentation of the play-within-the-play, and the 'staged' duel scene at the end of the film. In RICHARD III the second memorable disruption is that of Edward's death-bed scene, when Richard enters with the news of Clarence's death. The only similar scene in HENRY V is the disruption of the ceremony of ambassadorial presentation, when Exeter opens the casket to reveal the famous tennis balls.[25]

Another aspect of the film's spatial strategy which gives it a sustained theatrical stamp is the reconstructed geography of the City of London. Where cinema would normally find no difficulty in coping with actual geographical distances between filming locations, the interiors for this film involved the construction of a studio set which made the Tower, the palace and Westminster directly adjacent localities. (The diagram taken from the shooting script appears on page 77.[26])

If RICHARD III is not as complex a filmic articulation as HAMLET, it is probably true to assert that its aesthetic totality is more satisfyingly accessible through its neatness of structure. This compact neatness is achieved through two means: firstly through that spatial intention which sustains ideas visually, from one shot and locality to another, and secondly through a clear reiteration of the film's overall cyclical structure in briefer moments of action.

The motifs which link shots and localities are numerous. We have already noted the repeated use of arches and of symmetry in composition. Other specific details have the same function. The wine itself, in which Clarence is drowned and which runs over the floor of his cell, is taken up with wry irony in the following shot, as Mistress Shore places the King's pitcher in its niche. The bell, which Richard sets wildly ringing as he swings grotesquely down on its rope, becomes many bells swinging at his coronation. The blood which drips from the axe after Hastings's execution finds its development as a linking motif in the dripping rag used by a woman cleaning steps, in the next shot. The shot of Richard and Buckingham leaving for Ludlow after Edward's death ends with the framing of their shadows moving across the floor, and this links through a dissolve to the next shot of shadows on the snow-covered street as riders go to fetch the young Prince Edward.

Together with the recurrent visual concentration on the crown, there is the constant intrusion, onto various surfaces, of Richard's shadow. Both the crown and the shadow, as visual motifs, tend to suffer from a certain inflexibility of develop-

ment. The crown, particularly, becomes emblematic rather than symbolic, so that
Foster Hirsch writes of it as being 'obvious and unimaginative'. Of the shadow,
'which at one point or another overtakes all the principal characters', he asserts that it
is 'equally blatant, an example, like the prologue to H AML ET, of Olivier's concern for
making the material accessible to popular audiences'.[27]

If there is a lack of subtlety and an overworking of the shadow device, there is an
aspect of it which Hirsch overlooks: its spatial fluidity which affords a distortion of
shape, giving grotesque physical form to the advance of the tyranny which it
represents. As such, it is used to some effect to magnify the figure which casts it, and
to suggest the continuation of Richard's accomplices. Just as Richard's own shadow
engulfs the space on the screen as he moves to ensnare Clarence with the words
'Clarence beware! Thou keepest me from the light. / But I will plan a pitchy day for

7. R ICHARD III (Olivier). The set for R ICHARD III (Courtesy: British Film Institute)

Abbey and throne room

Since this script was written there has been a re-conception of its form. Originally there
was to have been an annexe to the abbey with a throne in it through the south transept (see
plan), and, therefore, the original movement was from left to right. It has now been decided
the action after the actual Coronation should take place in the throne room itself. It has been
found necessary to conceive the position of the throne room adjoining the north transept.

From this, it will be seen that any action around the throne after the Coronations of
Edward IV and Richard III, will, in nearly all cases have the directions right and left
reversed.

The plan is not to scale, it will not necessarily be built as a composite set, and is subject to
alteration.

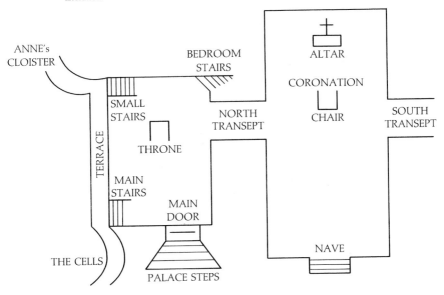

thee', so too, shadows become associated with Clarence's murderers as they enter his cell, and with Buckingham as he and Richard set off to Ludlow to ensure the dispatch to London of the young Prince Edward.[28] As they leave, the screen is filled with their two shadows stretched across the floor. Constance Brown, in her astute and penetrating critical essay on the film, disagrees with Hirsch on the effect of the shadow manipulation. She regards the shadow motif as both symbolic and metaphoric. 'The shadow is one of the most overworked cinematic devices, but Olivier's employment of it is fresh and sophisticated – symbolic and metaphorical rather than horrific . . . it swallows up the screen . . . just as Richard's tyranny will swallow up England: just as every tyrant swallows up the country he rules.'[29]

Just as these shadow effects are a refinement of those in HAMLET, so, too, this film's major structural cycle is given more pointed emphasis through reiteration within certain scenes. Singer notes four relevant scenes, the first being Richard's opening soliloquy, which begins with the opening of the doors to the throne room, and ends with the doors opening again, to reveal, both to us and to Richard, the progress of the funeral procession, with Lady Anne in mourning for her dead husband. The sequence ends with the camera moving back from Richard, through the doors of the exterior of the building. Secondly there is the brief scene in which Richard persuades King Edward of Clarence's threat to him. The moment of Richard's venomous admonition to the King is enclosed immediately before and after by a shot of the two monks who chant the missal. Thirdly, in the scene in which Elizabeth is warned that Richard will stop at nothing in his removal of obstacles to the throne, we are shown Elizabeth looking away from the camera, towards the Tower. The scene ends with the camera focused on her face from a point outside the window-frame, and we see her departure from the room, from this outside position. Finally, the summoning of Hastings to the Tower is enclosed cyclically. Stanley and a messenger arrive through an arched entrance. Hastings is roused and escorted through the same arch, to the Tower.

Thus far our discussion appears to suggest that the derivative links in RICHARD III come more evidently and consistently from HAMLET than from the earlier history film of HENRY V, and this is a fair judgement in terms of its cinematic technique. However, it is illuminating to bear in mind two aspects of RICHARD III which relate it to HENRY V. One very obvious one is the use of colour film and the pictorialism in the décor. The other is an observation, which Jorgens corroborates, that the manipulation of moments of action in the cinema frame in RICHARD III becomes a grotesque perversion of important spatial suggestions in HENRY V.

Foster Hirsch notes the relation of colour and style to HENRY V. 'The vivid colours and theatrical stylization of Roger Furse's sets, recall HENRY V. As in the earlier film, the recurrent tableau effects, the sharp colours . . . are based on *Book of Hours* illustrations; the historical drama unfolds before us like a series of pages from an illuminated Medieval manuscript.' But he then goes on to assert that the colours are out of place in relation to the nature of the drama that is being unfolded. 'There seems no particular thematic rationale for Richard to hobble through such airy, fanciful settings . . . Olivier doesn't use the pretty sets as an ironic counterpoint to Richard's dark deeds . . . the artful design of the film remains thematically neutral.'³⁰ These two observations suggest an oddly superficial stance on Hirsch's part. He seems to assess the use of colour and décor style as a purely presentational mode, and ignores the implication which the indulgence of colour makes that the monarchy is, by nature, historical, political and theatrical, and that colourful ceremony is the language of its expression. Richard himself does not constitute the wholeness of the monarchy's historical panoply. His occupation of the throne is a usurpation, and the juxtaposition of Richard's dark, twisted nature with the assumed nature of medieval kingship would seem to cry out for colour in the visual context. 'Ironic counterpoint' is surely the very effect which the colourful sets achieve.

The suggestion that Richard is a grotesque parody of Henry V is enforced on several occasions. The unexpectedly robust vitality of Richard's movement in the frame is a twisted echo of Henry's charismatic energy, his deformity making him always out of kilter with the lines of the set and the horizontals and verticals of the cinema frame. Jorgens sees the diagonal lines in the frame as being significant. Of Richard's figure, he remarks: 'His list to one side often makes him the most pronounced diagonal in the frame; the camera shows him askew in a world in which he does not belong.' He remarks upon this incongruity again in discussing the presence of Jane Shore in the court. Of the procession from Edward's coronation, he writes:

The pomp and circumstance, festive music, and carefully orchestrated symmetrical movements as the procession moves from one room to another are made silly by the coy glances of a sensuous and beautiful woman [Jane Shore, the King's mistress] who, despite the presence of the Queen, makes eye-contact with Edward and physically cuts a diagonal across the official flow as she passes through his followers.

Richard's wooing of Anne near the beginning of the film is a violent distortion of Henry's wooing of Kate at the end of HENRY V. The two elderly and sedentary monks in RICHARD III constitute a hollow echo of the vigorous monodic rendering of the Agincourt hymn sung by Henry's victorious soldiers, as they march from the battlefield under triumphant banners. These distorted visual reminiscences are thematically valid, for they reveal the changed relationship between ceremony and commitment; between physical action and spiritual context which has evolved between the reigns of Henry V and Edward IV. 'The ceremonies of Henry's world are dead – they are still decorative and colourful, but the corpse has indelicately begun to stink.'³¹

The rift which has widened between ceremonial order and real politics, marking, as it does, not only a social distance but a distance also in time, is reinforced in RICHARD III by visual comment on the symbols of ritual and their use. The use to which the sceptre is put is especially significant. After Edward's coronation, as the royal procession moves out, Edward pauses briefly to acknowledge the hovering presence of Jane Shore. Before moving on, he strokes her unobtrusively under the chin with the head of the sceptre. Later, when the sceptre is held by Richard, we see a very different employment of it, as a weapon. Seated on the throne, Richard consults Buckingham about the execution of the plot to murder the young princes. Buckingham, however, judging this to be an opportune moment, displaces that issue with a reminder to Richard that he has been promised a reward for his loyalty. Richard counters by asking 'What's o'clock?' Buckingham, finding his petition unanswered, finally answers 'Upon the stroke of ten'. Richard's shatteringly violent response 'Then let it strike!' is accompanied by his bringing down the sceptre with vicious force.[32] The sceptre's impact on the throne-arm is shot by the camera from behind the throne, and the shot captures most powerfully the nature of Richard's use of the absolute power he has at last secured for himself. 'The closeness of the camera to the throne and the suddenness of the cut contribute to a subjective impression of violence and emphasize the narrowness with which the sceptre misses smashing Buckingham's hand, which he pulls off the throne just in time.'[33] The estrangement between Richard and Buckingham is complete and irrevocable when Richard ends the discussion with his line 'Thou troublest me. I am not in the vein' and thrusts the sceptre violently into Buckingham's chest, pushing him away.[34] Both Richard and Edward abuse the sceptre, and in so doing, stress the abuse of royal power which has accrued behind the guise of ritual since the medieval harmony of the heroic kingship of Henry V. But the difference in their respective abuses of the symbol of power highlights the spectrum of corruption from lascivious privilege to violent tyranny.

If the use of the sceptre charts the change in the relationship of the monarchy to its subjects through time, and indicates the dissolution of medieval values, there is also, within the span of the film, a more obvious spatial signalling of the passage of time and the condition and control of the royal privilege. It is the visual underlining of the play's poetic references to the time of year, with outdoor glimpses which give to the action a seasonal context.

The theme of the fall and rise of the state is even underscored in good Elizabethan fashion by the changes in the seasons. The story begins with the 'glorious summer of this son of York,' moves through the deadly, sterile, yet perversely decorative winter of Richard's discontent, and ends on the parched plains of Bosworth Field, where Richmond's triumph heralds the coming of spring.[35]

Given the minimal exterior shooting in the film, up until the battle sequences, the seasonal reinforcement is not quite as strong as Jorgens would lead one to believe. There is no memorable establishing shot of the initial summer, though it is arguable that the prevalence of – and references to – Richard's shadow in the early sequences are evocative of the summer sun. There is only a short glimpse of winter snow falling on the streets of London. Certainly there is a most memorable visualization of the 'parched plains' on the battlefield of Bosworth – though only with a considerable disciplining of the imagination can they be constrained to evoke an English spring rather than a Mediterranean summer.

Both the seasonal shifts in the time-span of the film's narrative coverage and the use of colour recall Olivier's HENRY V, yet no sooner is that acknowledged than RICHARD III's more subtle spatial manipulations take us back to HAMLET. The grouping of figures in the frame at crucial moments in RICHARD III is strongly reminiscent of HAMLET. Apart from the deep-focus compositions which we have already noted, the use of encirclement is notable. The circle of soldiers who close in to kill Richard at the end of the film brings to mind the circle of guards with their spears pointing inwards towards the dying Claudius in HAMLET; just as Claudius in his final gesture holds aloft the crown, so Richard holds up in his deformed hand the sword, hilt upwards like a cross. In an important respect, both Claudius and Richard, at the centres of their respective death-circles, add a final coda to the development of their characters between their receiving the mortal stroke, and their deaths. But there emerges an important distinction in the effects of their final moments.

For Claudius it is the final convulsive and involuntary amplification of his ambition to die as king. For Richard, it is a much more complex amplification of his twisted psychological make-up. His death throes, Constance Brown argues, give physical expression to deep distortions in his personality, and the selective strategy of the cinema frame affords his movements a grotesque spatial articulation.

The convulsive twitching, which may pass for technical accuracy at first, has none of the irregularity associated with spasms. It is movement that is distinctly structured and rhythmed, a kind of grotesque ballet. In fact it is rather overtly suggestive – an orgastic consummation of a life characterized by the identification of love and violence. The fact that this time Richard is on the receiving end only intensifies the raw power of the effect, introducing an element of poetic justice and implying, as does the play, that a portion of Richard's destructive impulse is self-directed.[36]

RICHARD III is generally acclaimed as a film which is more substantially Shakespearean than either of the two earlier adaptations. There are two reasons for this critical response. The first is that by 1955 familiarity with Shakespearean film had allayed, to some extent, academic suspicion. The second is that RICHARD III is consistently sustained along lines much closer to theatrical presentation than is either HENRY V or HAMLET. The long, uninterrupted takes which allow Olivier to shape and modulate his delivery, together with his direct address to the camera, leave the viewer with a greater sense of the actor's control of the cinema frame – and therefore his control of space. It is a control only possible, perhaps, where the leading actor is also director and part-producer. If the specific filmic dimensions of RICHARD III are less immediate in their impact, their subtlety and their appropriateness remove the film unequivocally from the artistic sterility of mere photographed theatre. The primary articulation of Olivier's RICHARD III is essentially filmic.

When one views Olivier's cinematic achievement over the whole span of his three films, there emerges an interesting logic both in the choice and sequence of his adaptations. The shift in values which lies between the reigns of Henry V and Richard III, as Shakespeare conceived it, the great move from medieval feudalism, with its clear spiritual foundation and its harmony in the nature and function of the monarchy, to the Machiavellian politics of opportunism which was one of the consequences of the Renaissance, finds its encapsulation within the span of H AMLET. If the spirit of the Old King Hamlet evokes – as it arguably does – the old order with its charismatic warrior-king, and Claudius represents the new politics of opportunism, then Hamlet stands, an isolated figure of anguished doubt, between the old and new regimes, just as Olivier's H AMLET with its restless spatial strategy stands between the two history adaptations, both of which have less complex and more precisely directed spatial articulations.

5   Orson Welles's MACBETH

Shakespeare's *Macbeth* derives much of its dramatic tension from the choices and decisions made by the individual character within the framework of a medieval Christian universe. Welles's film inevitably reduces this dramatic intensity by limiting Macbeth's options, and by giving the witches a manipulative ascendancy, their power over Macbeth being visually established early in the film when they are depicted with a small crowned effigy at their feet. As a reflection of Shakespeare's play, the film fails more lamentably because of its deviation from the original dramatic perspective. Some scenes (notably the murder of Duncan, the banquet and Lady Macbeth's sleep-walking scene) are overblown and lose their impact while other important action is awkwardly compressed. There is an unsuccessful attempt to keep the Christian dimension of the drama alive through the ubiquitousness of the Holy Father (an additional character invented by Welles). There are seemingly pointless changes in the dramatic action. Macbeth is brought into the latter part of Lady Macbeth's sleep-walking scene, yet she is allowed the run off shrieking, to fall to her death despite the emphatically depicted bars on the castle windows. The ineffective nature of evil is lost when Macbeth appears personally to participate in the murder of the Macduff family. The film's dramatic power suffers, too, from a noticeable exhaustion of acting technique during those scenes which Welles films in long takes.

While all this is true, Welles's MACBETH is, in significant respects, a turning point in the development of Shakespearean cinematic adaptation. Its major effect upon the critical response to filmed Shakespeare was to confront critics with a new territory of adaptive endeavour which had to be accommodated. Many were aghast at the boldness of the assertion which Welles placed before them, and the debacle which culminated in its being withdrawn from the 1948 Venice Festival gives some indication of the strength and the nature of the feelings the film aroused, especially since its obvious contender (in whose favour it was withdrawn) was Olivier's HAMLET. Coming nearly ten years before Kurosawa's much acclaimed THRONE OF BLOOD, the significance of Welles's first Shakespearean film lies in its serving as the most 'positive . . . touchstone to discriminate the cinéaste from the Bardolator'.[1]

The film asserts for cinema an autonomous artistic claim for a valid expression and presentation of Shakespearean material in terms of a predominant spatial concept, and, in so doing, it is the starting point of that line of approach which culminates in

Kurosawa's THRONE OF BLOOD on the one hand, and in Kozintsev's two master-pieces HAMLET (1964) and KING LEAR (1971) on the other. The film's thematic integration of a specifically cinematic spatial articulation makes it unsurprising that its critical acclaim comes from French rather than English critics. Bazin in his study of Orson Welles writes of the younger generation of French critics, 'who were unstinting in their enthusiasm, and in retrospect I think they were right to prefer Welles's MACBETH, torn between heaven and hell, to Olivier's Freudian HAMLET'.[2] Claude Beylie, writing in *Etudes cinématographiques*, proclaims the film's importance:

The cinema is only then, the shadow of a shadow, printed upon the wall of a cave, the ragged garments of a clown ludicrously agitated before the light of a projector. Given this, Macbeth in the version of Orson Welles, must be considered one of the most beautiful films ever created, in that it illustrates, with maximum rigour and simplicity, this definition (in no way restrictive) of our art. I would venture to say that, at the least, we know of few films in the history of cinema which have come so close to what Shakespeare calls 'life's fitful fever'.[3]

The similarities between Welles's MACBETH and Olivier's HAMLET in fact lie closer to the surface than our immediate perception of the films, or their critical reactions, suggest. Both films were preceded by stage productions from which the films' respective interpretations were developed, yet each has a spatial strategy which is essentially cinematic. The architectural structuring of their settings is used to externalize psychological complexities, and the borderline between the conscious and subconscious worlds of the heroes is the major preoccupation of cinematic exploration. Both films exploit the stark contrasts of monochromatic film to present dramas of light and darkness.

Despite the evolution of both films from original stage productions, the evidence suggests that while Olivier had to evolve an entirely new spatial strategy for the effective transfer of theatrical ideas to film, Welles's theatrical conception of *Macbeth* was developed with the potential of cinema very much in mind. Where Olivier's film strove to present a *Hamlet* which was generally within the aesthetic expectations of its intended audience, and one whose textual cuts had to be pre-emptively excused, Welles found no cause to apologize for his approach – which he claimed was an experiment in filming a 'difficult subject' on a small budget and a short shooting schedule.[4] Nor did he advance any justification for the far more radical textual excisions which he made. Where Olivier's HAMLET was informed by the Freudian interpretation of Ernest Jones, and so based upon the interpretative concept of the Old Vic production of 1936, Welles's film grew from his own staging of *Macbeth* in Harlem in 1936 and later in 1947 at the Utah Centennial Drama Festival. Unlike Olivier, Welles had no traditional theatrical loyalties to subdue, and his staging of the play is in many ways reminiscent both of the late nineteenth-century melodrama, and of that film genre, the 'horror movie'. Richard France, in an article first published in 1974, writes of the Lafayette Theatre production of Welles's *Macbeth*,

Just as Welles was to take Herman Mankiewicz's script for CITIZEN KANE and turn it into a magic show, so too, did he transform Shakespeare into a spectacle of thrills and sudden shocks.

Audiences were drawn not so much to see the working out of Macbeth's tragic destiny, but to experience the same undefined responses which make horror movies both ridiculous and yet still exhilarating. The impression it left in the theatre was that of a world steadily being consumed by the powers of darkness.

He observes, too, the predominance of spectacle over dialogue which distinguishes Welles's theatrical concept, like the nineteenth-century melodrama, as ripe for cinematic development. 'His vision of *Macbeth* was hardly tragic. Audiences were aroused by the production, but, by stripping the text of its intellectual content, [Welles directed] their response . . . wholly to the spectacle.'[5]

In three further important respects Welles's theatrical conception of the play relates it to the melodrama and to cinema. Firstly, there is the deliberate concentration on fluid transitions which brought the stage as a space for action closer to the cinema screen. Welles's transitions were effected through both sound and lighting, and France regards both of these as staged 'dissolves'. The transition from the banquet scene (which Welles made into a coronation ball) to the world of the witches was accomplished through the fading out of sophisticated waltzes overlapping with the fading in of voodoo drums, which rose to their climax of volume only when the visual transition was complete. The visual dimension of the composite technique of the cinema dissolve was wrought 'by the use of light on the various levels of the set'.[6]

Secondly, while music is related to place, and therefore has spatial relevance, the considerable resources deployed for the generation of sound other than dialogue indicate unequivocally the relation in Welles's mind between cinema and theatre. 'There was a sizeable pit-orchestra and, backstage, a group of percussion instruments, made up in part of brass and kettle-drums, a rain box, a thunder sheet and a wind machine. This latter ensemble was not only for simulating storms, but also for accompanying some of the grander speeches.' The most significant result arising from this widespread deployment of sound resources is the actor's concession of control to the director. Virgil Thompson, the musical director for Welles's original theatre production, has commented perceptively on this. 'With all the percussion rattling, players backstage cannot hear the lines, but must depend on light cues; nor can an actor so accompanied change his reading much from one night to another.'[7] The relevance of this reduction of performance variability to the essence of cinematic presentation and control is clear, as is the implication carried by the credit line which was associated with Welles's Mercury Theatre productions: 'Production by Orson Welles'. The implication is that he not only functioned as the director, 'but as designer, dramatist and, most often, principal actor as well . . . The concepts that animated each of them [Welles's productions] originated with him and, moreover, were executed in such a way as to be subject to his absolute control.'[8]

Olivier's impulse was to delegate much more openly than Welles. On the theatre stage, Olivier has often been clearly aware of his own ability to dominate action, but he is not recorded as striving in the theatre for the total control which Welles sought and which found its fulfilment in cinema. Certainly it could not be said of Olivier, as it has been of Welles, that in his productions 'content served as little more than an obvious vehicle for . . . expressive form. Welles's real statement was contained in his violent imagery. Thus the actor became simply another facet of the imagery.'[9]

Finally there is the question of Welles's use of the space of the stage itself. In his theatre production of *Macbeth*, Welles transposed the setting from Scotland to the island of Haiti, since he felt that the force of the supernatural as a dominant and formative element would be more credible in a social context of 'voodoo'. In addition to making the stage a microcosm of a society with a genuine cultural commitment to a belief in tangible supernatural powers, Welles also brought the stage closer to the realism of cinematically depicted space at the point when Birnam Wood moves towards Dunsinane. The foliage used was tropical, and Welles arranged the effect so that the stage filled imperceptibly with jungle. At a given moment, the jungle fell to the floor, revealing a stage filled with people, and Malcolm seated on a throne.

What emerges consistently from Richard France's carefully documented record of Welles's theatre production of *Macbeth* is a staging conception of the play which is in essence primed to achieve its aesthetic culmination in cinema. Welles's impulse towards total control of every aspect of the dramatic presentation and impact results in a film which projects his own personal response to Shakespeare's play, as an orchestration of sound and spatial evocation rather than the development of character through dialogue. It is in the changed relationship between the dialogue and the visualization, and in Welles's drastic reduction of the dialogue's complexity, that his adaptive priority differs so radically from that of Olivier's HAMLET. Where Olivier visualizes for film an interpretation of Shakespeare's play, Welles visualizes his own perspective on issues that lie behind the energies of the play.

Both Welles's MACBETH and Olivier's HAMLET can be considered in terms of expressionism, if by expressionism is meant the 'shaping of the outside world from within . . . the building of a new world inside itself'.[10] Welles's expressionism is, however, much more forceful than Olivier's. Where Olivier projects an Elsinore which is a spatial expression of Hamlet's psychological complexity, Welles develops an entire cinematic style which relates MACBETH to classic expressionist cinema. His violently disjunctive editing rejects a world-view which is based on a 'chain of data'.[11]

Of the typical features of classic expressionism which are especially relevant to the MACBETH style are the isolation of the individual, the sense of endless simultaneity and disintegration, the obsession with death, and the vertiginous angularity of both the camera's shooting angles and of the line within the frame.[12] Welles's pronounced expressionist effects are consonant with the turbulence in his view of the *Macbeth* drama, and turbulence in which the character of space changes with the state of Macbeth's mind.

The opening of Welles's film employs a technique which, on first consideration, appears not dissimilar from that of the start of Olivier's HAMLET. The elements of HAMLET were shown as a collection of theatrical props, a castle wreathed in mist, and the movement of waves against a rocky shore; all suggestive of a metaphorical sophistication. With Welles's initial visuals, the film's compositional substance is introduced, but at once we are in a pre-sophisticated world of bare elements and stark juxtapositions rather than developed compositions. Where the opening of HAMLET invites an orientated if sombre contemplation, the pace of Welles's opening visuals promotes a cumulative sense of disturbance; of the flow of ideas being constantly interrupted and displaced by quick dissolves into unrelated images.

Like Olivier's HAMLET, Welles's MACBETH establishes its major poles of conflict through a spoken prologue. Unlike HAMLET, the conflict for which we are prepared is given an historical perspective. The psychological dimension is left for the film's spatial articulation to reveal. Welles's prologue runs as follows:

Our story is laid in Scotland, ancient Scotland, savage, half lost in the mist which hangs between recorded history and the time of legends. The cross itself is newly arrived here. Plotting against Christian law and order are the agents of chaos, priests of hell and magic; sorcerers and witches. Their tools are ambitious men. This is the story of such a man and of his wife. A brave soldier, he hears from witches a prophecy of future greatness and on this cue, murders his way up to a tyrant's throne, only to go down hated and in blood at the end of it all.[13]

The simple clarity of this spoken exposition is juxtaposed with a montage which evokes rather than establishes the textures of the film's spatial substance, and throughout the opening sequence of images Welles merges the technique of the cinematic dissolve with the natural revelatory and obscuring effects of the mist which swirls about the landscape. From the initial shot of cloud and mist effects in an otherwise vacant sky we move with the camera through a series of dissolves to a shot of the Celtic cross, which is obscured once again by mist and cloud. This clears to reveal the three witches standing on an eminence of rock, holding their oddly forked staves. The swirling mist engulfs them, clearing again to expose in medium close-up a bubbling surface of muddy liquid, a grotesque tree 'skeleton' and finally a shot of hands shaping from the muddy formlessness a figure of a child – a type of voodoo doll.

The juxtaposition of the mist and cloud effects with the glimpse-shots of outlines and symbols, and the final forming of a figure from the bubbling viscous liquid, taken together with the greater juxtaposition of the simple spoken prologue with the weird sequence of initial visuals, constitutes a clear suggestion that the essence of the film's thematic conflict is to be that of 'form' against 'formlessness'. In his merging of the controlled cinematic dissolve with what appears to be the natural action of the mist, Welles gives added emphasis to this polarity. It is as though the formative control in the film is more at the whim of nature than at the hands of the artist.

It is a significant achievement of the film that it sustains the tension in this polarity between form and formlessness by its suggestion of the world of the dream, with its nightmarish sequence of imagined reality without formal logic in a territory of unful-filled action, from which there is a desperate desire to escape. Joseph McBride, in his biography of Welles, has suggested that Welles's MACBETH 'evokes less a struggle of the will for dominance than the struggle of the mind for consciousness. The change in him [Macbeth] after the murder is almost indistinguishable; he seems to be sleep-walking from the beginning, and his blindness to the possibility of free choice makes it difficult for us to consider him a tragic hero.'[14]

S.S. Prawer, in his book on the 'horror movie' genre, observes that the elements of the horror film are pervasive. 'Terror . . . enters as an ingredient into many films that resist classification as "horror-movies" or "terror-films" in the narrower genre sense. It is an essential part of cinema.'[15] Olivier's HAMLET is one Shakespearean film which illustrates this with the long slow climb of Hamlet to meet the ghost of his father. There is one sustained shot just of Hamlet's feet as they move up the stone steps. Welles's MACBETH, however, holds more sustained generic affinities with the horror film and the *film noir*, partly because of the ripeness of the Macbeth plot for such treatment.

The hallmark of the *film noir* is its sense of people trapped – trapped in webs of paranoia and fear, unable to tell guilt from innocence, true identity from false. Its villains are attractive and sympathetic, masking greed, misanthropy, malevolence. Its heroes and heroines are weak, confused, susceptible to false impressions. The environment is murky and close, the setting vaguely oppressive. In the end, evil is exposed, though often just barely, and the survival of good remains troubled and ambiguous.[16]

The tendency, too, for the horror film to feature some kind of monster given form by unnatural forces in the world where time and place are accorded the dislocations of the dream, further relates Welles's spatial strategy to that genre.

The essence of the nightmare which pervades the film is evident in the a-logical and a-historical relationship of space and time. Dunsinane is, in fact, a papier-mâché agglomerate of walls, caverns and rough-hewn arches. In the context of the dream, however, its non-realism is no barrier to our acceptance of it as rudimentary, rock-hewn architecture without style or form, and therefore without period. Its labyrinthine suggestion of *psychological space* is a visualization which isolates and confines man in the torrid secrecy of his own most abhorrent ambitions. Its timelessness makes it universal. Jean Cocteau has observed most eloquently the relationship of spatial detail to time in the film, and of both spatial and temporal dislocation to the dream:

Coiffed with horns and crowns of cardboard, clad in animal skins like the first motorists, the heroes of the drama move in the corridors of a kind of dream underground, in devastated caves leaking water, in an abandoned coal-mine . . . At times we ask ourselves in what age this nightmare is taking place, and when we encounter Lady Macbeth for the first time before the camera moves back and places her, we almost see a lady in modern dress lying on a fur couch next to the telephone.[17]

Claude Beylie, too, perceives the stature which the film achieves through its temporal ambivalence:

Macbeth is a sanguinary madman, a modern Atilla who hears only his own demons and is vanquished by them; he appears then, on the screen dressed in animal skins or bound in a strange harness redolent of both the paleolithic and atomic eras – a cuirass reinforced with metal plates that look like hideous blisters, a steel helmet guarded by nightmarish electrodes, horns or antennas . . . His palace is carved into the rock itself, bored full of shapeless windows like the lair of a cyclops. We are transported with him into the very bowels of the earth, or perhaps into some other planet.[18]

Welles's refusal to locate the spatial detail of the costume and décor in space or time gives the film the power of the dream vision; shape without form, presence without rational interpretation and without relative place in the world of conscious perspective.

Olivier's HAMLET made Elsinore the psychological architecture of its hero. But it made Elsinore also a castle which could be accommodated within the conventions of dramatic expectation. Welles's MACBETH presents Dunsinane as a psychological externalization which is more complex, for it is freed from the Freudian symbolism which governs much of HAMLET's spatial deployment. In HAMLET Elsinore evokes an unequivocal presence of stone and its locations become identifiable as consistent, familiar places. In Welles's MACBETH, there are no familiar places. The spatial context for the drama has the disorienting properties of an endless elusiveness of form together with the suggestions of an unstable organism. The spatial substance, in some affinitive way, takes on the involuntary biochemistry of Macbeth. Its cavernous walls exude drops of moisture just as Macbeth's skin glistens with the torrid sweat of panic.

The film's affinity with the dream vision has a major consequence. It dissolves the moral polarities which categorize action, and in so doing it reflects the confusion of the 'fair/foul' dichotomy equated by the witches in the play's opening scene. In contrast to the suggestions of the prologue, the film's spatial articulation plunges the action into a universe which is not only a-historical but also a-moral, and as André Bazin has rightly noted, this dissolves the traditional distinction between guilt and innocence. He discerns the spatial suggestions of 'a prehistoric universe – not that of our ancestors, the Gauls or the Celts, but a prehistory of the conscience at the birth of time and sin, when sky and earth, water and fire, good and evil, still aren't distinctly separate'.[19]

The important dramatic potential arising from the cinematic presentation of such a universe resides in what it liberates through its refusal to define. In its emancipation from inherent moral judgement, action is exposed to the irrational response of instinct. There is no doubt that Welles's Macbeth finds his own action instinctively repellent and horrifying. Consequently, we are not presented with a Macbeth distanced from us because of his action, but one who remains human because of his instinctive and emotional power; a Macbeth 'who wallows in his crimes, but in whom we nevertheless sense a mysterious spark of innocence and something like the possibility of grace and salvation'.[20]

While Welles adopts the usual course of making his film a blend of interior and exterior sequences, there is an imbalance in the overall spatial strategy. The philosophical and interpretive dimensions that are brought into play by a *mise-en-*

scène which comprises papier-mâché, fur coverings, water, mists and cardboard give the film its unique stature, yet the interior sets are exploited to the very edge of their limits. While the exterior shots are effective, their relative briefness fails to give the film an aesthetic poise. As McBride observes, 'only in the foggy exteriors do we find the necessary naturalistic counterpoint . . . We are thrown back on our sense of drama as theatrical spectacle.'[21] Knowing the background to the film's production, one is tempted to see the cause of the imbalance as financial, yet it is also clear that Welles was at pains to avoid what he saw as Olivier's mistake in HENRY V, where the exterior location for the Agincourt battle was too obviously a counterpoint to the undisguised artifice and theatricality of the interiors. For Welles the spatial realism had to be a world consistent with the inner being of the character. Shakespearean characters are people for whom 'you have to make a world . . . in HENRY V for example, you see the people riding out of the castle, and suddenly they are on a golf course somewhere charging each other. You can't escape it, they have entered another world . . . What I am trying to do is to see the outside, real world through the same eyes as the inside, fabricated one. To create a kind of unity.'[22]

The landscape in Welles's film evokes a dramatic world of violent contrasts between the jagged angularity of wind-stripped trees, the spatial vacuity of the background and the formless, swirling cloud and mist which confuses clarity of outline. Up to a point, the movement of the vapour in the vacant sky asserts its own autonomous symbolic stature, suggestive of 'evolving nebulae at some primal phase of creation'.[23]

The exterior shots are clearly not time signals. Unlike the seasonal change depicted in HENRY V and RICHARD III which visualized the passing of time, the seasonal suggestion in MACBETH is static throughout the film and is an enforcement of the nature of the universe in which Macbeth is placed. Charles Higham, in his work on Welles, suggests that season in Welles's Shakespearean films is an externalization of the hero's souls. But his specific substantiation in MACBETH reduces both the meaning of Welles's symbolism and the stature of the hero's predicament. His assertion that 'rain and fog, and the dark colours of the dying year figure in MACBETH,' and that the mist evokes 'Macbeth's stormy soul, shrouded in despair', places Macbeth at the end of a process of judgement rather than at the beginning of the struggle towards the apprehension of form.[24]

The shortness of the film's duration is in part due to the substantial cutting of the dialogue, but also, and more interestingly, to Welles's use of montage which is responsible for the narrative energy and pace of the early part of the film's dramatic development. Montage here is effectively achieved through cinematic dissolves rather than abrupt cuts, so that the fusion of camera technique with the action of the mist, which we noted earlier, is sustained in the shift from image to image.

The movement of Macbeth from the encounter with the witches to his meeting with Lady Macbeth is given a compulsive energy through a means only available to film. The contents of Macbeth's letter are initially dictated by Macbeth to a scribe, and during the reading of this, the action's gathering pace is carried through three dissolves: from the momentary, static place of the dictation (a soldier's tent) to Macbeth's powerful and rapid horse-ride towards Dunsinane and finally to the shot of Lady Macbeth lying on her bed reading the letter. As Skoller suggests, the bracketing of the dynamic covering of geographical distance between two shots of static locality reflects 'in graphic energy, the power between the [unexpressed] plan to murder Duncan, and its execution'.[25] It is a means of visualizing a major theme in Shakespeare's play, the closing of the distance between idea and deed.

The function of the montage is not only to give narrative continuity a dynamic pace, but, more importantly, to achieve a level of dramatic complexity through the shifting of perspective. In the later parts of the film, the relative smoothness of the dissolved transitions is replaced by rapid cutting, especially cuts from long and medium-long shots to close-ups and the abrupt changes of camera-tilt to give vertical dimensions to perception. Both the close-up and the low-angle shooting serve the purpose of investing the character of Macbeth with cinematic stature in his self-centred isolation. McBride sees the close-ups as 'demonstrating the amoral egocentricity of the hero', and Skoller suggests that the recurrent low-angle camera framing of Macbeth is intended 'to give stature to the hero, but also to distort perspective on him . . . [and to reveal his] grossness and upwardly thrusting ambition'.[26]

The combination of low-angle shooting and montage gives to the moment of Cawdor's execution a memorable dramatic force. Lit from a source right of centre, the object of the camera's isolation is a drummer stripped to the waist, beating out a greeting for Duncan's return. In one of the few instances of camera movement, the frame closes in on the pounding drum-sticks as they strike the vellum, until the beating abruptly stops, synchronizing the final beat with the axe's fall on Cawdor's neck.

It is possible to trace the emphasis which Welles gives to the low-angle character shot through his whole canon, and to apply the often-cited theory that Welles's aim is to relate the looming force and upward thrust of the main character to the claustrophobic constraint of the ceiling's downward pressure. 'The ceilings descend to crush those they were meant to protect.'[27] Maurice Bessey, in his fascinating study of Welles the artist, suggests that the ceilings represent the imposition of the limited aspiration which society affords the individual. A distinctive feature of MACBETH is the absence in many of the low-angle shots of any roof at all, and in these shots the camera's main tendency is to relate faces to the formless, cloud-streaked, grey sky. Only in the 'Tomorrow and tomorrow and tomorrow' speech does Welles explore the visual potential of the sky with any persistence for an accompaniment of soliloquy.[28] The only scene in MACBETH in which the downward pressure of a ceiling is emphatic is the banquet scene. The action here takes place under a low-slung ceiling of animal skins, suggesting that only within the context of communal feast is there imposed upon action the constraints of custom and behavioural form. For the rest, the film stresses the openness of the vertical dimension by recurrently giving emphasis to the dense concentration of tall, slender crosses carried by the Holy Father's acolytes, and later by Macduff's army which moves in a long procession against the skyline in its march towards Dunsinane.

The vertical dimension in the film is further strengthened by high-angle shooting, sometimes to afford a wider view of action, but more importantly to assert relationships between Macbeth and other characters, and between Macbeth and his universe. A memorable instance of the combination of deep-focus and high-angle shooting is Macbeth's reception of the news that Birnam Wood has moved. With Macbeth's head and shoulder dark, huge and ominous in the right of the frame, the messenger reporting the movement of the wood is distanced and puny, and placed far below Macbeth's apparent vertical eminence. Again, Welles's spatial disposition stresses Macbeth's isolation and his inaccessibility in that isolation. He has taken refuge in his own importance. The shot is followed by another high-angle shot of Macbeth moving with uncertainty upon a strangely mottled floor-surface whose formless patches evoke the merest suggestion of a shadow-figure with arms outstretched. Macbeth, now small, distanced from the camera and alone, calls for Seyton, only to be confronted with the shadow of a man hanging from the rope of the alarm bell. Macbeth's isolation has led him ultimately into the disorientated, surreal landscape of the dream.

Only rarely does Welles move his camera in this film. Whether this is for budgetary reasons, as McBride maintains, or whether the nature of the film's derivation from the original stage production governed Welles's cinematic realization is a matter for surmise. But the theatricality of the film becomes noticeable where Welles films the action in longer, unbroken takes. One example of this is the long take during which Macduff is given the news of his family's slaughter. The décor comprises an area of open ground, with a stone cross and the trunk and branches of a leafless tree in the middle background. As the dialogue progresses, one becomes aware of that distinction between actors and scenery which relegates the scenery to the *aesthetic* background, so breaking the organic unity of actors and space which is essentially cinematic. Throughout this scene the composition remains static and the actors are held in medium-close shot. The long takes during Lady Macbeth's sleep-walking scene, too, dislodge the film from its earlier cinematic commitment so that the camera gives us a photographed theatre performance without integrating this into an overall spatial strategy.

There are moments during the film's later sequences when it becomes difficult to escape a sense that Welles's inventiveness is exhausted. The suppression of camera movement results in a spatial disorientation which seems to be a resort to sustain the film's cinematic stature. While this suspicion grows on the level of emotional response, it is nevertheless possible to argue the case for thematic validity, in one seemingly uninspired instance. When the doctor and nurse watch Lady Macbeth as she enters, in her trance-like state, the relationship of the characters is established through deep focus with the doctor and nurse in close-up on the right of the frame, and Lady Macbeth distanced, small and slightly left of centre. A little later, the camera gives us a reverse deep-focus shot with Lady Macbeth in the frame's left foreground, a flight of steps in the centre background, and the doctor and nurse in the right background. On first consideration, the deep-focus strategy here seems to achieve little other than to afford another angle on the movement which Lady Macbeth would make on the theatre stage. However, if this reversal of spatial proportion in the frame is considered as an articulation within the film's exploration of the worlds of the conscious and unconscious, then what occurs in the scene is ingenious. In purely spatial terms on the two-dimensional screen, the scene reveals a shift from a visualized situation in which the conscious mind – in the form of two minor characters – is dominant, to a spatial composition in which the unconscious overpowers the conscious world of restraint and discretion, and relegates it to the background. The spatial strategy in that sense is a microcosm of the psychological development of Lady Macbeth through the play. The doctor and nurse are left standing speechless beside the steps which lead back to the realm of the unconscious with its formless caverns and labyrinths, the world from which Lady Macbeth has just come, bringing with her the inverted relationship between instinct and reason.

Camera movement, when it does manifest itself, comes as a refreshing spatial resource. The most interesting camera movements are reserved for the final battle. Earlier in the film, the movement of the camera is used, sometimes with singular lack of technical competence, to prepare only for climactic moments. The following of the action as the murderers await and pounce upon Banquo is maladroitly handled. The tracking shot which holds Macbeth in the frame as he approaches the banquet table and the approach of the camera as Macbeth hears the witches' prophecy about the movement of Birnam Wood are more successful. In the latter shot the frame closes in on Macbeth from an overhead long shot to hold him in medium close-up, with only his upward-looking face illuminated in the midst of total darkness. In the closing moments of the film, the camera treats the approach of the army with rapid montages, affording only glimpses of Birnam Wood moving through the mist, though they are sufficient to reveal that Birnam Wood's trees are in full-leafed contrast to the gnarled, bare trees which have been part of the earlier *mise-en-scène*. With the heaving of the tree-trunks against the castle gates, the camera begins to track in on a low angle to frame the rhythmic thrusts of the battering rams, and with the rush of the incoming army the camera is at last liberated from its earlier constraint, following the action but never abandoning the dominant strategy of montage.

The battle is depicted against darkness and wind-driven violence, with the massed deployment of torch-flames to give the impression of formidable size to the invading force. Again Welles emphasizes the vertical dimension to give expanse to the scene, and to impart dominance to detail with angle-shots which glimpse the massed ranks of tall staves. Macduff's entry is shown in a most impressive silhouette which, despite the truth of Cowie's assertion that 'Welles's best effects are those that come and go before their artifice can be detected', cries out to be held longer to punctuate the hectic pace of the film's climactic sequences.[29] The penultimate sequence of the fight between Macduff and Macbeth is shot with a rapid succession of high- and low-angle glimpses against a background of light and shadow, with close-ups and medium close-ups of the characters in action. The fight ends with a swinging blow aimed to sever Macbeth's neck. The swing of the blade is interrupted by a cut to show the head of the voodoo doll rolling from its body, only then identifying the figure which the witches 'formed' from their muddy cauldron with Macbeth.

A further issue to be considered here is the relation of the camera to a narrative point of view. It was the camera movement in Olivier's HAMLET which established for the camera a clear 'persona' dimension. Welles is not concerned here to develop any such narrative identity. The insistent fragmentation of sequences into collages of shifted perspective and the spatial disjunction tend to break down any development of a consistent point of view. In this respect, the film has about it a surprising spatial ambivalence. On the one hand, the rapid succession of montaged perspectives is imposed upon the perception of the viewer, while on the other, the camera's agility affords a sense of omni-directional vision. The narrative function of Welles's camera is not limited, as Olivier's was in HAMLET, to the spatial laws of the presented work. Its revelations of quick moments of action operate upon the world of the film like flashes of lightning which create visual essence as they reveal it, and as such, the camera assumes the stature of a cosmic force. In three brief instances, however, the camera does take on a subjective identity. One such moment occurs when Macbeth is confronted by the illusory dagger. As the blade of the dagger is shown to pass across the eyes of the voodoo doll, it pulsates in and out of focus before there is a dissolve to a series of different perspectives on Macbeth, for his question, 'Is this a dagger . . .?'[30] The second is more direct when, during the banquet, Macbeth seated at one end of the long table confronts Banquo's ghost seated at the other. It is one of the rare moments in the film where Welles's camera uses a continuous movement through a spatial distance, and here he uses it to relate opposing forces preparatory to a dramatic climax. The camera focuses concentration on Macbeth's face at the mention of Banquo's absence. Macbeth delivers his lines: 'I drink to our friend Banquo, whom we miss. Would he were here', and as he lowers his arm after drinking, the shadow moves down over his features.[31] He rises unsteadily and points down the length of the table. The camera cuts to frame the dark shadow of the pointing finger on the rough wall of the chamber and then follows the movement of the shadow along the wall, to reveal for the first time the ghost of Banquo seen, as it must be, from Macbeth's point of view. Banquo's eyes stare forward and the camera, with a sudden cut, takes Banquo's point of view to study from the other end of the table Macbeth's reaction. It is a profound shot, for the camera shows Macbeth viewing the consequences of his action while he is viewed from the point of view of that consequence.

The third instance of subjective camera work recalls the technique used in Olivier's HAMLET when Hamlet first encounters the Ghost on the castle battlements. The rhythmic, pulsing shift in and out of focus is very similar to the pulsating effect

Welles uses at the point where Lady Macbeth waits for Macbeth to come down after murdering Duncan. Welles again takes the viewer into the perception of the character – an effect which Skoller suggests is 'very organic to the labyrinthine and animistic motifs that run through the film'.[32]

If the camera tends to eschew the exploration of horizontal spatial lines and concentrates its disjunctive potential in setting up a vertical consciousness of space through angle-shots, the oppositions established in this way are enriched by the opposed realms of light and darkness. Peter Cowie relates the interplay of light and darkness in MACBETH to Welles's use of light symbolism in his whole canon.

As so often in Welles's work, light is seen as a purifying element. Macbeth and his wife hatch their plans in semi-darkness (her 'Come, thick night!' is given visible form); there is an emphasis on the blackness of the branches from which Macbeth's men unsaddle the doomed Banquo. As Macbeth gasps, 'Is this a dagger which I see before me?' the images grow blurred, become suffused with gloom . . . Only at the end, with Macbeth decapitated after a fierce struggle on the battlements, does light assert its strength and honesty as hundreds of torches are brandished in the acknowledgement of Scotland's new king, Malcolm. But the off-screen lighting, so effective later in THE TRIAL, is flagrantly anachronistic in this production, with steady arcs where flickering light would be more convincing.[33]

To the charge of anachronism in the lighting effects, one might reply that a timeless universe, largely evocative of the unconscious, does not demand 'period' lighting. But Cowie's general premise that light has a symbolic value carries a more specific relevance in MACBETH than he appears to recognize. The recurrence of faces against the background of sky, or against the reflection of light from glistening and bright surfaces, results in a reiterative use of whole or partial silhouette: a suggestion that the knowledge and understanding of characters and matter is only partial. Skoller observes the implicit suggestion that the characters have 'passed over to a realm beyond light, with their dark side forward', yet this appears to make Macbeth's universe a post-lapsarian rather than a pre-formative one.[34] It is equally possible to suggest that the outlines and profiles which silhouette affords constitute the initial delineation of form, and that the film viewer is involved as a participant in the endeavour to make clear identifications, and to see more wholly the complexity of living organisms and inert matter. The inclination throughout the film to connect shadow and illusion with what is physically insubstantial but psychologically most significant is too insistent to dismiss as incidental. Macbeth's words when he is confronted with Banquo's ghost, after a concentration of shadow effects are 'Hence, horrible shadow!'[35] and it is one of the film's more subtle achievements that it explores, through a spatial juxtaposition of object and light source, the ambiguity of the shadow as form without substance.

Ironically, the combination of substance and form is most forcefully articulated in the film through a deployment of material symbols. The Celtic cross and the freakish, forked staves of the witches form a dominant semiotic dichotomy, giving an identity to the forces of order and chaos. It is also noticeable that the cross motif spawns a series of derivative configurations as the film progresses. The naked trees which recur as elements in the *mise-en-scène* have been seen as hinting at a crucifixion theme, with Macbeth's spiky crown suggesting the Crown of Thorns. Skoller takes this symbolic development further and relates the suggestion of felled trees rising to cleanse the world to the Resurrection. There are, however, grave difficulties involved in trying to integrate a logical development of Christian symbolism with the film's structure. While it is true that Welles introduces the Christian stance both in the spoken prologue and visually, there is not sufficient evidence to show that he really knew how to integrate it. Despite the inclusion of a character not part of Shakespeare's play, the Holy Father, there is no cinematically strong Christian statement in the film. Indeed the film works much better without any such statement, for the symbols are too readily evocative of a traditional philosophy of morality and they are too dynamic in their associative power. The Christian infusion in the film has an historic rather than a philosophical function. As a dramatic element it is something of a loose end, and any attempt to trace a symbolic evolution which is specifically Christian has two detrimental effects. Firstly, it shifts the interest away from Macbeth, and secondly, it bends the rugged strength of the film's imagery away from its stark, primitive impact. Spatial elements that are related within the film achieve a more positive effect. The metallic 'blisters' which festoon the upper part of Macbeth's costume sustain a connection between Macbeth and the mud-like bubbles framed in the close-up during the initial moments of the film.

Also interesting is a symbolic motif which recurs in the later part of the film, after the murder of Macduff's family. It is an inverted 'fish-bone' structure seen first as a window-barrier in Macduff's castle. It is later seen in a much more dominant form at Dunsinane, and its shadow forms a background to the final fight between Macbeth and Macduff. This increasingly pervasive metal configuration embodies features of both the 'Y' of the witches' staves, and the cross. Depicted as it is in increasing size towards the end of the film, it seems to represent the formation of Macbeth's own complexity: a being composed of the self-seeking will to power through destruction on the one hand, and of instinctive revulsion and remorse at his own inability to check the impulse and desire which motivate his action.

The failure of Welles's MACBETH to attract much favourable, or even penetrating, critical treatment lies partly in its refusal as a film to project sophisticated gloss, partly in its unorthodox approach and partly in its obvious dramatic and technical inadequacies. But the essential respect in which it baffled some of the critics who tried to approach it seriously lies in its inversion of the expected theatrical order. No Shakespearean film till then had, with such a bold sweep, communicated its thematic substance primarily through its spatial strategy. In this film the actors and the dramatic development of character are relegated to a secondary significance. In taking on the generic characteristics of the horror film and the melodrama, the film quite deliberately, according to Welles, does not arrive at tragic stature.[36] Rather, it presents the predicament of man in an equivocal universe, and it is at its best when it

8. MACBETH (Welles). The metallic 'blisters' on Macbeth's costume link him with the bubbles in the witches' cauldron visualized in the opening shots of the film. Orson Welles (Macbeth)

concentrates upon its essential preoccupation with the evolution of unsophisticated form as the basis of order, and with the privacy of self-perception in the unstructured world of the unconscious mind.

The film deals essentially with the insistence that man becomes a conscious perceiver and orderer of his place and priorities in a universe which does not necessarily present him with free choice to act. Its drama resides not so much in character as in the evolution and formation of the conscience. As an adaptation it demands the viewer's engagement in a way very different from Olivier's Shakespearean films, for the vigour and pace of Welles's montage and his refusal to identify or familiarize *place* in the film imposes upon the viewer the need to make connections.

Understandably, there are those who find the film a disappointment in its failure to achieve theatrical stature on the one hand, or to arrive at a filmic spatial realism on the other. To this latter criticism, André Bazin's enthusiastic and penetrating insight would seem to be the most articulate answer:

Those cardboard sets; those barbarous Scots, dressed in animal skins, brandishing cross-like lances of knotty wood; those strange settings trickling with water, shrouded in mists which

obscure a sky in which the existence of stars is inconceivable . . . Macbeth is at the heart of this equivocal universe, as is his dawning conscience, the very likeness of the mud, mixture of earth and water, in which the spell of the witches has mired him. Thus these sets, ugly though they may be, at least evoke Macbeth's metaphysical drama through the nature of the earthly drama whose metamorphoses they reveal.[37]

9. MACBETH (Welles). Welles's papier-mâché set takes on the characteristics of solidified mud and slime – the substance from which the *Macbeth* universe is formed. At the witches' feet stands the crowned effigy which suggests the power of the witches over Macbeth. Brainerd Duffield, Lurene Tuttle and Peggy Webber (the three witches)

6 Orson Welles's OTHELLO

Welles's OTHELLO raises basic questions about the nature of film adaptations of stage plays more incisively than his MACBETH. One reason for this is the fact that Welles's presentational concepts in the earlier film developed from his stage productions at Harlem and Utah. Another is that film's generic affinity with the 'horror film'. Thirdly, MACBETH was so much better in concept than it was in execution, that its initial impact on being screened failed to elicit much serious response either as Shakespearean or cinematic drama. Only the French critics, especially Bazin and Beylie, recognized the thematic articulation in the film's spatial strategies.

The techniques of OTHELLO are considerably more refined. The theatricality of constructed décor gives way to the realism of sea and sky, and to the architectural polarities of Venice and Mogador. For the first time in this examination of specific Shakespearean films, we are faced with a film which aims at reconciling theatrical drama with the realism of non-theatrical spatial elements. The sustained insistence with which the film achieves this reconciliation, and its integration of architectural realism not simply as a justification for cinema but as thematic statement, is the major distinction which distances Welles's OTHELLO from every other major Shakespearean film. The film gains its special adaptive stature, too, from Welles's cinematic language, which is fused with the dramatic energy of the play.

The guiding adaptive principle for OTHELLO was similar to that of MACBETH. Welles sought to base both films upon what he saw as the formative energies underlying the texts. Although Bosley Crowther's *New York Times* review of OTHELLO is unfavourable, he does engage himself with a central issue when he asserts that 'The text and even the plot of the original were incidental to the dark and delirious passions enclosed in its tormented theme' and that Welles's interest is primarily in 'the current of hate and villainy'.[1] Donald Phelps, in a much more tolerant review of the film for *Film Culture*, recognizes the same Wellesian audacity and observes of the relationship between the original text and the Welles adaptation, that Welles's commendable courage lies in his attempt 'not to make his film an accompaniment to Shakespeare's writing ... but to use to writing – what he saw fit to retain of it – as an accompaniment to the feeling of excited surprise with which Shakespeare apparently inspired him'. For Phelps, the significance of Welles's OTHELLO lies not in its success as a finished work, but in the witness it bears to Welles's refusal to 'attempt to act the good-will ambassador between Shakespeare and the film' and in the film's stature as a 'genuine adaptation'. Its genuineness, he maintains, stems from its being 'not a duplication, not a parallel, but a re-creation in cinematic terms, inspired by those emotions and images in the original to which the artist has responded'.[2]

Film historians in general credit Welles with establishing the long take and deep-focus perspective as essential expressive resources in the language of cinema. Yet, ironically, OTHELLO comprises an astounding total of some five hundred shots, of which the only long-tracking shot of Othello and Iago walking along the fortress wall is distinctly sustained. For the rest, the film is composed of brief, self-contained shots like a mosaic in time, each shot confronting the viewer with questions of relationship, the most important of which are:

1. The actor to the décor, and the spatial context to the dramatic action;
2. the camera to its composite object through angle and perspective;
3. camera movement to object movement;
4. character and dialogue to lighting contrasts;
5. objects to thematic development;
6. the individual shot to time, and to the flow of dramatic action.

The last of these gives rise to a further irony in the film, for while the spatial strategy of OTHELLO is more sophisticatedly cinematic than that of MACBETH, the actors Welles employed in the later film were more theatrically established. In MACBETH, for instance, Welles gave a sustained long take to Lady Macbeth's sleep-walking monologue, allowing a relatively unskilled actress to shape her presentation in front of the camera. The editing in OTHELLO, on the other hand, is so tight, that scenes involving experienced actors are insistently broken up into shots from different perspectives. Once again, one finds in an unfavourable review an important truth about the film. Tackling this very matter of the apparent conflict between acting and the film's idiom of expression, Eric Bentley asserts of Welles's own portrayal of Othello, that

he never acts, he is photographed – from near, from far, from above, from below, right side up, upside down, against battlements, through gratings, and the difference of angle and back-ground only emphasizes the flatness of that profile, the rigidity of those lips, the dullness of those eyes, the utter inexpressiveness and anti-theatricality of a man who, God save the mark! was born a theatrical genius.[3]

Bentley is essentially a theatre critic and he tends to denigrate the film for its failure to satisfy a specifically theatrical expectation. The truth of his perception here lies in the fact that Welles's understanding of cinematic space legitimately makes the actor part of the composition, or manipulated space, and not as in the theatre, a manipu-lator *of* space. The adaptation of *Othello* is achieved not merely by placing actors in a non-theatrical spatial context, but by treating both actors and dramatic space with the spatial resources of cinematic photography.

The language of the film is primarily the language of cinematic montage. The effects of this are, firstly, to suggest a depth rather than a flow in the action; secondly, to give the visuals a function that is not primarily narrative.

The clear consciousness of intention behind Welles's montage is revealed, as Skoller points out, in the closing shots behind the final list of credits. These last shots centre on the ship which will carry the bodies of Othello and Desdemona from the island on their ultimate journey. There is a sequential collage effect, with

1. fixed shots of the ship;
2. a shot of the fortress ramparts reflected on the water;
3. a series of angle-shots of the ship;
4. the shimmering water surface reflecting only light;
5. the rigging ladder and mast of the ship;
6. a reverse-angle shot of (5);
7. a close-up of the ship's prow in dark silhouette against the bright water surface.

There is about this a strong suggestion of cubist fragmentation, a 'resolution of the work through abstraction of its most essential presentational device'.[4] It is as though the idea must be dissected, probed and penetrated from many different angles.[5] As with the whole OTHELLO adaptation, so, with its component ideas, Welles's cinematic technique sustains an exploration in search of a dramatic centre.

While one must be circumspect in attaching too readily an artistic design – and more especially a conscious one – to a work whose images pass so fleetingly before the consciousness of perception, nevertheless, it is true to say that this film challenges the specifically narrative nature of cinema.[6] There is no doubt that Welles's intention is to move away from the conventional narrative flow to dissect dramatic action, and there is no doubt either that when Eric Bentley complains that Welles 'shows no sense of narrative, that is, of the procession of incidents, but only an interest in the incidents themselves – no, not even that, but only an interest in separate moments within the incidents' he has acutely, if inadvertently, identified the film's intention.[7] Unlike Olivier, whose objective is to make Shakespeare accessible in a narrative sweep to audiences with perhaps only the most naïve knowledge of the play, Welles addresses his OTHELLO to an audience whose familiarity with the plot, if not the text of the play, is assumed. It is therefore an adaptation at a more advanced aesthetic level, for the intention is to present visual relationships rather than to visualize narrative connections. A much greater responsibility devolves upon the viewer in forging the links which will make a coherent whole of the highly memorable visual moments in the film.

In this respect the film presents, with greater sophistication than MACBETH, a distinctly unusual relation of dramatic action on the screen – of spatial depiction – to time. Where Olivier's films integrate time and action so that one returns to the films again and again to confirm a response to movement, flow and effected transitions experienced within the duration of viewing time, one returns to Welles's OTHELLO in order to relate the detail of an encapsulated shot to connections which the mind has made since the impact of the viewing experience. Welles's film is a gallery of distinct visual memories presented in a very tight temporal structure and rhythm, but related also (because of their impact) to time outside the duration of the immediate visual encounter.

The nature of this relationship which Welles establishes between dramatic movement and time – between a flashed image and later contemplation – is in some respects the kind of relationship which Shakespeare's language accomplishes through the presentation of an artistic poetic image, which necessitating an aesthetic response, halts both the poetic and dramatic flow of the play's action. Othello's line 'Put up your bright swords or the dew shall rust them'[8] is one example of a poetic 'edifice' which momentarily freezes the action and dialogue both on the stage and also in the dynamic continuum of response. A more protracted arrest occurs in the sustained monologue which Othello speaks at Desdemona's bedside before she wakes for the last time. So frozen is the moment in time, that Desdemona becomes through the language, sculpted in 'monumental alabaster'. Even in the most rough-hewn play, *Titus Andronicus*, the speechless Lavinia is greeted by Marcus in words which fix her in the memory like the solidity of architecture:

> Alas, a crimson river of warm blood,
> Like to a bubbling fountain stirred with wind,
> Doth rise and fall between thy rosed lips
> Coming and going with thy honey breath.[9]

This is the effect of Welles's visual technique in O THELLO, and the force of Bazin's observation that 'the major achievement of Welles's adaptation . . . [is that] it is profoundly faithful to Shakespeare's dramatic poetry'[10] becomes clearest in this specific regard.

Like M ACBETH, O THELLO bears certain superficial similarities to Olivier's H AMLET. Like H AMLET, its first spoken words constitute an asynchronous prologue. However, the function of this prologue is diametrically opposite to that in H AMLET. Where Olivier's prologue was taken from the lines of the play itself and applied so as to give thematic guidance and to establish the film's narrative mode, Welles's brief prologue – spoken at a pace which precludes contemplation – is there to establish situation and character relationships in their rudimentary sense, and so to clear the way for a cinematic treatment released from its primary narrative obligation. Cowie sees this technique as basic to Welles's feeling for cinematic pace:

Welles reads aloud an introductory text telling of Othello's eminence and secret love for Desdemona. This serves a similar purpose to the newsreel in C ITIZEN K ANE, in which it places one at once in the surroundings where the drama is about to unfold. Welles in fact wastes very little time on niceties in any of his Shakespearean films.[11]

This shift away from the narrative mode is evident in the prologues of both M ACBETH and O THELLO, for what distinguishes these from Olivier's H AMLET is the relation of the visuals to the spoken words. In Olivier's film, the words are so dominant – and clearly intended as such – that they are printed on the screen as they are spoken. With the two Welles films the sequence of visuals dominates from the start.

Whereas MACBETH's initial visuals establish themselves as thematic ideas separate from the flow and action of the play, the opening visuals of OTHELLO are part of the dramatic action, for Welles opens the film with a prefiguring of its end, so making the dramatic development of the film a flash-back. The opening of Welles's OTHELLO, then, is a complete reversal of Olivier's strategy for the opening of HAMLET: for the OTHELLO visuals are taken from the substance of the film's action, while the spoken lines, making no pretence to poetic resonance, merely give narrative background. Furthermore, there is a much greater time-lapse between the opening of the film's visuals and the first spoken words of the sound-track.

The film runs for approximately eight minutes before there is any spoken accompaniment to the powerful dramatic images which explode with such pace, energy and angular variation upon the visual consciousness. To the accompaniment of wailing dissonances and heavy percussion rhythms, the shots appear on the screen with an initially deliberate disorientation. Othello's face is seen inverted on the screen as he lies on the funeral bier. The camera zooms close, and then away above the face to reveal the hands of those carrying the bier in procession. The bier begins to move forward and the context of the initial shot becomes clear so that the dissolve which follows and displaces the vertically subtended shots makes its connection. The funeral procession in long-shot silhouette moves slowly along the skyline, the insistent tilt of the horizon still denying the viewer any repose in the image. An immense, dark cross is carried by the processing monks, and this is taken up as a unifying motif some minutes later, after the sound accompaniment has changed to urgent, pulsating drum rattles and the tethered Iago is glimpsed – first from low angles and then from above – as he is dragged to a heavy iron cage. From inside the cage, the camera shoots a subjective, point-of-view shot through the eyes of Iago as he looks through the cross-shaped bars at the distant procession. After a shot of men operating a windlass and then of Iago's cage being hoisted high against the vertiginous wall of the fortress, the initial sequence of images concludes with the procession moving away and the camera moving vertically down behind the total black of the horizontal sightline to a final engulfing of the frame in darkness. (It is on this shot of an ultimate descent to subterranean darkness and oblivion that the whole film later ends. Its repetition articulates the film's major statement, of a world destroyed.) Only with the appearance on the screen of the film's title does Welles's spoken commentary begin, and the visuals which it accompanies quickly move the narrative situation through Desdemona's escape from her father's house, her marriage, the awakening of Brabantio and the shift of the play's action to the Venetian Senate. Only from this point does the dialogue assert itself as part of the intrinsic dramatic structure.

If the viewer has to accept a greater responsibility than is normally the case in cinema for making narrative connections in OTHELLO, it is not true to assume that Welles felt no obligation to his viewing public. Skoller is perceptive in observing the powerful surge of images at the start of the film, and their relation to Welles's spoken prologue:

[It is] as if the audience is being tuned in to the frequencies of graphic perception in this opening sequence, as if seniority of the eye were being promoted at the very start, before the attention of the ear and literary mind were solicited . . . The first words are a synchronous narration. Dialogue comes only after eye and ear are separately initiated.[12]

Welles himself, answering a question about his structural strategy at the start of OTHELLO, maintained that the initial depiction of climactic activity was not a device relevant only to this adaptation:

A film has got to open at a peak. It's not like theatre in this respect. A staged play can open serenely and build up to its climax. But a film must open with immediate impact, because this damned thing [the screen] is dead, so the 'riderless horse' must come in at the beginning. This is what this is [the initial prefiguring sequence of the film]; the riderless horse.[13]

While the disruption of the chronological sequence so forcibly announced at the start of the film shifts the mode from the narrative to the analytical, it is questionable whether, by virtue of the selective nature of the medium, it is possible in a dramatic adaptation to transcend entirely the narrative function of the camera. Skoller maintains that the montages in the film make the style one of 'perceptual' rather than 'conceptual' dramatic elements. This seems to suggest (as we have already noted) that the level of encounter is not simultaneously the level of understanding and that interpretation takes place after the film has been viewed. The pace and 'cascade' of images suggest a 'stream-of-consciousness' rather than a narrative mode.[14]

Nevertheless, there is a consistently identifiable intelligence behind the camera's selection and treatment of space, and once the flash-back is established, the dramatic development of the film is implicitly that of the play. Furthermore, there is an omniscience about the camera's intelligence so that in several instances the subtle foreshadowing of ultimately significant events can be detected in earlier shots. It seems safer to suggest, therefore, that in relinquishing a primary or conventional narrative function, the camera illuminates the architecture of the play and creates relationships between character, motivation, action and the world through the architectural articulation of space. This is not to say that Welles's film is a penetrating study of character psychology, however. Only Iago's character is of major psychological interest. For the rest, the film is, in Jorgens's words, 'a portrait of Othello's heroic world in disintegration'.[15] Welles's comment about the necessity of 'making a world' for Shakespeare's characters, of seeing 'the outside, real world through the same eye as the inside, fabricated one' is a more important guiding principle in this film than it was in MACBETH and it assumes a more subtle relevance in OTHELLO, for the making of Welles's *Othello* world depends upon what the camera creates from the locational options of real space.[16]

The *Othello* universe is created from a spatial strategy which visualizes G. Wilson Knight's critical analysis of the play in his famous essay, 'The *Othello* Music'.[17] Knight argues that there are two distinct and contrasting styles in the poetry of the play, and that the dramatic process is revealed in the change which overtakes Othello's language:

Iago is a different kind of being from Othello and Desdemona: he belongs to a different world. They, by their very existence, assert the positive beauty of created forms, – hence Othello's perfected style of speech, his strong human appeal, his faith in creation's values of love and war. This world of created forms, this sculptural and yet pulsating beauty, the Iago-spirit undermines, poisons, disintegrates . . . On the plane of poetic conception, in matters of technique, style, personification – there we see a spirit of negation, colourless, and undefined, attempting to make chaos of a world of stately architectural, and exquisitely coloured forms. The two styles of Othello's speech illustrate this.[18]

Just as Knight sees the reduction of Othello's language from poetic grandeur and simplicity to vicious, fragmented, a-rhythmic crudity wrought by Iago's infection of the Othello world-view, so Jorgens sees the compositional styles of Welles's film as being divided into two specific categories: the 'Othello style' whose features are simplicity, grandeur and hyperbole, and the 'Iago style' which infects the film's imagery with its 'dizzying perspectives, tortured compositions, grotesque shadows, [and] mad distortions'.[19]

The juxtaposition of the two styles is established in the initial shots of the film, as the camera frames Othello's face on the funeral bier at a contorted angle, following this with a long shot of the orderly, elegiac procession moving across the frame from left to right. These shots are abruptly cut to reveal Iago chained and dragged as he darts through the angry crowd and is forced into the small cage. The close-up shots of Iago through the cage bars and the vertiginous shots from the cage as it swings, prefigure both the grille-and-bar motif which recurs throughout the film, and the ironically elevated perspective of Iago's view of the world he infects with his acutely calculated manipulation. Just as the dark suggestion of bars and grilles breaks up the orderly composition of the frame so often in the film's visual development, so Iago, the victim of his own style, is isolated against the sheer perpendicularity of the fortress wall and visually disintegrated by the bars of his own ultimate prison.

The architectural features of Venice and Mogador not only reinforce the juxtaposition of the film's styles, but they also give a significant thematic relevance to the play's geography. In order to give the architectural statements in the film their due, it is pertinent to recall Welles's specific interest in Conrad's *The Heart of Darkness*, for which he once prepared a film script. James Naremore, in an article written in 1973, noted of MACBETH that it 'has as much in common with Conrad as with Shakespeare: the hero is fascinated by what Kurtz calls "the horror"' and he maintains that 'in the filmed version of *Macbeth*, as in the earlier script for *Heart of Darkness*, Welles is trying to show that the line between barbarous ambition and civil order is very thin'.[20] In fact these observations are not convincing, for MACBETH lacks an architecturally articulated starting point to dramatize Macbeth's movement into the darkness of the witches' prophecies, and the specifically *formative* theme in Welles's MACBETH has no relation to the Conrad impulse. The influence of Conrad on Welles is much more clearly discernible in spatial terms than in psychological ones, and the relation of architectural style to the geographical journey from Venice to Cyprus in OTHELLO reveals a far more interesting Conradian affinity. The fruitful area of overlap between Conrad's *The Heart of Darkness* and Welles's film OTHELLO is that area which explores the relationship of individual man and his moral confidence to established cultural order, and the importance of architectural style in Welles's OTHELLO lies in the recognition that architecture is the manifestation of culture.

A culture is made up, factually, of the activities of human being; it is a system of interlocking and intersecting actions, a continuous functional pattern. As such, it is, of course, intangible and invisible . . . The architect creates its image: a physically present human environment that expresses the characteristic rhythmic functional patterns which constitute a culture.[21]

The Heart of Darkness spends much of its narrative energy on the relation of architectural and non-architectural environments to the behaviour of men, and while Jorgens does not note the Conrad derivation in Welles's film, he does deal with the relation of cultural order to architecture, and of architecture to the shift within Othello from certainty to self-doubt.

The civilized order which holds Iago in check is symbolized by the rich, harmonious architecture, sculptures of heroic man, placid canals and the elaborate symmetrical altar at which Othello and Desdemona are married. Visually, people are dwarfed by an old and massive order which, if it cannot eliminate human conflict and suffering, can prevent gross injustice and provide a framework for happiness. Within this civilized order, Othello is completely in command of himself, moves and speaks to his own rhythms.[22]

To illustrate this, he refers to the narration of Othello's winning of Desdemona's love, which is filmed in sustained takes of Othello's profile, and to the initial love scene with Desdemona.

The Mogador architecture conflicts profoundly with the Venetian style. The abutment of the fortress situation against the sea suggests the strategic, defensive isolation of an island setting in which,

at the frontier of the civilized world, the restraints of Venice are lifted. Art, luxury and institutions, so evident in the galleries, rooms and squares of the canalled city, are absent. Armaments and fortress represent a cruder and in the end hopelessly inadequate way of dealing with the 'Turk' in man. Group leadership by white-haired civilians is replaced by the individual generalship of Othello . . . Glassy canals are replaced by vicious seas which pound at the battlements. And the longer we are in Cyprus, the more the involuted Iago style triumphs over the lyric, heroic Othello style.[23]

The truly Conradian influence on Welles's view of Shakespearean tragedy surfaces in the implicit suggestion that when Othello is removed and isolated from the physical and spatial manifestation of an historic cultural heritage, he is prey to ideas which dissolve every vestige of his own earlier certainties. The ordeal for Othello then becomes the ordeal of the search to discover the independent self. In Conrad's *The Heart of Darkness* the nature of that ordeal is spatially articulated by a journey up the endless 'snake' of the River Congo. In Welles's OTHELLO it is articulated by the labyrinth.

Welles maintains that his films 'are all for the most part a physical search' and claims that 'the labyrinth is the most favourable location for the search'.[24] The labyrinthine motif in OTHELLO is prefigured even before the film's action leaves Venice when, after the brief shots of the wedding in the church, Iago and Roderigo are seen walking alongside the dark lower levels of the canal system, where momentarily Othello and Desdemona glide past them in a gondola. The motif is taken up after the move to Cyprus when, after their initial skirmish, Cassio pursues Roderigo through the vaults of the fortress amid splashing water and the gathering smoke of torches carried by the disorderly throng of soldiers trying to follow and watch the action. The oppressive consciousness of the labyrinth gathers force as the later action of the film becomes increasingly enclosed. 'We move inside the labyrinthine bowels of the fortress, into vaulted halls, long staircases, sewers where the deceptively placid water mirrors endless arches, and the Turkish bath where the sweat and steam lead to a crescendo of rushing water at Roderigo's death.'[25]

With the progressive enclosure of the action, Welles deploys another source of photographic and thematic articulation within the space of the frame: the dramatic opposition of light and darkness. Skoller observes that the play of light and shadow constitutes a 'basic element of the visualization of OTHELLO', and unlike the constrained lighting range in MACBETH, Welles in using real locations for OTHELLO is able to exploit a wide spectrum of possibilities ranging from brightly lit outdoor scenes with natural shadow contrasts, to interior scenes in which action is depicted sometimes with the barest outlines etched by reflected light from mirrors and moisture.[26] There is, in fact, a progression from open, broad outdoor lighting to enclosed chiaroscuro and silhouette through the primary line of the action, from the arrival in Cyprus to the murder of Desdemona. But the overall pattern is not a simple progression, for the film opens in outdoor light, with the funeral procession shown in sunlight and then in silhouette against the sky. This is followed by Iago's being led to the cage and then hoisted with the glare of the sunlight falling upon him from varying angles as the cage swings on its chain.

Variations of outdoor sunlight open and close the film, but the initial and terminal outdoor light sequences enclose an inverse set of 'brackets' made of darkness – the initial awakening of Brabantio with the punctuation of darkness by torch-flames, and the almost total darkness of Desdemona's murder with light only etching in the outlines of Othello's face. Within these two sets of containing 'brackets' the progression from light to darkness is paralleled by the shift from exterior to interior scenes and by the consequent change from Mediterranean sunlight to controlled sources like windows, mirrors, torches and candles.

10. OTHELLO (Welles). The parting of Desdemona from her father: even at this early stage, the spatial motifs in the image foreshadow 'the net that shall enmesh them all'. Suzanne Cloutier (Desdemona) and Hilton Edwards (Brabantio)

After the heroic exaltation of Othello's arrival in Cyprus, with flying banners and sounding trumpets held aloft against the open sky with bright cloud formations, there are two later, open sky-lit shots. Yet these three shots suggest not simply a static, reminiscent light motif. There is a clear progression articulated in them, for if the arrival of Othello is a zenith of the film's bright hope, the later shot of Othello and Iago on the fortress ramparts is darkened by the juxtaposition of its open, elevated location and its free, sustained tracking movement, with the mood of its dialogue and its spatial dispositions as Iago first insinuates doubt in Othello's mind.

Iago and Othello walk along the parapet in a sustained tracking shot for eighty seconds.[27] The mood of the shot is governed spatially by a number of counterpointed and cross-cutting rhythms. The smooth horizontal movement of Iago and Othello is punctuated by the white breaking waves in the distance, by the darkness of rocks, by the dark barrels of cannons mounted along the sea wall and by the alternating blocks of shadow and strips of light thrown across the path of the two men. The variation of reflected light, the definition of objects as they enter and leave the frame and the simplicity of tonal contrast make this shot visually 'symphonic'. It is the point at which Othello relinquishes the view of the great harmony of the world he once believed in beyond doubt.

The importance of the lighting effects in this shot arises not only from the visual rhythms set up by the objects which the frame passes and by tonal contrasts. It emerges also from the spatial strategy of the tracking shot and of the shots which immediately follow in the same location. The location allows for a shot in great depth, yet for the sustained tracking Othello and Iago remain close together in medium-close shot, in the foreground. At Iago's line, 'Why then, I think Cassio's an honest man', he walks abruptly forward out of the frame and the camera stops its tracking movement to isolate Othello in the frame, standing still.[28] Iago has abandoned him at a moment calculated to leave him overbalancing on the threshold of curiosity and doubt, and Othello's next line is as much of an appeal for Iago not to distance himself as it is for him to explain what he has left unsaid.

> Nay, yet there's more in this.
> I pray thee, speak to me as to thy thinking,
> As thou dost ruminate, and give thy worst of thoughts
> The worst of words.[29]

The camera now turns away from the sea to frame a shot of the length of the path ahead, revealing in its frame Iago's distance ahead of Othello. As he continues the dialogue, Iago presses home his advantage, moving back to face Othello, coming directly towards him and then moving to the wall overlooking the sea. With the camera back, holding its earlier perspective across the path, Iago turns with the light falling obliquely so that his right side (frame left) is in light and his left side in shadow, and keeping his distance from Othello he delivers his cutting homily on the frailty of man's perception and the danger of jealousy. Othello's reactions are shot, first from a low angle with his profile against the sky, and then with his face darker and contorted with the first signs of paranoia and confusion, from a higher camera position – suggesting his submission and Iago's ascendancy over him. Iago and the wall stand between Othello and the surging waves of the sea, which are only glimpsed, as Iago speaks, through a vacant cannon-port in the wall. Welles's manipulation of the two men in space and in relation to the natural outdoor sunlight is part of the general strategy whereby Iago moves into oblique light and Othello into the trap of darkness.

The third shot in this outdoor progression is the subjective-camera shot of the sky, the inverted aspect of the fortress wall and the flying gulls, seen from Othello's point of view as he lies on the beach recovering from his fit. It is the least interrupted sky-shot in the film, with the inverted edge of the fortress wall and the long row of curious laughing faces peering down, shown upside-down at the top of the frame with the open expanse of sky *below* them. Its sunlit glare and vertical disorientation suggest an agony of confusion more grotesque than doubt resolved by action in darkness.

The darkness of the film's interior shots offers a great range of subtlety. The darkness of Othello's self-doubt is stressed by the spots of light which seem to press down upon his head as he lurks in the shadow, brooding on his paranoia. After the

arrival of Lodovico and the Venetian emissaries, and the striking of Desdemona by
Othello, the outline of Othello's face is lit merely by reflected light in an etched effect.
Often the border of the cinema frame itself is distorted from its accustomed rectangle
as pillars, windows and mirrors frame spaces of light in unusual shapes so that 'bodies
and faces [are] compressed' unnaturally.[30] The film reaches its nadir of darkness with
the strangulation of Desdemona. There is only the barest minimum of light in the
scene. It is, as Skoller suggests, a scene virtually shot in 'black-on-black', with the
merest suggestion of 'silhouetted close-ups with glinting points of light on Othello
and Desdemona'.[31] Othello, after the discovery of the murder, is framed in long shot
looking upward at the incredulous faces which stare down at him from a roof trap-
door, as though he were at the bottom of a dark well of isolation.[32]

Within the overall pattern of the film's lighting progression there is an ingenious
use of mirrors and of occasional shifts from front-lighting to silhouette. The use of
mirror reflection extends the potential for varying and distorting perspectives, for
isolating reflected light in the frame and for visually turning Othello in upon himself
in a revelation of his self-doubt. The strategic positioning of mirrors allows Welles to
move a character from front-lighting before a window across to silhouette against
reflected light, without moving the camera. He brings this effect off most successfully
when, after the failure of her plea for Cassio's reinstatement, Desdemona moves
away from Othello. The change in his view of her as he watches her go is articulated
with brilliant economy as she moves out of the light into a moment of dark silhouette.
The effect is reinforced later when Othello publicly rejects Desdemona in front of the
Venetian visitors. Desdemona comes directly up to the camera, and Othello's hand
comes from behind the camera to strike her across the face. With his bitter
denunciation of her, Desdemona moves back into the depth of the picture and stands
for a time in silhouetted profile against the bright background.

Shadow is used more effectively by Welles than by Olivier. This is partly because
composition in the Welles imagery is generally more complex, and partly because
the rapid pace of the montage does not emphasize particular shadow effects with the
same insistence as is found in Olivier's RICHARD III, for instance. Two particular
shadow effects are memorable in their effect on the frame's perspective. One is the
depiction of Desdemona's mortification at the first clear suggestion of Othello's loss
of trust in her. Instead of giving the expressive work to the actress, Welles articulates
the complexity of her confusion and her powerlessness through camera angle,
lighting angle and frame composition. Desdemona is seen in a high-angled long shot,
as a small figure dwarfed by two tall, dark-shadowed pillars which extend upwards
beyond the top of the frame. Between these dark, upward thrusts, Desdemona walks
on to a sunlit courtyard whose surface is decorated by a continuous pattern of white
semi-circles resembling a boundless network of chain. This horizontal plain of 'chain-
links' extends beyond the visibility of the frame on three sides, so that the small
dimensions of Desdemona are placed in a context of limitless space, both vertically
and horizontally. That is the visual effect of this remarkable shot with its striking

contrasts of direct line to complex pattern, of architectural expanse to the relative minuteness of the human organism, and of the merciless glare of the sun on endless surface to the huge shadowed elevations thrusting endlessly upward. (In fact, Welles has manipulated his architectural resources ingeniously, for the pillars are, in reality, the stone supports of a staircase bannister. The shot is taken in deep focus, through the supports.)

The second specifically memorable shadow effect follows immediately upon this last shot of Desdemona's isolation. As Othello moves under an arch in a tracking shot, the arch's shadow moves over his profile in a hint which prefigures the next shot of Iago's inverted shadow falling along the road as he comes towards Othello, and displacing the light from the top of the frame downward, as he confronts Othello to broach the idea of Desdemona's murder. The ingenuity, economy and natural flow of these three shots illustrate the subtlety of much of Welles's spatial strategy in OTHELLO. He is able to give to shadow an allotropic property so that at one moment its comment is fleeting and barely noticeable, while at others it assumes a heavy substantiality as it does in the great bars of shadow which fall across Othello and the bed after Desdemona's murder. Bars of shadow are, in fact, a constant reminder of the imprisonment theme which haunts the action of the film. The heavy encroachment of shadow is symbolic, in Cowie's view, suggesting that 'dreams are defeated once again by darkness in the Wellesian universe'.[33]

The effects of shadow and of shifts of light and darkness appear almost incidental in the sequence of Othello's narration to the Venetian Senate. Initially he is framed in clear profile against a light-coloured background. As he tells the story of his wooing of Desdemona, he moves confidently and smoothly in and out of shadow, against changing backgrounds. The rhythm of light and shadow seems to be subservient to Othello's movement. Only when the action moves to Cyprus does shadow begin to contain and encroach upon movement.

Finally, there is one brief sequence, the first love scene in the nuptial bed-chamber, where the subtlety of the lighting changes relates in microcosm the dramatic process of the play. Othello and Desdemona stand together, Othello in darkness and Desdemona brightly lit. Othello moves to close the window shutter and the frame dissolves to show their shadows on the bed-curtains and on the bedroom wall as they embrace. It is as though in that brief moment, both are united in an unconscious statement of the foreknowledge of the darkness of death. In the same way that Shakespeare prefigures the ending of the play in Act II with Othello's line 'If it were now to die, 'twere now to be most happy', so the lighting change in this brief scene and the shadows on the wall prepare us for the moment when, after Desdemona's murder, we are shown the great fortress tower with the bedroom window no longer the one spot of light amid the stone.

Camera movement is more evident in OTHELLO than in the earlier film, MACBETH, and it is a resource used adventurously and to great effect from quite early in the film's action. There is often a subjectivity in the camera's movement, so that in the early drinking scene, for instance, the camera pans around at waist level, suggesting the dizzying perspective of the dancers viewing their shadows on the walls, before it comes to rest and focus on Iago's signal to Roderigo to provoke Cassio. There is a surprising and effective development of this sequence, for the camera pans quickly to hold in the frame Roderigo's exit as he follows Cassio from the scene. At the end of the swivelling action, the camera actually moves along the line of Roderigo's departure so that the illusion is given of the impending action being prepared, with Roderigo 'being followed with the eyes, and then with the whole body moving forward'.[34]

The other specifically subjective movements are those which view the funeral procession from Iago's point of view in the swinging cage, and the movement of the camera as it takes on Roderigo's point of view, seeing the silver stabbing thrusts of Iago's sword as its blade moves in and out through the slatted drip-boards of the Turkish bath, to kill him. The movement of the camera also makes it partly a subjective shot of the sword's movement.

There is an effective use, too, of symmetrical camera movement to connect brief moments and so to give thematic force to montage. When Desdemona tries to plead for Othello's clemency for Cassio, she follows Othello, and her attempt to catch up with him and engage his attention is in itself a spatial articulation of her effort to reach his compassion, and of the distance between her intention and its result. The camera closes in on Desdemona's face in a rapid zoom as she follows Othello. In the next shot, the camera replicates this zooming close-in, but it is Iago's face which is its object. Not only does this reveal the connection which Iago's cunning constructs as he plans to use Desdemona's action, but it arrests the moment in the memory, encapsulating the whole sequence in a visual 'rhyming' device.

The sustained tracking shot on the fortress ramparts has already been dealt with at some length. Two further points may be made about it. Firstly, in addition to the visual rhythms already observed, the shot gains complexity and additional effect from its aural counterpoint, which sets 'the regular beat of the boots on the stone' against 'the uneven bursts of speech and silence', so that the auditory contrapuntal effect reflects and reinforces the visual ones.[35] Secondly, there is the relation of this shot to the major thematic weight of the film.

Joseph McBride proposes that the key camera movement in the film is the radial panning shot.

Several times in OTHELLO, when Othello first succumbs to the throes of jealousy and when he reels around after stabbing himself, Welles creates an hallucinatory centrifugal motion by panning rapidly around with Othello, from a very low angle, making the whole world seem to be swimming around behind his madly moving figure. These images convey an overwhelming sense of vertigo, of a world without a governing principle, and the surrender to chaos is at the centre of this film. Suicide, an act which Welles explicitly condemns in THE TRIAL, is the only course open for character as morally impotent as Othello, whose nobility is solely in the grandeur of his self-destruction.[36]

To suggest that the film's centre is one of morally impotent surrender to chaos and to self-destruction, and to base this interpretation on the recurrence of a brief camera

11. OTHELLO (Welles). The long tracking shot along the sea wall during which Iago
suggests the possibility of Desdemona's infidelity. Orson Welles (Othello) and Michéal
MacLiammóir (Iago)

movement which happens 'several times', with only two instances given, seems a
strange misunderstanding of the relationship between the part and the whole;
between structure and meaning. It can be more convincingly argued that the
interpretative key to the film lies firstly in the finale of the rapid paced sequence
which opens and closes the film, where (after the funeral procession and the
imprisonment of Iago) the camera makes its closing descent to total darkness, and

secondly – in more specific psychological terms – at the film's mid-point, the sustained tracking shot.

The long tracking shot has been considered so far in terms of its rhythmic effects and its lighting nuances. A third statement within this shot emerges from the fact that while the camera and the two men move with unchecked fluidity along the fortress wall, the camera's perspective laid out in depth remains constant. Part of the function of the camera's movement here is to give an emphasis to those spatial elements which remain constantly part of the picture, but which do not move with the camera. These compositional elements are sea, rock, sky and the assertion of man upon the natural environment in the form of architectural structure. The cannons which the frame accommodates as it passes, all point out to sea and the fortress is emphatically functional, asserting itself as the confident frontier of solidity and order before the surging sea of chaos. At this very point, as man walks, elevated and at ease, patrolling the established border, the enemy strikes from within the fortress, and the sea whose white waves roar in the distance becomes the internal dark sea of self-doubt. The spatial elements of the shot, the relationships it sets up and the metaphors it projects make it, in Jorgens's words, 'the centre-piece of the film', and in this shot lives the key to the film's thematic development, to Welles's concept of what Othello was and what he is to become.[37] The centre of the film is not a 'surrender' but a *fall* to chaos, and it is prompted not by moral impotence, but by malignant and subtle manipulation in an isolated frontier post with no manifestation of a cultural order from which Othello, the Christian convert, might derive moral confidence. The film's gradual shift to dark interiors is a spatial articulation of Othello's change from heroic simplicity to the sullen anguish of uncharted introspection.

The one spatial feature which might be expected to run against the grain of a film so editorially fragmented is the establishment and embellishment of character through movement within the frame. There is relatively little of it and what there is is given to the character in whom the greatest degree of theatrical interest is invested, Iago. One instance reveals Welles's ingenious ability to combine montage with character movement. The moment of Cassio's falling into Iago's trap is covered by three shots (cutting directly from one to another), the first of which reveals Iago and Cassio standing and drinking together. The second shows Iago walking forward to put distance between himself and Cassio, and the third shows Iago, from a different angle, backing away from the developing conviviality as if to cover his tracks. The strategy here confirms Skoller's observation that the 'recording of action is something that goes without saying; the *saying* is in the careful accretion of expressive angles and compositions' and it also establishes for Iago his distinct degree of theatricality in the film.[38] Both here and in his placing at other moments *between* the main action and the camera, the film viewer is treated like the theatre audience in a melodrama where the intention is often to make the audience aware of the villain's presence and impending action before the victim senses danger.

There is much in the film's treatment of Iago to suggest that he is the main

Wellesian interest in the play. His figure, make-up and movement assert a theatrical rather than a cinematic conception of the role, as do MacLiammóir's own observations on his work on the film.[39] Of Iago's movement, David Robinson in his review for *Sight and Sound* (1956) observes:

He glides about, constantly busy, curious, painstaking about his evil. His sinister figure is scarcely once absent from the screen. Even in the most intimate scenes between the Moor and Desdemona, a sudden movement will reveal Iago slipping from a gallery or behind a pillar . . . With his restless busyness, his drawn, unsmiling woman's mouth and its absurd pencilling of whisker, he is melodious, methodical, evil angel to Othello.[40]

Peter Cowie finds in the particular cinematic characterization and placing of Iago an affinity with other Wellesian film characters.

A terrible loneliness exists within him as it does within Arkadin and Quinlan. Welles shows him lurking at the back of the church where Othello and Desdemona are married in stealth . . . Time after time, the wind blows his hair about his face, making him look like some predatory animal; his headgear resembles a vulture's straggling hood . . . Welles shows him repeatedly in a superior position, forever gazing down on his victims from the battlements or a stairhead as if he held sway over them.[41]

There is, as we have noted, an irony in the elevated position which Welles gives so often to Iago, for the final view Iago has of the world whose collapse he has wrought, is from the cage in which he is held captive as it swings at the end of its chain. It is ironic, too, that Iago, the one character with considerable mobility in the film, is finally held by bars which inhibit all but the movement of his eyelids.

The recurrent presence of the cage at different moments is another constant reminder of Iago's presence, for it is associated indelibly with him in the opening moments of the film. Joseph McBride concentrates on this association of character and symbolic object in corroborating the theory of Welles's major interest in Iago.

The full extent of Welles's fascination with Iago is revealed at the very onset when Iago is dragged past the funeral procession of Othello and Desdemona, and thrown into a cage . . . The cage appears throughout the film – hanging outside the nuptial chamber! – and the emphasis given to it, like the emphasis on Iago at the beginning is a reflection of his control of Othello at the expense of his own life.[42]

Like Cowie, McBride substantiates his assertion by a reference to Welles's technique, noting that 'Welles usually reserves such metaphors for his hero.'[43]

Since the film articulates the relationship between man and culture through the symbolism of architectural style, it is not surprising that symbolic use is made of objects. The cage is a transitional object, for it is a reduction of architecture to its ultimate perversion, transforming the space of *domain* to the purely functional diminution of a prison. It asserts itself as one end of an architectural progression in the film, from the ornamented and artistic grandeur of Venice, to the high abutments of the Cyprus fortress, to barred enclosure. As such, it reflects a progression in the infection of Othello's world, from heroic joy in psychological response, to paranoia and finally to isolation and remorse. The cage is omnipresent. It is constantly recalled in grilles and gratings, in the dark horizontal spears which fragment, as it were, Desdemona's body and whose dark points seem to pierce her bright form as she walks behind them, and in the heavy barred shadows which fall across Othello as he sits on Desdemona's deathbed. The final agony of Othello's grasp of Desdemona's innocence is shown with Othello behind immensely tall vertical bars whose shadows extend across the floor to Emilia lying and uttering her last words, 'She lov'd thee, Moor.'[44] The disorientation of her face in the frame stresses the universal perversion which Iago has wrought. The bars that isolate and confine Othello in his dawning understanding suggest that his self-humiliation and Iago's public humiliation are counterbalanced and are as inevitably intertwined as was their initial complicity. There is a splendid irony, too, in Othello, the public man, being confined in the dark cage of shadows, silhouetted with the light behind him, while Iago, the secret man of shadows, is finally suspended with no shelter from the blazing glare of the Mediterranean sun.

The transitional nature of the cage lies in its being the final absurdity of architecture – a structure not built upon foundations but suspended at the end of a swinging chain, whose interior lighting and exterior lighting are identical – and its dual nature of being both *place* and *thing*. Its derivative motifs are all things or parts of things, and they all reflect the central idea of Iago's strategy: the trap, the snare, the mesh. 'With as little web as this will I ensnare as great a fly as Cassio',[45] he says, and

> So I will turn her virtue into pitch
> And out of her own goodness make the net
> That shall ensnare them all.[46]

There is an organic progression, too, in the derivatives of the trap motif. The grilles, gratings, bars and slats give way to barred shadows, to the rope ladders of the ship's rigging, to pieces of netting, and finally to the impenetrably close weave of the cloth fabric which is stretched over Desdemona's face to disfigure the beauty of her features into a horrifying death-mask. The cloth drawn over Desdemona's face is the final instrument used in Iago's imposition of the grotesque upon beauty, and the shot of Desdemona's features writhing beneath it becomes a graphic articulation of his ultimate cynicism.

Objects with a more obvious direct symbolic import are the bed, the handkerchief and the slowly descending ship-sails which accompany Othello's lament, 'Othello's occupation's gone.'[47] There is about their slow descent a sexual connotation, as there is about the repeated shots of cannons firing, after Othello's outraged cry, 'Cuckold me!'[48] More subtle is the removal by Iago of Othello's armour as an articulation of Othello's submission to Iago's persuasive power as he relates his suspicion of Desdemona's sexual affair with Cassio. 'The quiet, meticulous way in which Iago removes his master's armour while perjuring Cassio, [seems] thus to strip away the Moor's resistance to his cunning.'[49]

There is an interesting subtlety, too, in the dimension given to Roderigo's characterization by the small, fluffy dog which he carries about with him. As well as being a revelatory detail in Roderigo's characterization, it also takes on for a moment the stature of a commentary on him. The dog's relation to Roderigo reflects Roderigo's relation to Iago. It is almost always seen to be carried by Roderigo, just as Roderigo is 'carried' by Iago. At the point in the film's action where Roderigo turns – albeit ineffectually – on Iago with,

> My money is almost spent; I have been tonight
> Exceedingly well-cudgelled; and I think the issue
> Will be, I shall have so much experience for my pains;

it is Iago who carries the dog, and as Roderigo reaches out to take it, the dog nips his finger, thus underlining the unexpected and fatuous impotence of Roderigo's flash of recalcitrance.[50] The dog's commentary on the character of Roderigo reaches its climax in the prelude to the murder scene in the Turkish bath. Its uncertain but trusting trot along the boards in the bath-chamber prepares us for the neurotic and puerile distractions of its master as he sits drawing love-graffiti on the wall, then fails in his half-hearted attempt to kill Cassio, and finally cowers under the boards trying to solicit Iago's reassurance.

Welles's OTHELLO is a formidably dense film. The power of its articulation is not as readily accessible as is the more conventional force of Olivier's cinematic narrative, because the complexity of its images has so little time to make its immediate total impact. The editing, at times, borders upon the subliminal and André Bazin is right in regarding it as 'shattered like a mirror relentlessly struck with a hammer'. It is, in his view, 'carried to such a degree that this stylistic idiosyncrasy becomes a tiresome device'.[51]

The strength of the film lies in the successful aesthetics of its spatial strategy, for it accomplishes in a masterly way the shift from the centripetal microcosm of theatrical space to the inevitable centrifugality of cinematically 'real' space, without losing theatrical concentration or tragic resonance. In Bazin's words:

Welles has succeeded brilliantly by recreating a completely dramatic architecture, but one which is almost solely composed of natural elements taken from Venice and the castle at Mogador. Through the use of montage and unusual camera angles (which effectively prevent the mind from reassembling in space the disparate elements of the set), Welles invents an imaginary architecture adorned with all the salient features, all the predetermined as well as the unexpected beauties, that only real architecture – natural stone that has been worked by centuries of wind and sun – can possess. OTHELLO unfolds, then, in the open sky, but not in nature. These walls, these vaults and corridors echo, reflect and multiply, like so many mirrors, the eloquence of the tragedy.[52]

7   Orson Welles's CHIMES AT MIDNIGHT

CHIMES AT MIDNIGHT and Olivier's HAMLET are the two films which most successfully fuse the elements of theatre and cinema in the field of Shakespearean film. Some adaptations have more powerful moments and some are technically more polished, but these two films sustain an equipoise in their spatial strategies which makes them organic cinema, while still allowing the actor to shape delivery and to establish character. We have traced something of Olivier's move from theatre to cinema. The theatrical dimensions which surface in Welles's films, and which emerge fully in CHIMES AT MIDNIGHT, are most clearly traced if the film is seen in relation to the Welles canon, and then in relation to the two Shakespeare films that precede it.

Most critical surveys of Welles's films discern a clear division between the Welles of CITIZEN KANE with its forging of new dimensions in the language of the cinema, and the Welles whose camera sought to explore the contemplative and elegiac potentials of cinematic expression.

Clearly, there is the temptation to expect and so to seek a division between the early Welles and the late Welles: the period of vigorous brilliance and that of autumnal mellowness. Mike Prokosch, in an article on Welles published in 1971, sees TOUCH OF EVIL (1958) as marking a significant turning point which makes a neat chronological division between those films 'that analyse personality through dramatic conflict' and those that 'create atmospheres that speak for their heroes'.[1]

There is, however, substantial and convincing evidence to suggest that Welles's artistic evolution does not fit so readily into a chronological sequence, and that the film which comes closest to the organic balance and repose of CHIMES AT MIDNIGHT (1966) is THE MAGNIFICENT AMBERSONS (1942), separated from it by twenty-four years and seven films. Not only does the affinity of style and spatial manipulation strike the observer, but Welles himself saw in these two films a realization of cinematic intention which he acknowledged after the completion of CHIMES AT MIDNIGHT. 'THE MAGNIFICENT AMBERSONS and CHIMES represent more than anything else what I would like to do in films . . . what I am trying to discover now in films is not technical surprises or shocks, but a more complete unity of form and shapes.'[2] Both CHIMES AT MIDNIGHT and THE MAGNIFICENT AMBERSONS are elegiac; the former 'not intended as a lament for Falstaff, but for the death of Merrie England . . . as a conception, a myth which has been very real to the English-speaking world . . .' and the latter a lament 'not so much for the epoch as for the sense of moral values which are destroyed'.[3]

Prokosch himself, in writing of THE MAGNIFICENT AMBERSONS, recognizes in it the very qualities which come to mature fruition twenty-four years later in CHIMES AT MIDNIGHT.

Its dramatic integration is complete; its narrative and emotional progress, character development and thematic intensification mesh smoothly because Welles stages its 'action over continuous time and space . . . its characters are interrelated in sustained sequences. Their emotions develop gradually until they burst into action: . . . scenes last until they run out of energy.

He points, too, to the same theatricality which emerges in CHIMES AT MIDNIGHT and which concedes to the actor a greater degree of dramatic responsibility and control. 'By using long takes, Welles maintains an overall dramatic progress while the individual characters express and act out their motives.'[4]

Finally, James Naremore, in what is probably the most engaging study of the film, points to the affinity between Welles's view of Shakespeare's world perspective, and Welles's world perspective as it emerges in THE MAGNIFICENT AMBERSONS. He quotes Welles in conversation with André Bazin:

[Shakespeare] was very close indeed to another age, if you understand me. He was standing in the door which opened onto the modern age and his grandparents, the old people in the village, the countryside itself, still belonged to the Middle Ages, to the old Europe . . . his humanity came from his links to the Middle Ages . . . and his pessimism, his bitterness – and it's when he allows them free rein that he touches the sublime – belong to the modern world, the world which has just been created.

And he goes on to suggest that,

If the historical terms are changed, this becomes a fairly accurate description of the man who made THE MAGNIFICENT AMBERSONS – a film which draws its 'human' qualities from a nostalgia over the nineteenth-century Midwest, and its lyric pessimism from a bitterness over the modern age. Thus Shakespeare's links to 'the countryside' are very like Welles's own attachment to a vanished Wisconsin, and the bard's 'sublime' is very similar to the director's quarrel with industrialism.[5]

One other film gives substance to the suggestion that in CHIMES AT MIDNIGHT Welles found a satisfying structural and thematic expression for his profound dramatic impulses. Robin Wood maintains that Welles's film TOUCH OF EVIL is crucial in its revelation of the thematic centre of the Welles *oeuvre*. The governing dramatic development in Welles's films, he asserts, is between two men. 'One is old and corrupt, the other young and pure.' The films deal essentially with the betrayal of the older man by the younger, but the older is always 'the film's centre of emotion, and is played by Welles'.[6] The thematic affinity between TOUCH OF EVIL and CHIMES AT MIDNIGHT is very clear. Hank Quinlan is, like Falstaff, betrayed by his protégé and he dies in desolate surroundings. He has become out-dated by the world he finds himself in, and so he resorts to the misuse of police power in order to try to hold on to his position. The one person who mourns him is the lady of the brothel who, like Doll Tearsheet, stands alone and says, 'He was some kind of man.' In the

Falstaff plays, then, Welles found the centre of his Shakespearean interest: the tussle
between child and adult, between nostalgia for the past and the demand to adjust to
the coming age.

In the same way that it distinguished THE MAGNIFICENT AMBERSONS from the
cinematic muscularity of CITIZEN KANE, so this shift from explosive juxtaposed
editing towards sustained character and spatial interrelationships distinguishes
CHIMES AT MIDNIGHT from Welles's two earlier films. (Bazin, it will be remembered, diagnosed the major flaw in OTHELLO to be the editing which 'shattered [the
film] like a mirror relentlessly struck with a hammer'.)[7] Yet it is facile to suggest, as
some critics have, that the relative lack of visual energy in Welles's third Shakespearean film reflects an exhaustion of his artistic charge. The displacement of dislocating
perspectives by a more intense spatial concentration is essentially determined by the
nature of Welles's involvement with the hero figure. In the films that derive their
style from that of CITIZEN KANE, McBride maintains that 'Welles was obsessed with
the problem of construction, and solved it perfectly with a style which locked the
apparently powerful hero into an ironic vice of which he was almost totally unaware.
We could not be farther from the characters.'[8]

The alienation of the viewer from the central character, which McBride here
observes, is achieved by the interposition of Welles's complexity of expressive style.
We are aware of our emotional distance from Welles's MACBETH, and even from his
OTHELLO. One of the ironies in Welles's OTHELLO, as we noted earlier, is that the
major theatrical presence is given to Iago, and there is – partly because of a
fascination built on his theatrical character development in the film – something more
memorable and poignant in the withdrawn, haunted eyes of Iago peering through his
cage bars, than in any momentary shot of Othello or Desdemona. What has
happened in CHIMES AT MIDNIGHT is that Welles has closed the distance between
himself and his hero, and the film's style, 'though it is every bit as deliberate and
controlled as in KANE, no longer demands our attention for itself'.[9]

There are two reasons for examining in some detail Welles's intentions in
preparing to make the film CHIMES AT MIDNIGHT. One is that since the material
comes from a number of plays, the selection of central ideas and their ordering
become the responsibility of the film maker rather than the dramatist. The process of
adaptation, then, would start with forging an independent structure and perspective
in the material itself, rather than with the problems of transferring a given structure
from one medium to another. The other is that the intentions voiced by Welles afford
a rare revelation of the extent to which Welles thought as a dramatist for the theatre
and worked as a dramatist for the cinema.

Three weeks before starting the shooting work of CHIMES AT MIDNIGHT,
Welles spoke of the film and its envisaged departure from the style for which he was
known.

It will concentrate on the actors and there are going to be a lot of close-ups: in fact it will be my
close-up film. The number of sets available to me is so restricted that the film must be anti-

baroque, and must work essentially through the faces. When the camera moves away from the faces, it covers period settings and actors in costume who are only going to distract from the real thing. But the closer we keep to the faces, the more universal the story becomes.[10]

The implications of these intentions are significant in locating Welles in the evolutionary development of Shakespearean film. The desire to concentrate in close-up on faces invokes a visual idiom more appropriate for television than for cinema. As an intention, too, it pre-dates the style of much of Peter Brook's KING LEAR (1971) and, more emphatically, that of Peter Hall's A MIDSUMMER NIGHT'S DREAM (1969). Welles's wish to diminish the effect of a particular historical period on the location of action finds its most consciously sought culmination in the work of Kozintsev. The expression of these intentions, linking the thinking of Welles with that of Russian and English film makers whose work is widely divergent, gives Welles a position of central importance in the field of Shakespearean adaptation for the visual media.

More elusive and more interesting is the assertion that spatial detail will diminish the impact of 'the real thing'. It is an odd turn of phrase when one considers that cinema articulates so clearly in terms of 'real things'. What did Welles conceive to be 'the real thing'? It is nowhere made specific, but an interesting conclusion can be drawn from a further statement by Welles: 'FALSTAFF owes it to itself to be relatively undistinguished on the visual plane because it is above all a very real human story, very comprehensible, and very adaptable to modern tragedy. And nothing should interpose itself between this story and the dialogue. The visual elements of the film ought to remain a backdrop, something secondary.'[11]

The major interest in this statement lies in the extent to which it is uncharacteristic of Welles. The massive Welles presence has abdicated in favour of the character, situation and 'very real human story' of Falstaff. The proposed work of presentation has, as it were, assumed its full stature. 'The real thing' would seem to be an amalgam of three elements: a concept of modern tragedy, the presentation of it essentially through narrative and dialogue, and a readiness to bend the medium, if not emasculate its natural and proper priority – the visualization of abstractions through concrete spatial substance – to the requirements of artistic concept.

It would seem that Welles has come full circle. Where in MACBETH he stretched theatrical techniques in the direction of cinema, and where in OTHELLO he gave, through architecture, a theatrical resonance to what remains essentially cinematic, here in the concept of CHIMES AT MIDNIGHT he seems to have intended 'the visual elements' merely to 'remain a backdrop, something secondary', thus disrupting the organic reciprocity between actor and décor, and deflecting cinema back towards theatre.

It is ironic that Welles, in moving away from the entity and form of a complete Shakespeare play structured and written for the theatre, should have considered defusing the dynamics of the filmic image and shifting his spatial strategy towards theatre – and yet not been satisfied that theatre itself afforded a complete articulation of the material. (CHIMES AT MIDNIGHT evolved from Welles's stage production of *Five Kings* staged in Belfast in 1960.) Ironic, too, is Welles's association of the Falstaff story with 'modern tragedy' – unlike Shakespeare's plays, which he considered to be melodramas rather than tragedies – and his intimation that the presentation of a 'modern tragedy' was not compatible with the technical and spatial resources of cinema. On this latter point, however, Welles's view has an alluring consistency with that of Nicholas Vardac who argues convincingly that the link between theatre and cinema was not forged out of the most highly developed theatrical forms, but out of the theatrical melodrama of the late nineteenth century. Indeed, the evolution of Welles's production of *Macbeth* from the stage to the screen is a microcosm of the whole movement which Vardac charts.

Welles's intentions, voiced with such obvious seriousness before the shooting of the film, were not carried through. Though very different in style, CHIMES AT MIDNIGHT is as cinematic in essence and total impact as MACBETH and OTHELLO. The expressed intentions are significant in their revealing the extent to which the spatial articulations in CHIMES AT MIDNIGHT emerge – as they do with such telling force – from the encounter between the artist and his material during the process of artistic execution. CHIMES AT MIDNIGHT gains immensely over Welles's earlier Shakespearean films through the muted subtlety of the relationship of character to spatial context. The directorial consciousness which is so difficult to evade in the earlier films – making itself felt in the jagged shifts of perspective in MACBETH and the great bravura juxtapositions in OTHELLO – is nowhere obtrusive in CHIMES AT MIDNIGHT.

In relating Welles's intentions to his execution, Pierre Billard in his 1965 review of the film succinctly observes: 'That was before. During the course of shooting, the sleeping cinéaste in Welles was awakened.' With specific regard to Welles's intention to relegate spatial detail to 'a backdrop', Maurice Bessy confirms the organic importance and cinematic stature which Wells ultimately accords it: 'He makes this "backdrop" a complex correspondence between things and people, between shadows and light, and from which a Middle Ages emerges that is immense, turbulent, baroque, and bawdy, ready to burst its heart on the battlefield.'[13]

Inevitably, a character with the distinct physical dimensions of Falstaff must find a fully developed cinematic expression in an organic relationship with things and with characterized space. Inevitably, too, the nature of the spatial context which Falstaff calls into being will generally suggest an historical location. Welles's fear that spatial detail would fix the action in historical period and so deprive the drama of its universality is offset, partly by the development he allows in intercharacter relationships in long takes, but mainly by the dynamic way in which the spatial elements and textures are made to work in the film.

The relationship of spatial context to character is as dynamic in CHIMES AT MIDNIGHT as it is in MACBETH and OTHELLO, but there is in CHIMES an important distinction. In the two earlier films, the respective heroes are increasingly confined within architectural structures which close in and isolate them. The particular domains which had become integrated with the characters of the heroes triumphed over them. The castle and the fortress, once controlled respectively by Macbeth and Othello, became their prisons and, in a sense, their tombs. For these two earlier films, Prokosch is justified in observing that 'Welles puts his characters into single unified space . . . which contains their conflicts. When his heroes die, this space is left as the only permanent reality.'[14] If this is less true of OTHELLO than of MACBETH, that is because the spatial elements of the OTHELLO composition are more diverse; nevertheless, it is true enough of the film's conclusion. In CHIMES AT MIDNIGHT, too, there is a process whereby architectural space profoundly affects, it if does not govern, the individual human spirit, and there is an ultimate sense – though it is both more subtle and more complex in this film – in which space vanquishes the hero. But what gives CHIMES its distinction is its early establishment of clearly separate interior worlds, two of which assert themselves in a parallel development throughout the film. In this film there is a clearly defined sense in which characters have their own architectural and social ecologies. For the King it is Windsor and the formality of the court: for Falstaff it is the Tavern. The film expressly refuses to unify space. Indeed, the moment of the hero's destruction is wrought precisely by his own mistaken attempt to unify space. Falstaff's cry to Hal, 'God save thee, my sweet boy! . . . My King! My Jove! I speak to thee, my heart!' and his momentary disruption of the ceremonial procession constitutes a proclamation of the values of the Tavern in the precincts of the Abbey.[15]

It is the parental roles of both Henry IV and Falstaff that Welles stresses in the film. Ann Birstein's observation that Welles's Falstaff 'is no boon companion, but the boy's father, a truer one in many ways than Gielgud's chilling, dispassionate, though noble king', is right not only in discerning the conception of the character but also in its grasp of the way Henry and Falstaff relate to the film's décor.[16] The two fathers pull Hal in opposite directions. The separate worlds in which each of the fathers is most wholly himself are irreconcilable, impregnated as they are in tone, structure and substance with the personalities and world-views of their respective incumbents. As respective projections of Falstaff and Henry, the Tavern with its beams and Windsor with its high, cathedral-like walls work for the characters they project. Hal's first hint that he will ultimately reject Falstaff is as out of place in the Tavern as Falstaff's misjudged final cry to Hal is in the high-walled environment of his late father. When in the play-within-the-play acted out in the Tavern, Falstaff protests, 'Banish plump Jack, and banish all the world!' Hal's reply, 'I do. I will' disrupts joyous theatricality in the same way that Falstaff later disrupts state solemnity.[17] What saves the Tavern moment from moving beyond poignancy into melancholy as Hal, hands at his sides, palms turned back, confronts Falstaff in silence, is the arrival of the Sheriff seeking Falstaff for his complicity in the Gadshill robbery.

Welles's major achievement in CHIMES AT MIDNIGHT is his balance of the power of character with the power of place. To appreciate the dynamics of his spatial correspondences, it is helpful to examine in detail the separate locations he chose.

The hall in which the king sits has the architectural style of a cathedral. Indeed Charles Higham in his study of Welles's films notes the irony of this: 'Henry IV, whose relationship with the church was never easy, would have been astonished to find himself, incarnated by John Gielgud, holding court in the resplendent Catholic apse of Cordova.'[18] The setting is given depth and vertical emphasis by the great slanting beams of light which come from the high, unseen windows beyond the upper-right limits of the frame. There are steps which the supporters of Mortimer have to climb to approach Henry in the opening scene. The action is given a sepulchral tone by the high pillars and arches, which are prominent in the frame and which effectively dwarf the Percys, in their assertion of the King's remote majesty. There are no doors, yet the great sense of space and the deployment of characters at different levels place the King in elevated and cold isolation even when he is surrounded in his court. The humiliation of the Percys is given added effect by tilted camera angles which give the King his authority, and which make so understandable Hotspur's outburst of resentment when the Percys leave the palace.

The expansive, uncluttered spaces allow the King a slow, majestic fluidity of movement, the upward angle of the camera sustaining Henry's stature in the frame. The sense of high, open, vertical space above the King affords these shots uninterrupted power, for there is no ceiling to suggest that the King is in any way 'contained' or diminished by the world, with which Welles so often oppresses the individual's power. The King's presence is essentially one of cold immobility. He is either sitting in state, or he is walking forward with clearly controlled strides as the camera tracks away before him holding his head and shoulders in an up-tilted shot. The most pronounced movement the King makes within the frame is to move away from the camera and recede rapidly into a long shot as he leaves one room and enters another. It is as though he deliberately disregards the camera set-up, so imposing on the viewer the chill brusqueness which characterizes his attitude to all who try to approach him closely. Only in the latter part of the film, after the Battle of Shrewsbury, is there a tendency to study the King's face in close-up shots – most noticeably in the sustained soliloquy on sleep.

There is nothing to mitigate the echoing detachment of stone in the King's palace. It stands in its cold austerity for the concept of medieval kingship which Henry Bolingbroke embodies: sobriety, remoteness, lofty inscrutability, clear-minded decisiveness. Only one part of the palace has its wall softened by a curtain, the King's bed-chamber, the curtain even there decorated only with a heraldic motif. The chill stone verticals, the open, unfurnished floor spaces, the tendency towards an almost ascetic frugality, make the palace also a spatial articulation of Henry's penance for his own guilt at having seized the crown from Richard II. The man and his dwelling are one, and Hal is as much affected by the palace and its pressures, as by the expectations and disappointments of his father.'When King Henry receives his son Hal, he stands well in the background, gaining his majesty from the high walls around him. Motionless, he lets the freezing rigidity of the setting work on Hal until it breaks him down.'[19] Yet the stone perpendicularity of the King's palace functions as something more dynamic than mere setting for Welles. The interior spaces and the attendant pillars 'are actors themselves, not merely settings'.[20]

The construction of the Tavern is dominated by wood. The camera moves about the interior, always capturing in its frame the heavy timbers which support the roof structure, the wooden slats and rough-hewn logged walls, and the rough, ladder-like staircase which connects the upper and ground storeys. The staircase is used to sustain the consciousness of wood by intervening between the camera and the characters, or asserting itself in direct background, or being caught in the low-angle shots behind the heads of the characters. The furniture in the Tavern, too, is very much part of the important space within it. There are wooden tables and chairs, so that for the 'play extempore' the massive chair is lifted on to the long table and Falstaff is, in turn, hoisted into the chair. This is a fine parody both of the assistance which Bolingbroke secured from the Percys when he first displaced Richard II, and of the lofty elevated isolation in which King Henry sits at Windsor, when the Percys first approach to sue for Mortimer's ransom. One of the first shots in the Tavern shows Hal moving out from among the great tubby roundness of the wine-casks — their shape and recumbence anticipating Falstaff himself.

James Naremore does not find in the Tavern a sufficiently warm ambience to pose a really effective opposite world to Henry's palace.

The Boar's Head is a vast, oak-beamed, bawdy house, lined with narrow corridors and occasionally filled with revellers. The stench of old beer seems to hang in the air, and Welles has done nothing to give the place the artificial charm of 'merrie England'. It is a bare, rough, excremental atmosphere filled with pansexual displays of affection, where in the latter parts of the film, imagery of disease and death predominates.[21]

Yet there is comfort and softness in the Tavern. There are cushions — Falstaff initially chooses one for his 'crown' — and there is genuine warmth in the laughter of the women as they watch the impromptu play. There are beds in the Tavern, too. Falstaff sleeps in them; others lie in them. The presence in the Tavern of women is an important respect in which this world differs from the court of Henry IV and the 'exclusive male world of camaraderie, politics and power'. Mistress Quickly, simply because she runs the hostelry, stands just upon the threshold of being a mother-figure. Doll Tearsheet is both a lover and, at moments, a sister in her concern for Falstaff. But the Tavern by its very nature cannot afford a female role which is at once powerful and loving. Femininity finds its most complete expression within the character of Falstaff himself. 'In a sense . . . Falstaff acts both as a substitute father and as a displaced mother, being associated throughout with softness, earthy affection, and nourishment . . . He is the figure who stands for the child's need of love, intimacy, and human contact.'[22]

The establishing sequence of the Tavern interior ends with an early foreshadowing of the parting between Hal and Falstaff, and more subtly, of the film's conclusion. Hal moves through the Tavern door, closely followed by Falstaff. There is a cut to a shot of Hal from outside the Tavern door, as he pauses there by the trunk of a substantial tree with a sprig of ivy leaves in the foreground. There, with Falstaff in close background, Hal delivers his calculating soliloquy, 'I know you all, and will awhile uphold / The unyoked humour of your idleness'.[23] The speech is essentially presented as a soliloquy, but the words are said in Falstaff's hearing, so that he is visibly affected by them. He is left standing, dressed in his nightshirt, as Hal moves away from him, across barren, flat open ground towards the great stone walls of the distant castle. The camera holds in its frame the receding of Hal into the distance in extreme long shot, for it is Hal moving away from the world of wood, warmth and mirthful companionship, to the world of kingship, isolation, duty: the world of stone.

If the house of stone – the King's palace – is the house of Hal's one father, the Tavern is the house of his other father, with added undertones of femininity within it. Yet Falstaff does not relate to his home space in the same way that Henry does to his. The King is isolated and controlled and his spontaneity is deadened by the public figure he has to be. He controls the relationships within the palace as he does the distance between himself and any other man. Unlike the King, Falstaff cannot control the relationships and the space around him. His prominence in the Tavern arises more from his own desire for it.

Falstaff in the inn . . . is constantly moving, shouting, cajoling, approaching Hal. Only a guest, he cannot let the Tavern work for him; it contains too many others independent of his will. For money and favour – but even more for self-expression as a way of free survival – he keeps waddling into the foreground, bullying himself into prominence, but never dictating the subservience of the others.[24]

Yet the Tavern, like the King's palace, is more than merely a setting. The wood of the Tavern's interior does articulate in its substance, its texture and its association with warmth, an affinity with the seasoned yet supple spirit of Falstaff. The interaction throughout the film of wood and stone as seminal spatial elements sustains the central conflict between the waning world of organic spontaneity on the one hand, and the emerging world which is to be rational, detached, opportunistic and essentially inorganic, on the other.

Welles achieves a superb effect in his spatial strategy by making the house of Justice Shallow, in the substance of its structure, the meeting point of wood and stone. Kozintsev has written of Shallow as Shakespeare's 'man in the street':

No matter what happens in the world, he senses the passing of time only by the changes in the price of livestock . . .' To be or not to be' interests some; others only care how much bulls bring now at Stamford fair . . . Shallow is not only an insignificant man, he is the Great Insignificance. This figure embodies all the inanity of existence of a man who lacks the gifts of thought, desire, action, pleasure and pain.[25]

While this is certainly not convincing as a total assessment of the character of Justice Shallow in Shakespeare's play, it is the direction in which Welles's film pushes him. Shallow's fondness for reminiscence suggests that, in his way, he has like Falstaff tasted the sweetness of the lost Paradise. Welles's omission from the film of Shallow's orchard – an important garden setting in Shakespeare's play – makes Falstaff's friendship with Shallow less readily comprehensible, and it reduces Shallow to a state official (whence he gets his title 'Justice', and his authority to conduct the conscription formalities for Falstaff's army) with only the vaguest nostalgic reminiscence of 'the mad days that I have seen'.[26] The confused conflict between Shallow's nostalgia for the former world of largesse, and his function in imposing uncomprehended control over the lives of the lowly conscripts, is articulated in the construction of his house.

It is a house in which the wood supports for the roof splay out like the unruly branches of a tree. Unlike the clear-cut wooden structure of the Tavern, Shallow's house seems to be supported by a confused network of wooden struts. The walls of his house are clearly shown to be stone, but, unlike the orderly, cold stone of the King's palace, Shallow's house is built of stones which have not been specially shaped and which give the impression that, like Shallow's mind, they are in a state of disintegration. Like the King's great hall of state, Shallow's house is noticeably lacking in furniture. In the most sustained shots of the interior the floor is bare and in the empty moments when time seems suspended before the news of King Henry's death, Falstaff moves the only chair into the depth of the frame, placing it under the great tangle of wooden roof supports, and sits in it in relative obscurity, his diminution in size stressed by the wide-angled lens of the camera. It is an abdication from his normal prominence, and the foreground of the frame is left to the intoxicated collapse of Shallow during his absurd dance with Silence. Only in the scene where the conscripts are mustered is there a deployment of furniture. Yet it is not the furniture of comfort. It is the furniture of formality. Shallow and Silence sit at desks while the unfortunate conscripts rise from a row of seats and stand before them.

Like the architectural progression in Welles's OTHELLO, there is a progression of ceremony in CHIMES AT MIDNIGHT, where groups of individuals have to stand before a figure of authority. The film's narrative opened with the Percys presenting their suit to Henry for the ransoming of Mortimer, in the King's hall of state. The opposite extreme of this serious formality is projected in the 'play extempore' in the Tavern. It is fitting that the ceremony of conscription, with its uneasy mixture of the comic and the life-and-death serious, should take place in Justice Shallow's house with its structural amalgam of wood and stone. The most important dramatic movement in the film takes its starting point from the melancholy inanity of Shallow's inebriated hospitality at Falstaff's last visit to him. The dejected mood of the scene is accentuated by the unusual set-up of the camera. It is placed low, so that the frame suggests the proscenium frame of the theatre stage, and there it remains so that all movement comes to a stop until Pistol arrives with the news of King Henry's death. The message takes a little time to sink through the gloom of the moment, but as Falstaff realizes the truth of it, he comes forward from the melancholy distance at which he has been sitting and approaches the camera until he looms and towers, immensely huge, above it. The extreme upward tilt of the shot captures, too, the woodwork of the rafters above Falstaff. For the last time, Falstaff and the organic

12. CHIMES AT MIDNIGHT (Welles). The palace at Windsor: stone as Henry's affinitive element

substance of his world are glimpsed together. 'Is the old king DEAD?' repeats Falstaff as he grasps the significance of the news. The melancholy is gone. Falstaff is galvanized into action 'In one temporally unified shot, Falstaff has moved from dejection to joy, his steady progress forward in the frame marking his lifted emotion, the wide-angle lens making him seem a dot at the beginning and colossus at the end.'[27]

As Falstaff sweeps all before him in his great confident eagerness to mount his horse and ride to Westminster, he moves past a section of brightly lit wall. Given the film's elemental associations, it would seem legitimate to suggest that the brief shot of the wall surface comes as subtle warning that Falstaff will find Hal committed to the cold, stone-like duties of being a king. In a flash, it foreshadows the finality of the rejection which Falstaff will meet in his demand for affection and recognition from Hal when he disrupts the solemnity of the coronation procession as it moves between protective ranks of guards with tall spears, who in turn are 'contained' within high monastic walls of stone.

Falstaff is isolated, silenced and finally broken in the world of stone. He kneels

13. CHIMES AT MIDNIGHT (Welles). The Tavern: wood as Falstaff's affinitive element. Orson Welles (Falstaff) and Jeanne Moreau (Doll Tearsheet)

while Hal, his back still turned to Falstaff, utters the terrible words of rejection. Only with the words 'How ill white hairs become a fool and jester', does Hal half turn to Falstaff.[28] The camera shoots Hal in medium close-up, framing his head and shoulders from a low angle as it had once so emphatically done in the shots of King Henry, so stressing the difference in levels between the new King and Falstaff. The facial expression of Falstaff makes his silence most eloquent. As the deep pain of rejection cuts into him, all the lines of his face sag. Finally he accepts the inevitable estrangement with what is in part a smile and in part an expression of understanding that the priorities of the world in which he now finds himself are irredeemably incompatible with his own. His acceptance and his humanity are given an unexpected poignant dignity by the camera as it finally frames Falstaff's face from a low angle, according him in the silence the same stature as the King.

The last shots of Falstaff reveal a heavy old man casting an immense and lonely shadow across the stone which is now everywhere about him. Shallow's voice pipes out from the shadows, pressing Falstaff to pay him his thousand pounds. The warming fire that at the start of the film had burned in Shallow's grate, by which he and Falstaff had found respite from the bitter cold snow, has long since lost its flame. Coldness, darkness and isolation close in upon Falstaff as he hobbles off through the dark stone archway. 'I shall be sent for soon' is his last line in the film.[29]

In the same way that Mistress Quickly's threnody about Falstaff with its reprise of 'cold as any stone' gives to the film's world of stone its bitter epitaph, so, too, the great cumbersome coffin which is wheeled out of the tavern and which contains the body of Falstaff constitutes the culminating union of Falstaff with his affinitive spatial element in the film.[30]

Like the other interior settings, the interior of Warkworth Castle is both a projection of its occupant and an integrated component within the film's whole spatial strategy. It establishes elements of composition which later achieve an organic correspondence with the character of Hotspur. Unlike the interiors of Henry's palace and the tavern, however, which concentrate on associating the King and Falstaff with major single affinitive elements, the interior of Warkworth sets up an arresting incongruity in its dissonance of military and domestic assertions.

Hotspur, still smouldering from his humiliating encounter with the King at Windsor, emerges from an absurdly small bath tub. He holds a letter in one hand and tries maladroitly to keep a towel about his body with the other. His imminent nakedness is in superbly humorous contrast with the huge suits of armour which stand against the wall. His ireful vocal swagger has a laughably childish ring to it as he steps out of the tub and walks away from the camera, shouting warlike imprecations which reach their height as the towel falls about his ankles to reveal his bare buttocks.

The shots of Hotspur in his bath-tub are punctuated by exterior low-angle shots of trumpeters who swing their trumpets in varying directions against the sky as they sound fanfares out from the topmost towers of Warkworth. The abrupt oscillations from interior to exterior shots heighten the sense of incongruity, and Charles Higham observes that 'the intercut shots of fanfaring heralds effectively presage and summarize Hotspur's warrior ambitions against the King, ironically contrasting with his farcical lack of impressiveness as he steps clumsily from his bath, the pomp of wished-for office illustrating the extent of human folly'.[31] There is a flashy flamboyance about the Hotspur shots. His farewell to Kate follows quickly upon the bath-tub sequence. The process of parting takes them both outside to the flight of stone steps upon which Hotspur, in his haste, stumbles and falls so that the last farewell kisses are given by Kate who lies on the steps vainly attempting love-play with him.

This brief, hectic Warkworth sequence is thematically integrated in the film. Firstly, it reiterates in the parting of Hotspur from Kate the recurrent 'farewell' motif which runs so poignantly through the film, and gives it an added dimension by implying that an obsession with military heroism results in a displacement of eroticism. Ungratified sexuality is a sub-stratum which lies beneath all the relationships in the film. It surfaces in the casual promiscuity of Doll Tearsheet, in the cold, repressed masculinity of the King's court, in the innuendos of homosexuality between Poins and Hal and in the absence of any clearly identified mother-figure.

Hotspur's brusque refusal to delay his departure from Kate is the most blatant projection of this thematic undercurrent, and it finds a purely spatial development sometime later, near the end of the battle.

In one shot . . . we see the legs of two men writhing in slime, the figure on the bottom jerking spasmodically as if in parody of sexual climax . . . Early in the film, Welles has suggested that a passion for military derring-do is a displacement of sex (the dialogue between Hotspur and Kate is intercut with buglers blowing pompous calls to arms), but here the underlying eroticism of the chivalric code ('Yet once ere night / I will embrace him with a soldier's arm / That he shall shrink under my courtesy') is exposed in all its cruel perversity.[32]

Secondly, while the interior spatial contradictions of Warkworth do parallel the simpler contradictions of Justice Shallow's house interior, the nature of the cluttered detail which surrounds Hotspur and his movement within that context place him as the very antithesis of Shallow. Where Shallow's life has become a senile confusion of rambling reminiscences interrupted by incompetent function, Hotspur's is a confusion of domestic inadequacy interrupted by the romantic impulse toward heroic action.

The action at Warkworth is further integrated through its combination of interior development with exterior conclusion. Both the initial Tavern scene and the Warkworth scene generate their action inside and carry it outside to conclude it with a parting. Where Hal leaves Falstaff and walks slowly away over open ground, Hotspur rides off in a flurry of hectic enthusiasm. The movement from interior setting to exterior location is repeated and insistent during the first half of the film, as momentum gathers for the decisive meeting on the field of Shrewsbury, and the Warkworth scene with its intercut shots of high-positioned trumpeters gives a powerful thrust to this cumulative process. In the heavy predominance of metal in its compositions, this scene with its trumpets and its dark, brooding suits of armour points ominously towards the Battle of Shrewsbury, and simultaneously highlights the emotional immaturity of Hotspur in his ill-judged eagerness for the glory of war. When at his death he says to Hal, 'O Harry, thou hast robb'd me of my youth', the earlier composite image of the naked Hotspur in his bath amid massive suits of armour achieves its full relevance.[33]

The trumpets, too, as they proclaim with airy blasts the challenge of Hotspur to the sky, develop an associative relevance at the beginning of the battle. In addition to the auditory reminder of the trumpet calls on the battlefield, there is subtle manipulation of the frame's space in the shots of Hotspur and the Percys immediately before the battle. As they prime themselves for the fight, they are filmed from an extreme low angle, the camera being placed virtually on the ground so that they loom over the frame with only the sky as background. The shooting angle cuts their feet out of the frame, so that they 'appear to be standing on air', recalling the earlier trumpets 'echoing Hotspur's flatulent bravado'.[34]

When it was put to him that the landscape in CHIMES AT MIDNIGHT did not convey the conviction of real space, Welles replied:

But it musn't seem *perfectly* real . . . One of the enemies of the film is of course the simple, banal fact, the tree or rock that looks as it looks to anybody who takes a picture of his family through a camera on Sunday. So we have to be able to invest what is real . . . with a character, sometimes with a glamour, sometimes with an allure or a mystery which it doesn't have. To this extent it must be treated as a décor.[35]

The function of the landscape in CHIMES is specific. The exterior scenes provide the bitter alternative to the interior worlds presented in the film. Welles makes the exterior world of CHIMES what Shakespeare makes it in *King Lear*; the arena where man preys upon man (as he does comically at Gadshill, and viciously in the Battle of Shrewsbury) or the great space where nature preys upon life as it does in the ruthless freezing action of winter. Like Lear, Welles's Falstaff has inevitably to assert himself in a community whose values are no longer his, he is cast out in isolation, on the unsheltered world of nature. The last we see of Falstaff is his great coffin being wheeled out on to open ground, and that is where the film leaves it.

The wintry essence of the natural world and its amoral inhospitability is established at the start of the film, with the long shot of Falstaff and Shallow moving with all the cumbersome slowness of age, across the snow-covered ground, towards the warm fire which burns in the grate of the barn-like building associated with Shallow. Once the warmth of the fire is established as an antithesis to the cold of the outside world, there is a cut to the credits, behind which the bitterness of exterior reality with its indications of the dying age is taken up and reinforced. A long, straggling procession shuffles wearily across the skyline, leaning into the teeth of the winter wind, 'a cold wind, an English wind; a wind that forebodes the end of a whole period'.[36] The procession pauses in front of a series of gibbets whose hanging figures swing in the gusts, before going heavily on, with one man moving back with the wind, to retrieve the hat blown from his head. It is a spatial suggestion of desolation and death, yet it strikes a chord consonant with the chill reality of political ruthlessness of the reign of Henry IV. Consistent with his strategy in MACBETH and OTHELLO, Welles has articulated his thematic priority before the narrative action of the film begins. The fire and the snow, the reminiscences of Falstaff and Shallow and the wind-blown procession past the gibbets are all irreconcilable opposites. 'Falstaff is a fire set against the cold that pervades the film – the cold of Henry's castle, the chill wind of the battlefield, the snows that prompt Shallow to recall "the chimes at midnight", and the autumn woods of Gadshill.'[37]

The exterior world of the film is the wider context within which the aspirations of Henry and the Percys, Hal and Falstaff interact, and the exterior action builds with increasing pointedness to its climax in the Battle of Shrewsbury. The tone of some of these scenes, in keeping with the general tone in the early part of the film, is essentially playful. The darker moments are there, but they do not deflect the humour of Gadshill, for instance, with its ridiculous ambush and its pursuit through 'a forest of skinny trees' which has the comic effect of magnifying by contrast the cumbersome rotundity of Falstaff as he runs in his monk's robes, slashing wildly and ineffectually behind him with his sword.[38] In the spirit of its action in the organic correspondence of the trees with the 'world of wood', Gadshill is an extension of the Tavern. Yet, like the 'play extempore', it is a foreshadowing of more serious things to come. Apart from its parodying of battle, there are such visual portents as the tall leanness of the trees which is recalled later in the strong vertical clusters of spears before the battle and in the upright spears held by the guards in Henry's palace and at Hal's coronation. The tricking of Falstaff by Poins and Hal at Gadshill is mutely recalled in the final rejection scene, as Falstaff stands, humble and alone, against a background of tall spears, listening to Hal's dismissal of him. There is, too, the moment when Hal throws a handful of autumn leaves over Falstaff in his white robe before the robbery. It is an emphasis of the autumnal poise of the epoch, and a wry comment on the aging of Falstaff and his distance from Hal.

It is with hindsight that these hints of seriousness assume their darker complexion. Only in the context of the whole film do they show for what they fully are. In the context of Gadshill alone, they are but puzzling moments of play. A general air of jollity is carried forward in the processions of soldiers mustering for the battle, and only with the shots of battlefield preparation do the ominous hints of war's seriousness begin to shift the mood of the whole film. A still composition dominated by a mobile cradle carrying four spears (possibly unusually barbed lances), their points silhouetted against the sky, splaying out towards the camera, strikes the note of unrelieved bloody intent which will inform the coming shots of the battle. The specifically metallic dimensions of the film's deployment of elemental images begins to assert its importance in the concentration on weaponry and in the trumpet calls which mingle with – and are displaced by – the moan of the wind sweeping over the plain. The battlefield assumes a prospect of bitter desolation, setting the low-angle shot of Hotspur's final swagger in a context which makes his confidence suddenly fatuous.

Hal, shot in medium close-up against the sky, listens silently and enigmatically to Falstaff's speech about 'honour', and the last moment of comedy comes as the heavily armoured knights are lowered from trees and derricks on to their horses. Momentarily the suspended riders recall the bodies hanging from the gibbets, but as Falstaff in his massive armour is hoisted to the top of the pulley, and then let fall before a horse can be got under him, the comedy arises from the imagination's perception of Falstaff inside the vast metallic figure which sits expressionless on the ground.

The battle in CHIMES AT MIDNIGHT is a hideous and ferocious onslaught, and in its sustained realism is quite unlike any battle in any other Shakespearean film. There are derivative influences. The montage effects derive from Eisenstein's battle sequences in ALEXANDER NEVSKY, and the great cloud of dust which dims the outlines and gives the combatants their anonymity is a device used in the battle sequences of John Ford's earlier films. Only the mounting of the armoured knights is reminiscent of the preparatory scene for the battle in Olivier's HENRY V. But where Olivier's Battle of Agincourt deals chiefly with formations and with the fusion of

spectacle, colour and music in a rhythmic development, and where his Battle of
Bosworth in RICHARD III selects recognizable individuals isolated at moments of the
action, Welles's battle photography concentrates with unmitigated directness on the
furious brutality of war. He refuses to allow history to gloss its unrelieved horror or
its universal relevance. There is no distancing medieval 'tapestry' effect afforded by
the colour and pictorial idiom which Olivier employs. Welles's battle is meant to be a
major aesthetic disruption from which neither the tone of the film nor the perceptive
mood of the spectator returns to its former equilibrium.

The wide-angle lens of the camera captures a broad expanse of the plain with
mounted knights in broken formation charging over it, dust fading the outlines, as
the charge continues. Intershot with the charge are glimpses of Falstaff in long shot,
looking like an immense, ungainly, armourplated beetle, walking alone and incongru-
ous in open ground. The opposing armies meet and the pace generated by the cavalry
charge is taken up in the montage of blows given and received, wielded clubs,
swinging chain slings, spiked maces and swords. The viciousness of the hand-to-
hand combat is unrelenting, and it is punctuated with high-angle shots of groups of
archers bunched by the seething activity around them, shooting their arrows with
clean efficiency and skill, followed in turn by rapid close-up glimpses of men pierced
through with arrows and of horses impaled and collapsing in convulsions. Welles
uses soft-focus silhouette in his close-up concentration to maintain the refusal of
identity and so to isolate the raw brutality of man and weapon from any partisan
sentiment, and his pace of montage is hectic and sustained.

The editing of the battle shots presented less of a problem than might be
supposed. One reason for this is the shooting method which Welles employed.
Instead of shooting short bursts of action and building them into a sustained
sequence, Welles reversed the process and shot long, uninterrupted takes of action,
from which he selected short lengths. He found that this method gave him the realism
he sought. 'They didn't seem to be really fighting until they had time to warm up.
That's why the takes were so long, since there was no way of beginning the camera
later and cutting. But I knew I was only going to use very short cuts.' Welles further
increased the sense of pace and the variety of movement by shooting the battle
action from a continuously moving point of view. 'We shot with a big crane very low
to the ground, moving as fast as it could be moved against the action. What I was
planning to do – and did – was to intercut the shots in which the action was contrary,
so that every cut seemed to be a blow, a counter-blow, a blow received, a blow
returned.'[39] In fact the final effect is not quite what Welles suggests. There is far more
variety in the sequences than a mere exchange of blows. Another reason for the
effectiveness of the editing of the battle sequences is that unlike those parts of
Welles's films where dialogue had to be a major consideration, these takes could be
edited with only the ultimate visual effects in mind. 'For the only time in the movie,
he can edit, not to cover gaps and defects, but as an artist.'[40]

While the battle section is a remarkable achievement in purely visual terms, there is an important aural dimension to it. Welles has observed that 'The danger in cinema is that in using the camera, you see everything. What one must do is succeed in . . . making things emerge that are not, in fact, visible.'[41] Welles achieves this by juxtaposing the frantic montaged action of the battle and its concomitant sounds of clashing metal, whinnying horses and grunting men on the one hand, with a dissonant choral accompaniment sung by treble voices on the other. What Welles managed in counterpointing visual rhythms in the long tracking shot in OTHELLO, he manages here by counterpointing the slow, stressed beats in the choral chant with the hectic rhythms of the battle, so that the comment of the treble choir upon the action of war gives the entire sequence cosmic dimensions approaching those in Britten's War Requiem. We do not merely see a battle: we are given an apocalyptic vision of humanity's regression. The slowing of the pace of battle, after nearly ten minutes, as soldiers wrestle, coated in mud and find it impossible to rise, is the visual culmination of this regression. The battle has reversed the process of evolution and man has returned to the slime from which he emerged, writhing rather than walking upright.

Only in the encounter between Hal and Hotspur does the level of personal identity in the battle surface. When Hotspur falls after the brief duel, Hal removes his helmet so that Hotspur's head falls back. He looks upward as he accuses Hal of robbing him of his youth, and the oblique framing of his face during his last words is the camera's comment on his incompatibility with Hal, a comment which is given final emphasis with the immediate return to a normal upright framing of Hal's face in his brief lament. This is the one moment in the battle when individual man is more important than the mass.

Critics have not been unanimous in their response to the battle sequence. Ann Birstein is one who considers it 'pointlessly bloody' but most regard it as one of Welles's supreme achievements.[42] Pauline Kael maintains that the battle in CHIMES AT MIDNIGHT

is unlike anything he [Welles] has ever done, indeed unlike any battle ever done on the screen before. It ranks with the best of Griffith, John Ford, Eisenstein, Kurosawa . . . The compositions suggest Uccello and the chilling, ironic music is a death-knell for all men in battle. The soldiers, plastered by the mud they fall in, are already monuments.[43]

The end of the battle brings about the reunion of identified individuals on the desolate plain strewn with bodies in the distance. Welles has omitted the gross moment of Falstaff's stabbing the dead body of Hotspur, so that we do not experience a major deflection of sympathy. Nevertheless, the occasional shots of Falstaff peering from behind bushes and trees during the latter stages of the battle tend to prompt an ambivalent response in their context, and like everything else in the film, Falstaff, as he arrives carrying the body of Hotspur, head down, is not essentially funny. The major eloquence of the scene arises from the silent exchange of looks which pass between Hal and the King, followed by the very deliberate departure of the King as he turns – characteristically – away from the camera and strides into the distance, his cloak flowing out behind him. It is a highly ambiguous statement. Is it a judgement of Falstaff? Does the King's withdrawal suggest that he doubts Hal's claim? Is it Henry's moral disapproval of the cheap desecration of Hotspur and the Percys? Is it the final moment in which Hal turns from Falstaff to commit himself to the inheritance of the throne? No doubt it is all these as well as being emphatic statement – impossible for Hal or the viewer to ignore – about Henry Bolingbroke, his inscrutability and remote coldness.

The change which the battle has wrought in Hal is darkly underlined by the sequence in which Falstaff, now shown in medium close-up and surrounded by Bardolph, Nym and Pistol, utters his eulogy on sack. He holds out his mug to Hal in a toast. But, for Hal, the moment is charged not with the resuscitation of an earlier innocence, but with a recognition of the seriousness of history. Instead of acknowledging Falstaff's toast, Hal walks away (once again over open ground) and lets his mug fall as he walks in long shot. 'Welles does not have him dash it to the ground with theatrical emphasis; the casual, almost automatic gesture carries far more force, as if Hal were sloughing off his past.'[44]

The battle shatters irrecoverably the mood and tone established in the first half of the film. Apart from the changed perspective of perceptual sensitivities, which darkens the viewer's response to the later action, the pace of the film slows noticeably as nostalgia, melancholy and sickness debilitate action and govern the relationship between characters and spatial detail.

The King's melancholy is accompanied by his own sickness, which strikes him with sudden force as he rides from the battlefield, and by his guilt at having been – for all this ascetic penance – inescapably an usurper of the crown. In the palace he collapses, is carried to his bed by monks, and insists that the crown be placed beside him on the pillow. His soliloquy on sleep, with its ending 'Then happy low, lie down / Uneasy lies the head that wears a crown', is given over a cyclic visual structure, the King first standing before a barred window, his whole body in full shot, a heavy shadow falling across his brow and face.[45] The camera moves in, giving the soliloquy dimensions of both speech and silent reflection, and for most of the speech the King's face is held in close-up. At the last lines, the camera pulls away again to hold the King once more in full shot at the window.

The last shots of the King highlight the fact that for him life can only end when the legitimacy of the crown is secured through direct, unquestionable succession. Hal, believing his father to be dead, takes the crown from the bed. The King wakes, rises with urgent vigour and strides about demanding to know who took the crown. At the end of his final recognition of Hal's allegiance, he dies with virtually no noticeable collapse. He merely becomes still.

Falstaff's melancholy is established by his heavy, weary arrival at the Tavern and his muttered aside, as he sits before a small round table, that he must 'turn away' some of his followers. The suggestions of sickness are insistently made through the camera's concentration on the interior lavatory at the Tavern, on its easily identifiable wooden door, on Falstaff's visiting it, on others visiting it and on the page coming from it with a sample of Falstaff's urine.

For much of the duration of this interior scene, Falstaff lies on his back on the floor with Doll Tearsheet who clambers over his immense stomach, giving, as Jorgens suggests, a simple visual articulation of Falstaff as 'a huge hill of flesh'.[46] There is, too, an arresting reminder of the 'inverted' shot in OTHELLO, when Falstaff on his back looks upward to catch sight of Hal and Poins. The camera takes Falstaff's subjective view so that we see Hal and Poins looking down from the 'bunk' above, their heads inverted at the top of the frame, their conversation derisive of Falstaff's aged sexual desire.

The last shot of the Tavern interior indicates a final dissonance between its social conviviality and Falstaff's dejection. To the accompaniment of merry music, the camera moves with smooth sweeps along and among the beams and rafters as though stroking them, to frame the whole dance scene from above. Falstaff thrusts his way through the throng and out, to head for the house of Justice Shallow.

William Johnson in an article for *Film Quarterly* (1967) has observed of Welles that 'He is not content with the straightforward flow of time – four of his films (KANE, OTHELLO, ARKADIN, CHIMES) begin with the end of the action before leaping to the beginning.'[47] The cyclical structure in CHIMES is complex, and there is a sense in which Johnson's assertion is not true. The start of the film showing Falstaff and Shallow coming through the snow, with Shallow's piping, 'Jesu, the days that we have seen!' and Falstaff's reply, 'We have heard the chimes at midnight, Master Shallow', is not the end of the film's action.[48] This dialogue is recapitulated when Falstaff and Shallow again sit in Shallow's house, immediately before the climactic 'farewell' of the film. With Pistol's arrival with the news of Henry's death, the pace and anticipative vitality of the film is resuscitated, so that the line of action sets off on a new tangent which splays out on the one hand to the young King's preparation for war with France; on the other, to Falstaff's final isolation and heavy shuffle towards death.

By combining substantially the material from the two parts of *Henry IV* together with pieces from *Henry V, Richard II* and *The Merry Wives of Windsor*, Welles is able to form an organically durable structure which knits together correspondences and presents its dimensions through polarities which do not arise within the structure of the individual plays. The dented cooking pot and the cushion – both of which Falstaff wears as 'crowns' in the first half of the film – develop a progression from ridiculous parody to implacable seriousness in their profound contrast with the real crown which the young King wears and which gleams so prominently as he turns to press home his rejection of Falstaff, who finally stands bare-headed before him. The progression of crowns is also a statement about Falstaff and Hal. The preposterous adornments which Falstaff wears tend to make him bigger, to magnify him in parody. The crown which Hal wears as the new King, on the other hand, seems unnaturally large. It weighs him down and makes him physically smaller. It is part of a process of 'diminution' for Hal. The trees at Gadshill, as has been noted, have their connection with the Tavern-world through their organic correspondence, and with the later ranks of vertical spears at the coronation. In Act II of *Henry V,* before sailing from Southampton, Henry instructs Exeter to

> Enlarge the man committed yesterday
> That railed against our person. We consider
> It was excess of wine that set him on.[49]

With ingenious and powerful effect, Welles is able to give these lines a specific reference to Falstaff and his earlier disruption of the coronation procession, the word 'enlarge' carrying its wry ambiguity and giving the moment a fleeting dimension of wit. Both the coronation scene and the brief scene at Southampton place the young King in perspectives reminiscent of his father's remoteness. The former associates him with high stone walls; the latter with emphatic difference in levels, as Henry addresses his embarking army. Finally there is the antithesis already noted, between Hotspur's bustling preparation and swagger, and Shallow's senile disintegration. The welding together of the material enables Welles to accelerate the pace of the film to its culmination in the battle and then to slow the action down to its final stillness. The mid-point where the pace changes is placed within the battle sequence and is spatially articulated through the change from dry, dusty earth upon which horses charge, to mud where men are immobilized in their heavy armour.

There is, then, a cyclic pattern to the shifts of pace in the film, as there is, too, in the transitions between interior and exterior locations. In this latter respect, William Johnson's assertion of this film's cyclic completeness is more convincing. The film starts with the slow, painful movement from exterior long shot of Falstaff and Shallow, to interior close-up as they sit before the fire. The dominant movement throughout the first half of the film is, from that point on, an *outward* one, culminating in the battle. Thereafter, all movement is *inward,* from exterior to interior locations – the King to his palace; Falstaff, Hal, Poins, Bardolph and Nym to the Tavern – or from one interior to another – Falstaff from the Tavern to Shallow's house; Falstaff from Shallow's house to the Abbey at Westminster. The final movement in the film is the trundling of Falstaff's coffin from the Tavern, out over open ground into distance exterior long shot, reversing the initial movement of the film, and giving to it a spatial and dynamic symmetry.

By framing the entire action of the film between an initial inward movement and a closing outward movement, Welles manages to accommodate the dramatic conflict within a form which – unlike MACBETH and OTHELLO – gives it poignancy without abrasiveness. The inner cyclic framework formed by the reiteration of the snatch of dialogue between Falstaff and Shallow has a less obvious function. In an ingenious way its importance lies in its very refusal to enclose the whole action. By enclosing much of the film between the echoes of aged nostalgia it gives that part the complexion of 'action embedded in reflection'.[50] But in excluding the King's final rejection of Falstaff, it places that climactic moment outside the muted context of remembered past and gives it an unexpected immediacy. There is no longer any retrospective comfort, as Shallow's piping plea for his thousand pounds makes clear. Nostalgic particularity is effectively counterpoised by universal predicament.

The range of original dramatic unities from which the material is drawn, together with the separate and autonomous worlds which the film accommodates, provide Welles with the opportunity for considerable cinematic variety. The camera movement in the Tavern, as it ranges about exploring with an accustomed freedom different levels along the horizontal and diagonal lines of the woodwork, and where it 'dances' about like a dog anticipating a game, pulling back in front of Hal, Poins and Falstaff as they set off for Gadshill, is in clear contrast with its constraint in the palace at Windsor. Like everything else, the camera is governed in its movement by the King and the architecture which surrounds him. Except in those moments where it takes on the subjective point of view of the King, the camera films insistently from a low angle. It is either still, filming action in long shot with a wide-angle lens placing people in the immense architectural perspective, or it tracks back along straight lines between the Gothic pillars. In Cowie's words, the camera is 'inert when Henry speaks . . . in Eastcheap, it roves, glides and swings in time with Falstaff's mirth'.[51]

Movement within the frame is similarly varied, in accordance with the characters of the King, Falstaff, Hotspur and Hal. The King and Falstaff are given emphatic spatial antithesis. Henry gives the impression of consumed greatness. 'From the beginning he is depicted as a dying man, a wraith garbed in ornamental clothes; in contrast to his rival, Falstaff, he is bodiless.'[52] Yet when he moves, Henry does so with dignity, or with decisive firmness of spirit so that his physicality functions purely as the embodiment of his mission. Falstaff, on the other hand, draws attention to himself less through clothes – or even dialogue – than through his body, and the anonymous reviewer in *Time* gives him justified emphasis in describing him as 'immense, waddling, jowly, pantomiming with a theatrical strawberry nose and crafty, porcine eyes', and in ascribing his dramatic assertion less to 'spoken English' than to 'body English'.[53] Given the striking physical evidence of uncontrolled indulgence, it is, as Naremore points out, paradoxical that Falstaff's death will result 'more from a broken spirit than from bloated flesh'.[54]

For Hal, the in-frame movement is altogether more complex. His movement is related to the conflict of loyalties within him, and to a deeper unpredictability of his personality. Always enigmatic in his sudden changes from action to reflection, from conviviality to introverted solitude, Hal's most consistent characteristic movement is the long, slow, deliberate walk away from the camera and into the distance, as a reiteration of the film's 'farewell' motif. His rapid diminution as he recedes into the far distance, filmed through the camera's wide-angle lens, suggests that in leaving Falstaff and moving toward a life of public propriety Hal does diminish himself inevitably. The statement is too insistently made for it to fail to recall the more abrupt move, away from the camera, of Henry. Only on the last occasion does Hal turn back to face Falstaff, making clear the finality of his rejection. There, heavily cloaked, with only his head and shoulders framed in medium-close shot, Hal seems to recall the 'bodiless' nature of his father. It is Welles's final articulation of the composite 'distance' between Hal and Falstaff.

Unlike the dispassionate work of the camera in MACBETH and OTHELLO, the camera in CHIMES AT MIDNIGHT has a more committed subjectivity about it. It does not have the independent narrative identity which Olivier gives the camera in HAMLET, but the Falstaff story is told from a point of view which elicits an enduring sympathy with Falstaff himself. In trying to connect what is seen with what is felt, the camera identifies not infrequently with Falstaff. The shots of Hal walking away are all taken and sustained from Falstaff's point of view. William Johnson suggests that there is in fact an expressionist tendency in the camera's treatment of space. The expansiveness of the film's spaces is, he maintains, a product of Falstaff's personal vision. 'The Tavern, for example, is enlarged beyond probability, in much the same way that a childhood haunt is enlarged in one's memory: this is how Falstaff, the perpetual child would remember it. Similarly, the wide horizons of the film's outdoor scenes . . . evoke the spacious, innocent Olde Englande that Falstaff imagined he lived in.'[55]

The camera makes its statements in CHIMES AT MIDNIGHT, but in casting the film with actors who are well able to shape delivery and to use with effect the duration of a long take, Welles has conceded some of the director's prerogative for manipulating space to the performers. To that extent, the deliberate theatricality of CHIMES places it in a different class from MACBETH and OTHELLO. However, in the sense that the décor is organically expressive and thematically integrated, it is no less cinematic. Jorgens and Higham draw attention to shots which are reminiscent of both MACBETH and OTHELLO: 'the gallows with hanging traitors, the castle high on the rocks, the briarlike bar in the window' recalling MACBETH, and the 'sunlit flowing banners, forests of spears . . . close-ups of blaring trumpets' recalling OTHELLO.[56] Higham more convincingly draws attention to the initial shots of the film — the procession along the skyline against the background of gibbets, the style of the credits — and suggests that Welles's three Shakespearean films present a seasonal trilogy: MACBETH, OTHELLO and CHIMES being associated respectively with autumn, summer, and winter.[57] The CHIMES landscape is certainly a projection of winter, but there is one arresting inconsistency at the moment of Hotspur's death. There is summer leafiness behind Hotspur as he rolls slowly back, and Naremore argues that this is deliberate irony, 'a sign of his premature death'.[58]

Spliced into the structure of CHIMES AT MIDNIGHT are three spoken passages of narration, read by Ralph Richardson. The function of this narrative monologue is quite unlike that in MACBETH or OTHELLO (whose introductory narration Welles himself compiled and spoke, merely to give the action a contextual relevance) or that of the narrative prologue to Olivier's HAMLET (which isolated a thematic and interpretative priority). The 'narrative voice' in CHIMES presents a commentary upon action and character, and has a vigorous new dimension to it, for the commentary passages are taken from Holinshed's Chronicles, the source material for Shakespeare's histories. The Holinshed material introduces the historical placing of the action, heralds the change of mood after the battle and comments finally upon the character and reputation of the new King, as the film ends.

Aesthetically, the voice-over commentary has an integral function well beyond the informative level, for it juxtaposes the dramatic material of Shakespeare with its source, thus pointing the differences between chronicle, play and – by implication – the film. The difference in the world-views of the dramatist and film maker on the one hand, and of the chronicler of history on the other, is given telling emphasis in the ironic detachment of Richardson's voice as it speaks of Hal as having 'put on the shape of a new man' and as one who 'left no friendship unrewarded', while the camera holds the wide view of open ground as Falstaff's coffin is wheeled through the Tavern gate and away into long-shot distance.

The integration of Holinshed's material as a dispassionate level of commentary given by a voice associated only with the function of documenting apparent fact, makes CHIMES AT MIDNIGHT, in the last resort, something more than simply a cinematic adaptation of high dramatic calibre. The film becomes implicitly, too, a revelation of the symbiosis of art and history. As such, it eludes easy categorization. Maurice Bessy considers it 'not formally speaking a period piece, but rather a great documentary, a clandestine reportage, hidden away and protected for centuries, and now brought to light by a film archeologist'.[59] It is not an unperceptive placing of the film, except in its failure to point to its continuing relevance, the fact that childhood is a world of innocence inevitably displaced by the adult world of disillusionment. For that must surely be what Welles meant when he spoke of 'the lost paradise' as being 'the central theme in Western culture'.[60]

8 Peter Brook's KING LEAR and Akira Kurosawa's THRONE OF BLOOD

Peter Brook and Akira Kurosawa have both made films which are, in their very different ways, logical extensions of the endeavours we have so far discussed, to accommodate Shakespearean drama in cinematic space. The plays involved here (*King Lear* and *Macbeth*) both demand a juxtaposition of the world of nature with the world of man, yet the directors are at opposite ends of a spectrum in the spatial strategies they employ. While Brook's KING LEAR seeks a spatial selectivity in order to heighten the effect of dialogue, Kurosawa's films RAN and THRONE OF BLOOD find a spatial articulation which almost dispenses with the need for dialogue. Both directors incorporate deliberate theatricality in their films, in pursuit of very different cinematic effects. Like Olivier, Brook has directed films yet he is most strongly associated with the theatre. Like Welles, Kurosawa is best know for films he has made. Both Brook and Kurosawa stand apart from Olivier and Welles in that neither is an actor. Their spatial strategies are, therefore, likely to be more objectively developed.

Like Olivier, Brook emerges from an eminent theatrical involvement with the works of Shakespeare. Like Welles he has shown himself to be original, unorthodox and experimental in his cinematic work. Of his five major films, only one is an adaptation of a Shakespeare play, and in all his work, he has expressly attempted to push forward the frontiers of cinematic potential.

With MACBETH and OTHELLO Welles broke away from the narrative cinema of Olivier and delivered jarring shocks of perspective, dislocated angles, bravura contrasts of light and dark, delocalized space and distinctly untheatrical acting. His cinematic language gave his adaptations explosive power by juxtaposing simple and complex compositions, and by alternating the long take with rapid montage successions. Brook's KING LEAR was a more drastic innovation. It broke away from cinematic tradition – and from a substantial Shakespearean tradition – by rebelling against its romanticism. The film makes Shakespeare's play a revelation of the grotesque rather than a tragedy, and there is some justification for the suggestion that in this film Beckett and the critic Jan Kott come dangerously close to displacing Shakespeare.

It is little wonder, then, that Brook's film has provoked a more profound critical division than any other Shakespearean film, suggesting that by 1971 the field had reached a level of maturity which engaged the minds of Shakespearean scholars and film specialists in lively debate. The most searching criticism separates clearly into favourable and unfavourable response. Several critics, among them Frank Kermode, and Charles Eidsvik in his book *Cineliteracy: Film among the Arts*, champion the work as a significant cinematic achievement, while others, notably Pauline Kael, and William Johnson in his review for *Film Quarterly*, regard it as a limitation and a distortion of Shakespeare's play, and consequently an unsatisfactory adaptation.

The film explores complicated aspects of the relation of theatre to cinema. In some respects the film has a clearly theatrical commitment, yet there are dimensions of its spatial strategy which remove it from the kind of theatricality which the films of Olivier and Welles acknowledge. There is a duality of treatment in the film whereby the camera tends to treat the actors and the environmental spatial detail separately, and in this conventional sense cinematic commitment, which occasionally promises to develop from the landscape shots, fails to mature. More specifically, the reasons for the film's lack of conventional cinematic poise centre on a suppression of camera movement and transitional flow. In the first place, the presentation of the play as primarily a drama of faces brings it closer to television than to cinema, as does the relation of dialogue to visualization. The spoken lines consistently dominate in the total impact of word and picture, so that the visuals increasingly take on the function of illustrative rather than expressive development. Secondly, when faces are not held in close-up the frame composition is consistently limited to the medium close-up shot, holding characters – in either sitting or standing positions – from head and shoulders to waist. Sometimes only one character is held thus in the centre of the frame for a sustained shot, as is the case when Goneril and Regan speak their respective opening speeches to Lear. Sometimes two characters balance the frame composition, standing or sitting side-by-side, as Lear and the Fool do, or as Goneril and Regan do, travelling in the covered wagon. Very occasionally a third face is recognizable holding the centre of the frame in soft-focus depth, as Cornwall's is when Lear and Regan discuss the earlier violent departure from Goneril's castle. These compositions, so recurrently emphatic in the visual style of the film, achieve the effect of isolating characters from their spatial background so that the important reciprocity between actor and décor is broken, and the dramatic energy of cinema vitiated.

Furthermore, certain items and details which the camera frame reveals take on a theatrical rather than a cinematic significance because their integration with the film's development is not dynamic. The animal-skin costumes, the flames in the hearth, the landscape in the exterior shots – all these suggest stasis rather than process. They indicate the relationship and the distinction between man and beast, and the hostility of bleak 'nature', but they hold these ideas within and around the action as monolithic statements whose significance, like a fixed stage set, becomes apparent in the dialogue. One means of investing an object with cinematic development is to vary its relation to a light source, but the uniform grey diffused light in which the film's action is bathed throughout eliminates this possibility as it does the dramatic contrast-effects which offer to cinema such powerful resources. The cinematic possibilities of

14. KING LEAR (Brook). Framing for dialogue. Paul Scofield (Lear) and Annelise Gabold (Cordelia)

presenting either cosmic or expressionistic dynamics within the universe of the action are deliberately eschewed. Only in the brief distanced shot of the duel between Edgar and Edmund is there a low sun in the background.

Nor are there many instances where movement of the camera makes any cinematic statement. For the most part, the camera is held still. Where it does move, the most memorable shots of the film are produced. One such shot is the slow moving-camera exploration of the feet and sodden bodies of dead rats drowned in the storm flood. The close anatomical detail which is revealed to accompany the great breadth of Lear's prayer gives specificity to the 'houseless poverty', while the generalizations of the prayer give a wider relevance to the sodden fur of a rat.[1] It is superb cinematic synthesis. The opening sustained shot in the film, too, is effective. The camera pans and tracks, moving slowly across a deep composition of still faces while the opening credits appear on the screen. Taken without interruption and in complete silence, this shot establishes the importance of faces in the frame composition, and the diffused uniformity of light.

Like the adaptations of Welles, Olivier and Kurosawa, this film exploits a

15. KING LEAR (Brook). Framing for dialogue. Alan Webb (Gloucester) and Susan Engel (Regan)

combination of interior and exterior locales. Unlike the other films, though, Brook's KING LEAR does not integrate the exterior shooting to liberate the action, nor does Brook exploit the varied spatial relationships which outdoor locations afford him to any marked degree. Like the skins, the fire and the grey light, the bleak expanse of snow-covered undulations presents a pre-eminently static image; one of unrelieved, bitter desolation. Most of the outdoor shots could be 'stills', but they establish one important motif in the film, the *travelling* motif which gives the film a dimension of space which no stage production could have.

Finally, the relation of sound to the visuals is unusual. Sound effects and vocal projection only occasionally evoke a sense of spatial realism. For most of the film, the closeness of the voices and the lack of resonant acoustics suggest an oppressive containment of space. The amplifications of whispers and the silence together with the vocal restraint in speaking the dialogue tend to dislocate utterance from character. Most striking in the abnormal restraint of the sound-track is the total absence of music. Film as a medium of expression almost always incorporates music. Brook's KING LEAR is the only Shakespearean film which relates action to spatial realism, and which refuses to include a musical dimension. Given the cinematic convention of a musical component and the music associated with and intrinsic to the plays of Shakespeare, Brook's exclusion of it must stand as one of his most emphatic statements.

All of these will, on first consideration, give strength to the argument that the film remains 'very much a stage play', and that in failing to move away from the stage, Brook even imposes its lighting dimensions on the screen by plunging 'that stage in darkness'.[2] They also support William Johnson's impression that 'the action seems to be forced into unnatural shapes' and that this unnatural constraint is inimical to the spatial freedom which can clearly distinguish cinema from theatre.[3] The uneasy sense that the film is not removed from the theatre stage with clear commitment is given substance by the comments of the film's producer, Michael Birkett. Four important points emerge from the decisions taken about the making of the film.

Much time and experiment were given to the dialogue (considered purely as dialogue and not as part of a total aural and visual cinematic structure). Recognizing that Shakespeare's poetic complexity is not easily accessible to the modern audience, Birkett and Brook asked Ted Hughes to prepare a modern 'translation' for the film. Hughes's script was later abandoned because 'the greatest passages in the play . . . have a force and emotional power that no translation, no paraphrase can possibly match . . . Once using some of Shakespeare's text, it seemed unnatural not to use it throughout.' Hughes was not asked to prepare a film scenario or a shooting script: he was asked to treat it 'exactly as if it were a foreign classic'. Such detailed consideration of dialogue without its integration in a predominantly visual context must invite an ultimate seniority of word over visuals.[4] Such a deliberate decision not to abandon Shakespeare's language would seem to imply a reluctance to abandon the original mode of expression.

The major concern about the visuals appeared to be the danger of their displacing the dialogue by intruding 'between the audience and the power of the words'. Most ironically, the challenge became one of almost eliminating visuals, of trying to find a way of producing a blankness on the screen without suggesting a total technical collapse of medium, and this is a major explanation for the reductiveness of the film's spatial strategy.[5]

The two final points concern the décor and the actors. The décor of the film was evolved less to allow the creation of dynamic metaphoric development and more to 'invent a setting which has a period and a flavour of its own'.[6] Birkett's words here seem to imply that interior shots will dominate, and that the function of the décor is theatrical rather than cinematic: a spatial context which reflects dialogue rather than a spatial development which expresses drama. Like much that is important in the film, the casting of the key roles was the direct result of Peter Brook's stage production of the play at Stratford-upon-Avon in 1962. Not only were theatre actors considered eminently suitable for the film, but to some extent the making of the film was dependent upon 'Paul Scofield himself [who] was one of our reasons for undertaking KING LEAR in the first place'.[7]

Birkett's very frank discussion gives an insight into the formative thinking which launched the making of the film, and suggests that while on the one hand the intention was to make a film, on the other the priorities that emerged were strongly theatrical as they resolved themselves in the process of crystallization. Indeed Brook's own remarks further substantiate this conclusion. In a letter to Kozintsev, he writes:

What happens when the close-up on Shakespeare carries material through another vehicle? As the speech ceases to be dialogue and becomes the vehicle of inner meanings, I then recognize that in Shakespeare, speech is the carrier . . . Then [if] you destroy the speech rhythm, the power of the Shakespearean text is destroyed.

A commitment to verbal priority and to the predominance of close-ups emerges clearly from this. The implicit intention to restrict the specific development of the drama through spatial detail and context becomes explicit when Brook later writes of his desire to reduce the compositeness of the image, and to give the actor's face almost total dramatic responsibility within the shot. 'Is the best we can achieve a safe compromise in which our close-up is longer than "normal" film, but short of "boredom length"? I say "close-up" – but what is the relation of close-up to full-shot – when full-shot always reveals background? . . . I want to avoid background.'[8]

An arresting question arises at this point, for it may be recalled that Welles's intentions before he started shooting CHIMES AT MIDNIGHT were identical with Brook's as implied here. The same conscious desire to concentrate on faces and to exclude background detail moved both directors as their respective films took shape in their minds. Why, then, are the films so very different in their spatial priorities? Differences in creative temperament and in the value given to dramatic character seem the most convincing explanations. Welles is clearly a director for whom spontaneity is important. Brook, on the other hand, is much more intellectual in his approach, refining his material and his conception of it through prolonged experimentation. The centre of Welles's CHIMES AT MIDNIGHT clearly gathered expressive richness to itself in the journey from conception to presentation, while the central assertion of Brook's KING LEAR finally arrives as a distillation. Since Welles concentrates in his film upon the development of characters, it is logical that he should do this through spatial correspondences. Brook de-dramatizes Shakespeare's play, and in removing the richness of character, also removes the spatial particularities which would naturally be its cinematic expression.

Thus far it has been argued that Brook's KING LEAR is essentially unsatisfying as cinema and that the cause of the film's failure to achieve the orchestrated fluidity of conventional cinematic expression lies in a stubborn theatrical rootedness. It is, however, possible to argue that what appears to be a major flaw is in fact deliberate intention and to accept – on a purely intellectual level – the film's ambivalence of spatial commitment as intrinsic to Brook's especial exploitation of his medium. This is to argue that the film's tightly organic structure demands that Brook's interpretation of Shakespeare's play must be understood before the spatial strategy of the film can begin to make sense. Such an argument is given substance by the fact that the major critical divide is consistent. Those who praise the film find Brook's interpretation of *King Lear* legitimate; those who find dissatisfaction with the film also find Brook's view of the play repugnant.

In an article which deals with the lighting dynamics of the film, William Chaplin maintains that these constitute a significant articulation of an interpretation which centres on bringing into the open that inalienable 'barbarism [which] resides still at civilization's centre'.[9] Chaplin discerns a clear cinematic logic in the progress of Lear from the dimly illuminated interior court scene where the action is motivated by Lear's initial 'darker purpose', to his destination on the white beach with the blinded Gloucester and finally with the hallucinations of Cordelia.[10] If barbarism is concealed at the centre, then its exposure means bringing 'the puzzling inner landscape of feeling in the King himself' (hinted at in the prolonged dark facial close-ups at the start of the film) into harmony with the most open natural landscape, so that 'the dark *style* of the inner landscape is sprung open into a cancerous visibility: the animal is driven out into the open'.[11]

Lilian Wilds, in an article published in 1976, admits that while Brook's interpretation of the play is arrived at through 'slanted editing' of the text, she considers the interpretation acceptable and finds the film coherent in its own terms. The spatial strategy of the film is, for her, a logical articulation of 'the Lear-world Brook has created – a world of complete negation'. The landscape of the film is therefore static, 'a physical universe that is forever winter; frozen, bleak, inimical to man', with the positioning of dead Gloucester's body starkly reminiscent of the dead animal carcasses glimpsed during the storm.[12]

Frank Kermode accepts that an original line of interpretation will necessarily result in some distortion, but he claims that creative adaptation depends upon a 'violent process' of imaginative engagement with the original text. For Kermode, then, the film maker will no longer seek to make an adaptation which sets out to satisfy traditional expectations. Nor, indeed, should he. Rather, he will strive to disturb an audience in the same way that his insight into the play disturbs him. The 'new maker's' authority is grounded not so much in the text as in the nature of his own engagement with the play. Kermode discerns this painful process of reconstruction to lie at the heart of Brook's film, which he consequently judges to be 'the best of all Shakespearean movies'.[13]

Those critics who take issue with Brook's interpretation of the play clearly also challenge Kermode's view of the film. For them it is wrong in principle to subordinate the complexity of a dramatic classic to a limited line of philosophical exposition by editing the text to fit an interpretation. Whatever coherence may be attained by such means is no compensation for imposed distortion. There is a significant critical consensus which finds the restrictions of Brook's interpretation responsible for a spatial reductiveness which emasculates the film from the start.

Of Brook's conception of the play, Pauline Kael writes, 'The world's exhaustion and the light's having disappeared may open up new meanings in Shakespeare's play to us, but as the controlling metaphors in this production they don't enlarge the play, they cancel it out.' In addition she finds cinematic development undermined by a 'theatrical conception [which] kills not only the drama but most of the poetry'. When the spatial strategy does move away from its theatrical emphasis, it remains locked in with Brook's interpretation so that it can only further insist that the world of the characters is a 'glacial desert'.[14] William Johnson, too, finds the spatial strategy of the film to be trapped within the confines of interpretation so that the bleakness of the exterior locations and the unrelieved 'slow, dry, deliberate voice' of Scofield combine to suggest 'the place beyond hope where Beckett's characters live'.[15]

Both Kael and Johnson find what in dramatic terms is the most serious result of Brook's vision of the play, the film's failure to develop character. Kael's sense that the 'unified vision' of Brook demanded a rigidity of control which deadened performance is supported by Johnson who finds the characters appearing 'only as Brook's puppets instead of the puppets of fate'.[16]

As Johnson goes on to point out, the problems of characterization are not the same in the cinema as they are on the theatre stage. As we have seen, characters on the screen gain their dramatic stature and vitality through their relation to the details of their spatial context, for the camera objectifies the actor and the décor in the same way.[17] Power and authority on the screen are qualified by 'whatever objective signs are visible', and Brook's refusal to incorporate objective signs 'reduces Lear's predicament to the dimensions of a family quarrel'. The particular vitiation of character development in this film arises, in Johnson's judgement, from a combination of Brook's deliberate reduction of character 'to fit his desired world-view' and his failure to realize that 'the objectifying power of the film will shrivel them still further'.[18]

Finally there remains the argument that identifies the significance of Brook's KING LEAR as residing not in its stature as a Shakespearean adaptation, but in the originality with which it exploits the resources of film's impact on the viewer. The central relationship becomes not so much that of the camera to its object as that of the rectangular cinema screen to its viewers.

In an interview with Geoffrey Reeves, Brook maintained that the devices for alienation on the Brechtian stage had their technical parallels in the cinema. He identified the freeze-frame, the caption and the sub-title as examples of these and claimed that alienation was the only means whereby the flexibility of cinematic visuals could be brought to match the versatility of blank verse.[19] Alienation would be achieved by the repeated dislocation of cinematic identification so that the viewer would be constantly reminded that he was in the cinema. An effective example of this in the film is observed by Lilian Wilds. At the moment when Cornwall blinds Gloucester, Brook blacks out the screen so that the viewer too is blinded. The effect here is initially to establish an identification with Gloucester, but at the same instant, the black screen alienates the viewer by frustrating his desire to see what is happening. The major effect is to remind the cinema audience that 'the film is a mechanical projection, not a window looking on a real event'.[20]

Equally conscious in its alienating intention, though more subtle, is Brook's use of dialogue conventions. Paul Acker, in an illuminating article published in 1980, observes that cinematic convention normally associates the frontal two-shot in medium close-up with intimacy. Brook uses this frame composition with Goneril and Regan sitting in their wagon, and elsewhere 'primarily in contexts of complicity'.[21] Two-shots in profile, on the other hand (with faces looking in toward the centre of the frame), are conventionally associated with 'contexts of dialectic'.[22] Brook stretches the convention so that in the flash-shots during the storm, close-up profile shots of Lear facing opposite directions follow each other in rapid succession, giving Lear's disintegration the implicit dimension of self-examination by argument. The third dimension which Brook employs is the alternation of shot with reverse-shot, a device used to follow the frontal shot of a speaker with a frontal shot of the listener, or to hold the camera on a first speaker and then to shift it to the second who replies. This is most consciously sustained in the opening court scene during which the exchanges between Lear and his daughters are so statically framed in medium close-up that even at this early point in the film one is made uncomfortably aware of the mechanics − the separate components − of the medium of film.

Peter Brook's K I N G L E A R emerges as a complex work whose engagement is almost exclusively with the intellect. Viewed with expectations induced by conventional cinema (and by the most satisfying films of Olivier and Welles) it will frustrate anticipation by seeming to miss all opportunities for cinematic development. Viewed as a critical interpretation of Shakespeare's play, it must be judged both intellectually narrow and aesthetically impoverished. Viewed as a film 'about what it means to watch a film [with] a self-reflexivity which will require the active participation of the aware and cinematically literate viewer', its segmented self-denials and apparent aesthetic masochism can be seen as part of a broader cinematic intention.[23] Fusing the mechanics of Brook's objective to the greatness of Shakespeare's play is not a particularly attractive aesthetic challenge. Why, the question remains, does Brook choose to perpetrate with such dispassion his cinematic deconstruction on *King Lear*? As Pauline Kael asks, 'Who wants to be alienated from Shakespeare's play and given the drear far side of the moon instead?'[24]

Charles Eidsvik sets out to answer this question by seeing the film as an extension of Artaud's concept of the Theatre of Cruelty. Brook's intention, in Eidsvik's judgement, is to 'dissect Shakespeare and what Shakespeare has become for many, a source of insights'. Brook's K I N G L E A R presents a view of man which is intended to be an attack upon the sensibilities. While Shakespeare's view of man and action encompassed personal choice, personal action, personal redemption, Brook's view of Shakespeare's play denies the personal dimension. In an age which is clearly not in essence 'personal' Brook seeks a relevance for Shakespeare's play by depersonalizing it and posing it as a question. 'The result is an impersonal film, in which Shakespeare's language is made to serve something other than the stages in Lear's narrative move toward personal redemption.' The question which underlies the film is whether there is any redemption of the world of barbarism, and if the final verdict of the film is ultimately one of 'fatigued incomprehension', then the potential for redemption must lie in a refusal to accept that verdict, 'to strike back, to think, to act so that Brook's version stands as a challenge rather than a condemnation'.[25]

Eidsvik does in fact confirm the initial sense that the film is in essence theatrical. There are theatrical elements in its spatial strategy as many critics have found, but the film has about it a theatricality of a novel kind. Brook treats the cinema audience in a way which is outside the cinematic conventions. In regarding the primary relationship as that between the screen's rectangle and the spectator/listener, he seeks to ensure the shared participative experience of the theatre. The film is not only frustrating in the sense that Brook intends, but in another sense, because where response to a theatrical assertion is corporate, that to a cinematic challenge is individual. Where the theatre unites its audience, the cinema isolates in darkness those who occupy its seats.

Of the two Kurosawa films, the one which most rewards intensive discussion as a Shakespearean film is THRONE OF BLOOD, released in 1957. Any objective review of Kurosawa's RAN, released as recently as 1985, will probably have to be awaited for some years. This is partly because of the stature which the work of Kurosawa has assumed in contemporary film studies, and partly because the film has had such brief and recent exposure that assessments of its affinity with Shakespeare's King Lear are still critically tentative.

There is an essential stylistic typicality about Kurosawa's work, and the basic ingredients which comprise the dramatic structuring of THRONE OF BLOOD are soon evident in RAN—horses, castles, warriors, hills, trees, mist and quiet moments of great dramatic intensity within enclosed space derived from the Noh theatrical tradition. Yet this film has a less substantial claim to be an adaptation of a Shakespeare play than does the earlier film. Lear's daughters are made into sons in RAN, and the feminine dimensions in the drama are therefore provided by the daughters-in-law. Their distance from Hidetora (the Lear figure) tends to vitiate their dramatic effectiveness, for the whole issue of marriages, dowries and the particular significance of Cordelia's rejection loses its force. Furthermore the most vicious action against Hidetora (the Lear figure) is motivated by the eldest son's wife, Kaede, through her husband. Such indirect action is wholly consistent with Shakespeare's Macbeth, but it reduces the weighty questions about 'nature' and the family which are central to Shakespeare's King Lear. Having no secondary Gloucester plot, the film lacks, too, the particular dimension of vindictiveness which Edmund brings to the Lear world.

The rigid ritualization of the culture within which Kurosawa places the action, with its restrained expression of feeling, reduces the drama of individual confrontation between father and offspring so profoundly embedded in Shakespeare's play.

The repressed aggression which finds many complex outlets in the Lear family expends its energies in RAN, undoubtedly with more spectacle but with less psychological subtlety, in open warfare. Kurosawa dramatizes his universe historically. As he did in THRONE OF BLOOD, he places the Lear action within a sixteenth-century Japanese warrior culture. Macbeth is a warrior and he is established as such early in the play. Shakespeare's Lear, however, is not. That, I believe, is why RAN depends much more than did THRONE OF BLOOD upon substance which lies outside the centre of Shakespeare's play.

The dramatic presentation of the world of nature, no less important in Shakespeare's *King Lear* than it is in *Macbeth*, is not integrated with anything like the same force in the later film. The extent to which it invades the minds and compulsions of the characters is suggested only with ambiguity in RAN. Certainly there are carefully placed reminders of its presence – the boar hunt at the start of the film, the sounds of birds and insects accompanying, sometimes with oppressive stridency, certain moments in the drama, and the shots of darkening clouds in the sky (a recurrent device to indicate the cosmic correspondence of the action). Much of the setting for the action, too, is on outdoor locations. The opening sequence of the film, for instance, establishes a relationship of man with nature, with four mounted archers riding over lush grassland on mountain slopes in pursuit of the wild boar. Initially the photographing of this landscape, with its deep valleys extending into the far distance and the impact of its colours, appears more scenically dramatic than anything afforded us by the monochromatic forest in THRONE OF BLOOD, but these dramatic qualities in the later film are visually arresting rather than structurally assertive. Where the forest becomes the projection of psychological space in THRONE OF BLOOD the nature signals in RAN tend to be reiterated rather than thematically developed and the dimensions of the natural world run parallel with the developing drama of human relationships rather than being interwoven with it.

Tom Milne, writing the review for *Sight and Sound*, has pointed to the infusion of Buddhism in the film, and to the resigned acceptance that the fate of the characters is decided in their past lives. 'Where Shakespeare's play is focused on future consequences as Lear discovers the extent of his folly . . . RAN is rooted in past causes. Where Shakespeare's tragedy is that of a foolish, fond old man . . . Kurosawa's is that of a monster . . .'[26] And Peter Ackroyd, in his review for *Spectator*, rightly maintains that 'this is essentially Shakespeare . . . stripped of its human dimension, and forced within a schematic framework derived from quite different attitudes or preoccupations'.[27]

All this is not to diminish the cinematic stature of Kurosawa's latest film as a film in its own right. But the film does not gain substantially from an attempt to trace specific correspondences with Shakespeare's play. Nor is it easy to find memorable moments in the film which are directly derived from dramatic high points in *King Lear*. On the contrary, the dramatic rise and fall in THRONE OF BLOOD bears a remarkably close relationship with the dynamics of Shakespeare's *Macbeth*. Dramatic peaks in the play are consistently reflected in the film. Moments like the arrival of Duncan at Dunsinane, Macbeth's move off to murder Duncan, his confrontation with Banquo's ghost at the banquet, Lady Macbeth's attempts to clean her hands and the moving of the wood to Dunsinane are all directly part of the film, and they develop the drama of the film with the same structural force that advances the action in Shakespeare's play.

Those like Geoffrey Reeves and Peter Brook, who argue against the consideration of THRONE OF BLOOD as a Shakespearean film do so on the grounds that Kurosawa is 'doing what every film-maker has always done – constructing a film from an idea and using appropriate dialogue; where the story comes from doesn't matter'. Like RAN it deals with human action set in a religious and philosophical framework very different from that of Shakespeare's plays. Despite the occasional echo of a Shakespearean image in the lines, THRONE OF BLOOD, like RAN, is further from Shakespeare than the films of Kozintsev, who clearly took Shakespeare's dialogue and his characterization as starting points. While Reeves and Brook have recognized THRONE OF BLOOD as 'a great masterpiece', they discount it as a Shakespearean film 'because it doesn't use the text'.[28] On similar grounds, Frank Kermode in an essay called 'Shakespeare in the Movies' pointedly excludes THRONE OF BLOOD on the grounds that it is 'an allusion to, rather than a version of, Macbeth'.[29] However, in the thirty years since THRONE OF BLOOD was released, the film has become, for those who have seen it, a part of our thinking about Shakespeare's Macbeth. It has extended the frontiers of discussion on the play and has made Western scholarship more aware of the universal appeal of Shakespeare's dramatic material. The two most authoritative surveys of Shakespearean film give it substantial coverage.

The initial reception of the film in the West was not enthusiastic. Reviewers found difficulty in taking the film seriously at all. Bosley Crowther, who had reviewed with acuteness and sensitivity Olivier's HAMLET, had, in 1961, no compunction in reviewing the New York showing of THRONE OF BLOOD as follows:

If you think it would be amusing to see Macbeth done in Japanese then pop around to the Fifth Avenue Cinema and see Akira Kurosawa's THRONE OF BLOOD. For a free Oriental translation of the Shakespeare drama is what this is, and 'amusing' is the proper word for it . . . Probably Mr Kurosawa . . . did not intend it to be amusing for his formalistic countrymen, but its odd amalgamation of cultural contrasts hits the occidental funnybone – that is all one can say – and the final scene, in which the hero is shot so full of arrows that he looks like a porcupine, is a pictorial extravagance that provides a conclusive howl.[30]

Whilst it is certainly true to say that there has been an important change of attitude since 1961 in the way North America and Western Europe look at Oriental culture, there remains – however serious we accept its artistic intentions to be – a substantial interpretative problem, and this is especially true where an original work is taken from one culture and articulated through conventions of another. It is deceptively easy for a Western observer with a knowledge of Shakespeare's play (and therefore with certain expectations of his own emotional response) to impose that response upon the unfamiliar idiom of the film; to make the unaccustomed semiotics of the film fit the known textual and sub-textual signals of the play.

Because this film dispenses with all but the most essential dialogue to carry forward the narrative, we are placed in the position of having to rely wholly on the manipulation of spatial detail within the screen's rectangle – upon movement, gesture, facial expression, décor and the reinforcement given to these by non-verbal sound – for all subtleties which go beyond the information of the story. It is therefore natural to assume that the expressions on the faces of Washizu and Miki when they receive their swords of promotion from their 'war lord' articulate the very feelings and emotional complexities of Banquo and Macbeth when, after hearing the prophecy of the witches, Macbeth is greeted with the title of Thane of Cawdor. It is a trap into which J. Blumenthal falls, notwithstanding the valuable contribution which his essay for *Sight and Sound* in 1965 makes to an appreciation of the film, when he suggests that Washizu is a fully valid equivalent of Macbeth.

> When Macbeth hears of his wife's death he delivers the famous speech beginning, 'Tomorrow and tomorrow, and tomorrow . . .' Washizu, looking into his wife's chamber, sees part of the result of his folly huddled in the centre of the room; his whole being sags and he moves off heavily to his own chamber. We follow him there. He enters the room and lets his limp body drop to the floor. 'Fool!' he cries. 'Fool!' These are the only words he speaks. Occupying the frame with his seated figure, however, are two other objects: his sword and the throne. Kurosawa holds this eloquent shot for a long time. It is as good an indication as any that Washizu is not a brutish man incapable of reflection. He is rather the spirit of Macbeth distilled into almost pure materiality.[31]

Kurosawa has not, however, created dramatic equivalents in the film's character-izations. Among other things, *Macbeth* is a drama about the power of choice, and the exercise of that power. THRONE OF BLOOD, on the other hand, is a drama about inevitable prophetic truth, and the film is more accurately titled THE CASTLE OF THE SPIDER'S WEB. Where Macbeth has choice, Washizu has only destiny, and this distinction between Shakespeare's play and Kurosawa's drama is forcibly announced at the beginning and the end of the film, by the chanting chorus which rings out the inevitable fate of ambitious men and proclaims it to be a truth which transcends particular circumstances of history. This major difference between Shakespeare's *Macbeth* and Kurosawa's THRONE OF BLOOD is succinctly propounded by John Gerlach, in his riposte to Blumenthal.

> Most of Kurosawa's changes are gauged to increase our sympathy for Macbeth so as to involve the viewer in an experience more psychologically acceptable. Although we are not likely to admit we would do what Macbeth has done, we can conceive ourselves being trapped, as was Washizu, by a deceiving set of circumstances. What Shakespeare has done is all the more difficult – he has made us find something of ourselves in a character whose avarice estranges us. In the words of Alfred Harbage we 'attach' ourselves to Macbeth because he is as 'humane in his reflections as he is inhumane in his acts'. Kurosawa eliminates the contrast between act and reflection and gives only acts performed in mitigating circumstances.[32]

If Washizu, Asaji and Miki (the representative character figures for Macbeth, Lady Macbeth and Banquo) are not specifically invested with the psychological complex-ity of the Shakespeare characters, that is certainly not to suggest that the film does not project its own artistic complexities in a tightly structured and forcefully integrated way. It does this through its spatial strategy, which might be described as 'symphonic' in that it selects four clearly established and autonomous elements and then, through a process of combination, development and modulation, achieves an aesthetically satisfying form in its finished composition. The four essential elements are the mist, the forest, the horses and the castle; elements which also constitute the dramatic world of RAN.

Kurosawa's films operate within more rigidly controlled conventions than do Welles's Shakespearean films, but their presentation of dramatic opposition is very similar in concept. The films of Welles and Kurosawa assert their dramatic conflicts through organically different spatial elements, and through the spatial development of separate worlds. It is least easy to find vital elements in MACBETH, partly because it is a film which deals with the evolution of form, but in OTHELLO the elements are stone, water and iron: in CHIMES AT MIDNIGHT they appear most clearly to be wood, stone and iron. In OTHELLO the worlds of Venice and Cyprus are opposed; in CHIMES, the Tavern and the Court.

The major conflict in THRONE OF BLOOD is presented through the spatial polarity between the castle and the forest; the world of man and the world of nature. The opposition between these two worlds is made more starkly dramatic by the subtle pointing of those simplest of contradictions, the vertical and the horizontal. Where the forest is a maze of great, immovable tree-trunks growing upward so that their tops are outside the space of the frame, the castle interior suggests wide space, expansive, uncluttered floors, ceilings supported by clean-cut, evenly placed beams. Even the vertical wall in the background has upon it a painted decoration which suggests long, horizontal cloud shapes. Further evidence of Kurosawa's affinity with Welles comes from his remark on the interior designs and the horizontal stress. 'To emphasize the psychology of the hero, driven by compulsion, we made the interiors wide with low ceilings and squat pillars to create the effect of oppression.'[33]

The castle and the forest interact throughout the film, but they do not merely represent opposite ends of a spectrum. Their interaction is subtly interwoven so that the ultimate triumph of one over the other is as organically inevitable as the process of evolution. On the purely narrative level, the process is simple enough. Washizu visits the forest twice, and then through a dramatic reversal the forest visits him with devastating finality. The finer details of the interaction are, however, very subtle, for Kurosawa establishes connections between the forest and the castle which cut across the stark opposition he had earlier established. Firstly there is a military connection; secondly a material connection; thirdly a connection whereby each is composed of opposites which reflect the greater opposition between the two.

Both the castle and the forest have strategic importance in the war-torn situation of the realm. The film opens its narrative action (after the initial chorus) with a desperate and weary soldier beating at the gates of the fortress within which the war lords sit making their tactical decisions. The soldier is a dispatch messenger bringing news of the battle, and in this early dialogue the strategic importance of the forest is identified. It is a maze of deceptive trails in which an invading army will lose its bearings, its cohesive unity and its morale. The military impregnability of the castle (and therefore the stability of political order) depends in the last resort on the forging of a successful alliance between the castle and the forest, the world of man and the world of nature.

The material connection of the castle with the forest is so obviously natural, that it is apt to pass unnoticed. The forest is not merely a military resource. It provides a natural building material for the assertion of the world of man. Nor is the fact that the castle is essentially a wooden structure simply a demand of the film set. Kurosawa's insistence on accuracy of detail is evident. Donald Richie, in his comprehensive study of Kurosawa's work, quotes Yoshiro Murali (the designer) as saying: 'We studied old castle layouts, the really old ones, not those white castles we still have around.' Kurosawa's own standards about material accuracy are uncompromising. He refused to make do with a 'false-front' set, because, he said:

I wanted to get the feeling of the real thing from wherever I chose to shoot . . . About sets, I'm on the severe side. This is from I K U R U onwards. Until then, we had to make do with false-fronts. We didn't have the material. But you cannot expect to get a feeling of realism if you use, for example, cheap new wood in a set which is supposed to be an old farmhouse. I feel very strongly about this. After all, the real life of any film lies just in its being as true as possible to appearances.[34]

The insistence on accuracy of design and material is paralleled in the searching choice of locations. The castle was constructed on the upper slopes of Mount Fuji, because only there could Kurosawa be assured of the kind of soil he wanted, the sweeping mists and the forests. Even where the interiors and castle courtyard shots were filmed in a studio, the organic material correspondences were sustained with meticulous care, volcanic soil from Fuji being transported to the Tokyo studio. Not only is the castle made from the natural resources which the forest provides, but so also are the protective shields which Washizu's armour has over the upper arms and shoulders, and so are the weapons which Washizu's soldiers use to destroy him.

The organic correspondence between the forest and the castle is made emphatically clear when, shortly before the final battle, the birds from the forest fly into the castle. The flight of the birds to the castle fulfils a complex function, but their arrival on the eve of the battle is prompted by the cutting of the trees, and their blundering flight into the repose of the interior geometric design makes two statements about the castle. They link wood with wood: and their haphazard intrusion juxtaposes the unregimented world of nature with the mathematically restrained world of man. The birds carry the suggestion that in the very nature of its organic composition, the wood of the castle – and of the artefacts within it – is ultimately allied with the wood of the forest.

As the trees move through the mist towards the castle (they are photographed in slow motion to give them an ominous fluidity of movement), Washizu's men turn against him and pin him to the wall with volley after volley of arrows. His groping attempt to move along the wall through the ever thickening cluster of arrows which stick into it is like a man clawing his way through a forest, and reiterates in metaphor Washizu's earlier disorientation in the forest, after his initial military triumph. The forest of arrows lodges in the wood of the castle and of Washizu's protective armour with a cumulative suggestion of organic affinity. The attempt to retain military and political control through allying the world of nature with the world of man has eminently failed.

The third level on which the castle and the forest are connected is on their accommodation of contradictions within themselves. While the forest imagery is dominated by the density and rooted strength of tree trunk verticals, there are paths and trails between the trees, and it is along these Washizu and Miki ride with mounting panic in the early minutes of the film, as they try to find their bearings. The invading army which finally moves in to capture the castle is only assured of success when they obey their commander's instruction to move directly through the forest and deliberately to ignore the paths.

Similarly, while there is an insistent emphasis on the horizontal dimensions of the castle interior, the final sequences of Washizu's preparation for the siege, his keeping watch on the forest, his exhortations to his men and his derision of the attempts of the invading enemy are all filmed to suggest a nervous and precarious vertical elevation of Washizu. The arrows that pin him against the wall and which lodge in his armour are all loosed from below. As the arrows render him increasingly helpless, he comes down from the upper storey to the castle courtyard. The final moments of his dying show him moving towards his men along the same horizontal level as that on which they back away, and collapsing forward away from the camera.

There is a suggestion, in both of these developments, that conflict between the world of nature and the world of man results ultimately in the destruction of both worlds. In both the castle and the forest, the horizontal defeats the vertical. Both man and the trees are brought low: reduced to a level with all things and gradually obscured from sight by the mist. The swirling and opaque clouds which seem to rise from the ground after Washizu's collapse and which obscure the outlines of the wide circle of Washizu's mutinous soldiers, move us back to the mist which so dominated the opening of the film and which recurs to accompany the closing repetition of the chorus, which tells of the once mighty fortress, where

> Lived a proud warrior
> Murdered by ambition
> His spirit walking still.
> Still his spirit walks, his fame is known,
> For what once was is now yet true,
> Murderous ambition will pursue . . .[35]

In a horizontal movement, the camera pans across and dimly discerns, through the mist, the ruins of the castle. The panning shot across empty, mist-shrouded desolation is identical with the opening shot of the film's action, and it is accompanied in the same way by the unmelodic drone of the chorus. The only upright which the camera explores vertically downwards is the wooden stake whose Japanese script commemorates the site of the ruin. With these simple camera movements, the dramatic opposition between the vertical and the horizontal is articulated at the very start of the film, and implicit in its cyclic return is the philosophic frame of the world's futility when power is the object of ambition.

If the major conflict in the film is that between the castle and the forest, it is a spatial and organic articulation of the philosophical conflict which lies beneath it; that of Asaji's – and later of Washizu's – view of the world where achievement and success are won through opportunism and the cunning abrogation of trust, set against the kind of world that the forest witch cynically describes – a world of vain ambition, of futility of action, of reductive mutability and ultimate insignificance. The film does not present an alternative world of moral goodness. Because the story of Washizu is not one of choice but of prophetic inevitability, there is no alternative for the man of ambition. The only hint of another priority in life comes in the reluctance with which Washizu accepts Asaji's persuasion that Miki (the Banquo figure) is not to be trusted. 'Washizu can only answer that somehow or other "we must have faith in our friends". It is a weak answer but it is after all the only one.'[36]

The dimensions of dramatic conflict are expanded through three other spatial articulations. There are juxtapositions between movement and stasis, geometric design and natural shape, horizontals and diagonals. The most elaborately developed of these oppositions is that between movement and stasis, and, like the contrast between the hunt and the sedate ceremonial order in R AN, it is established at the start of the action.

One messenger after another rushes into the fortress enclosure to report on the state of the battle. Each one, approaching the seated row of war lords, assumes the crouching posture of obeisance and then gives his report. The description is of frantic and precarious military actions, but the war lords sit unmoved in their long line, raised above the ground on a dais. The only movement in the scene, as each speaker pours out his words, is the fluttering of pennants in the wind. Later, when Washizu and Miki encounter the forest witch, they find this strangely asexual figure sitting within a flimsy enclosure. Her eerie stillness of body while she sings, set in the frame against the spinning movement of her wheel and its flow of thread, gives a visual dimension to the conflict between the flow of her prophecy and the unmelodic monotone which carries the words.

The first meeting between Washizu and Asaji (the Lady Macbeth figure) takes place within the cool respose of the castle's interior design. As Washizu relates the details of the encounter with the witch, he and Asaji sit very still on the floor. Asaji is expressionless in both voice and gesture, and so in apparent harmony with the simple stillness of the room. The tension in Washizu's facial muscles suggests the repression of violent conflicts within himself, while outwardly he is controlled in both posture and gesture. As Washizu's instincts begin to yield to Asaji's rational persuasion, our attention is drawn, by the intrusive sound of galloping hooves in the silence, to that part of the courtyard visible through the open door in the depth of the frame. A horse gallops wildly round within the courtyard stockade. In its evocation of powerful instinctive forces unnaturally contained, it is a most eloquent commentary on Washizu's emotional confusion. The shot achieves an effect very similar to that following Welles's sustained tracking shot of Iago and Othello as they walk along the fortress wall. Iago, it will be recalled, first invades Othello's instinctive trust with a rational argument about Desdemona's affection for Cassio. Iago, his back to the sea wall, pushes home his advantage facing Othello and the camera, so that through a vacant gun-port behind him we see the breaking waves rolling in towards the fortress.

There is a very subtle development of the opposition between stasis and movement in the characterizations of Washizu and his wife, Asaji. The conventions of movement through which each of these characters is revealed are drawn from separate artistic traditions. Marsha Kinder, writing specifically of character movement in the film, observes the consistent stillness of Asaji. She seldom moves in the frame, but when she does, it is with smoothness and control so that she 'glides across the screen as a unified presence, totally committed to ambition'.[37] Donald Richie maintains that her movement, gesture and expression are highly conventionalized and shaped within the choreographic discipline of the Noh drama. 'She moves heel to toe as does the Noh actor', and the shape of the actress's face is 'used to suggest the Noh mask'.[38] According to Richie, too, both the frame composition in the scenes when Washizu and Asaji are together, and Asaji's 'hand-washing scene' are wholly stylized within Noh conventions.

The movements of Washizu, on the other hand, lie distinctly outside the stylization of Noh. Indeed, according to both Kinder and Anna Laura Zambrano (who relates the film to a context of Japanese art in general), they do not rise from theatrical tradition at all, but from the depictions of the Yamato-e picture scrolls. Washizu moves like an animal. He paces up and down, he breathes heavily, he flexes his facial muscles rhythmically and bares his teeth. He gives the illusion of a capability 'to move simultaneously in several directions as he considers various courses of action'.[39] The disruption of the banquet, for instance, is articulated through the juxtaposition of Washizu's violent movements with a symmetry of reposed composition which reflects both architectural and social order. The stillness and mathematically precise positioning of the guests within the room and within the frame is shattered by Washizu's frenzied response on seeing Miki's ghost.

It is Washizu who forges and sustains the link in the film between exterior and interior space, and Zambrano observes the logical extension of the scroll influence to exterior composition. She notes the similarity of those compositions in many of Kurosawa's films, in which 'Samurai horsemen are often set against a natural background of fog or sloping hills', with the scroll paintings of battle action. 'The horses charge at full gallop, mouth agape with tension while their riders hold their weapons defiantly, moving in clusters along the landscape as had the samurai of the Kakamura era.'[40]

The clear distinction between the style of movement of Asaji and that of Washizu has a further important dramatic function. There are moments of intensity when the influence and power of the dominant character reveals itself in the 'infection' of the posture, movement and gesture of the submissive partner. As Marsha Kinder notes, there is a flow and recoil of influence between Asaji and Washizu during the tense silences which precede and accompany the murder of Tsuzuki (the Duncan figure). Washizu sits motionless, in the posture which we have come to associate with Asaji. Washizu's unaccustomed bodily stillness suggests that Asaji has invaded his character, 'temporarily suspending his identity'. Asaji returns to the room, bringing a spear which she places in Washizu's hands. He then rises and leaves the lighted area on his way to murder Tsuzuki. The camera holds Asaji in its frame while she waits in silence. Suddenly, to the accompaniment of shrill, dissonant music, Asaji rises and begins to dance with frenzied and ecstatic movements, 'as if acting out the violence'.[41] Her own frantic dance movements suggest the reciprocal invasion of Asaji's character by Washizu. The balanced transfer of the dominant role from Asaji to Washizu in this central scene is consistent with the change in each character from observer to agent; from one *waiting* to one *committing*. It is also consistent with the wider shift of dramatic dominance from Lady Macbeth to Macbeth, in the developing action of Shakespeare's play.

Finally the purely technical resources of fast- and slow-motion are used to heighten the disparity between the approach of the forest, filmed in slow-motion as it advances through the mist, and the fall of Washizu as he is unceremoniously toppled with sudden speed down the stairs, in the last minutes of the film. The intricate organization of this polarity between movement and stasis and between controlled movement and frenzy justifies itself thematically in the culminating overthrow of both man-devised and natural logic: the fulfilment of the prophecy that something as rooted as a forest will move. The movement–stasis polarity can be seen to have an implicit relevance to the medium in which Kurosawa works, for 'Making a forest move is no more miraculous than creating the appearance of motion out of still photographs – the illusion that lies at the centre of cinema.'[42]

The film's spatial strategy announces the world of man through geometrical design. Horizontals, verticals and diagonals are prominent as structural supports within the castle. The world of nature, on the other hand, is in its essence totally unregimented by the straight line. Only in man's perception is nature made up of verticals and horizontals. The strategic value of the forest resides in its refusal to be a geometrical system, and in the predictable certainty that man will impose his own perception upon it and consequently lose his way.

The dramatic conflict between the world of nature and the world of man, broadly expounded through the opposition of the castle and the forest, is elaborated through the collision of shape and design. One instance of this (the blundering flight of the birds into the castle rooms) has already been noted. A second and more important instance is encountered in the room which Washizu will occupy during the favouring visit of Tsuzuki. It is a room once occupied by a traitor who killed himself and left, upon its floor and wall, an indelible bloodstain. The room is therefore a centripetal spatial articulation of time in its pulling together the past and the future. In being prepared for Washizu, it ominously heralds his own act of betrayal. In the silent eloquence of this still, interior shot of the wall with its explosive, irregular outline of the bloodstain so at variance with the quiet angles and lines of design, prophecy and destiny become irrevocably knit. The repeated cry of the screech owl links the establishing shot of this room with its later location as the place from which Washizu and Asaji move to accomplish the murder.

A final instance of the aesthetic collision of shape with design emerges at the end of the film when Washizu – all too clearly a human shape – is trapped and cornered within the lines of the castle's interior design. As the volleys of arrows are shot into and around him, the camera shifts past diagonal, upright and horizontal beams to peer at Washizu, establishing an alliance between the camera and the archers in their common need for straight lines of access to their victim. The final shots of Washizu, pierced and penetrated with arrows, are the culminating ironic interaction between line of design and shape of natural organism.

Because it distinguishes with such finality the cinematic image from the darkness which surrounds it, the rectangular frame is highly appropriate for the articulation of dramatic opposition through linear emphasis. The conflict expressed through the vertical and the horizontal has been explicated at length. The geometrical system, however, incorporates a subsidiary element, the diagonal. In many of the shots in THRONE OF BLOOD the diagonal introduces a negative force which cuts across the dialectic of horizontal and vertical. Marsha Kinder relates the horizontal line across the frame to stability and order, and the diagonal to the disruption of that order.

The initial order is asserted at the start of the film's action by the horizontal line of war lords seated on their raised dais. The sequence of messengers who arrive to report on the battle is punctuated by horizontal wipes across the frame to indicate time lapses. The dramatic significance of the diagonal first asserts itself in the long shots of the arrival of Tsuzuki's procession. The line of the procession is first shown along a horizontal moving from left to right across the frame. Suddenly it makes a sharp angular turn to continue diagonally down the frame toward the lower-left corner. This angular turn coincides with the arrival of Washizu's opportunity for treachery and for the realization of ambition. During the sequence preceding Tsuzuki's murder, the guards outside Tsuzuki's chamber sit initially in an orderly horizontal line. The disintegration of this orderliness is wrought by Asaji so that they later sprawl haphazardly in their drug-induced sleep. Washizu waits for Asaji's return when she comes and places in his hands the murder weapon, a long spear which is accommodated diagonally within the frame.

16. THRONE OF BLOOD (Kurosawa). The lines of Washizu's body stress the conflict of diagonal with horizontal as he looks toward the castle and considers the prophecy of the forest witch. Toshiro Mifune (Washizu)

The antithesis between the horizontal and the diagonal dramatizes, too, in spatial terms, the distrust which has arisen between Washizu and Miki after the murder. When Washizu ultimately gains entrance to Miki's castle, with the coffin of the murdered Tsuzuki, he is confronted by Miki and his followers ranged in a horizontal line, 'supporting the authorized order of [the] deposed ruler'. The moment is awkward and tense and Washizu's horse stands at an oblique angle to the line of men. Miki rides forward to Washizu and turns, so that both men ride abreast away from the camera. 'By restoring the horizontal and making this truce with his rival, [Miki] re-establishes a temporary stability.'[43]

One further emphatic use of the diagonal is the prolonged sequence during which Washizu is shot with arrows. The volleys of arrows which pin Washizu to the wall of the castle fly along a diagonal line. The shooting by several archers is consistently from one specific direction, so that the arrows come from below and slightly across the plane of the picture.

It is possible to argue that this constitutes a cyclic use of the diagonal, and that the diagonal stress in the flight of the arrows redresses the initial downward diagonal in the path of Tsuzuki's entourage. Zambrano, however, makes the point that the forces which destroy Washizu do not constitute a just retribution. The cycle of betrayal and murder is not broken, for the soldiers who kill Washizu are as guilty as he. They rose to power by accepting his leadership, and they kill in order to save themselves. 'Washizu is destroyed not by his judges, but by his peers who suffer the same malady. Order is not established because it springs from men who are themselves without order.'[44]

The incorporation into THRONE OF BLOOD of the Noh theatrical conventions invites comparison, in this respect, with Olivier's HENRY V. Olivier did not regard cinema and theatre as opposites, yet within HENRY V it is quite legitimate to consider the staged presentation, for instance where the bishops justify Henry's claim to the throne of France, and the wholly cinematic presentation of the French cavalry charge as extreme ends of the dialectic between theatrical and cinematic drama. Both at the start of the Chorus's prologue and at the end of the film where the actors acknowledge the audience's applause it is clear that their gestures, movements, costumes and vocalization are subject to theatrical conventions, while no such theatrical constraints operate when the King rides his white charger. Olivier's inclusion of explicit theatre as part of the film's overall spatial strategy sets up a polarity between theatrical and realistic space, yet by incorporating theatre and realism within the medium of film, it reconciles them both in the film's presentational development and in its structural cycle.

The incorporation of the Noh conventions within THRONE OF BLOOD is much more complex, and the levels of its aesthetic operation are multiple. In the first place, like the theatrical conventions in HENRY V, the Noh in Kurosawa's film constitutes one extreme of conventionalized movement, gesture and vocalization, but here it is part of a tripartite structure rather than one of direct binary opposition. THRONE OF BLOOD is a film of very dense stylization. All character movement in the frame is stylized in terms of artistic convention, as is the frame composition itself. The only movement which can be considered natural is the movement of a riderless horse, and in this lies the importance of the shots of the ungovernable horse in the stockade, and of the return of Miki's horse without its rider after his assassination. The Noh choreography, therefore, is in direct opposition to natural movement, but it is also, as has been noted, at a clear remove from the frenzied – but nonetheless stylized – movements which characterize Washizu throughout most of the film.

Secondly, the Noh stylization in Kurosawa's film makes particular statements about the character of Asaji. In its conventional limits, the Noh is capable of presenting perfectly finished expression. Richie suggests that Asaji's characterization within Noh's rigid conventions is a reflection of her own limitations. The resemblance of her face to the fixed expression of the Noh mask is an indication of her refusal to become anything more than she is. Just as the world of the Noh is 'both closed and artificial', so too is Asaji 'the most limited, the most confined, the most [obsessively] driven' of the film's characters.[45] Within the spectrum of this film, Noh suggests the futility of perfection and the denial of nature in the distillation of personal potential down to the mere achievement of ambition.

17. THRONE OF BLOOD (Kurosawa). The dramatic opposition of shape and design: the blood-stains in the traitor's chamber disrupt the clear geometry of interior design. Isuzu Yamada (Asaji) and Toshiro Mifune (Washizu)

Any connection which might be seen to ally Lady Macbeth with the witches in Shakespeare's play is tenuous. However, in THRONE OF BLOOD, Noh clearly relates Asaji with the forest witch. The stillness and postural repose, the 'husky and unintoned' vocalization, the subdued but distinct ambient sound are all elements peculiar to Noh, and all are common to the presentations of Asaji and the forest witch, whose faintly clattering spinning wheel is later paralleled in the quiet swishing sound of Asaji's kimono as she walks in the silence before Tsuzuki's murder.[46] While both women are dramatized within the Noh conventions, there remains nevertheless a degree of ambiguity, for if they are both articulators of Washizu's unexpressed wish, their dramatic functions differ. The comment of the witch embraces a wider perspective. It is not only a specific prophecy about Washizu and Miki, but has universal relevance in its cautionary cynicism. She is, as Zambrano maintains, a 'warning of chaos', and this is visually emphasized in the piles of skeletal remains which surround her flimsy enclosure.[47]

The Noh stylization of the banquet scene is especially important, for it is here that the opposition between choreographic styles reaches its climax. The banquet scene in THRONE OF BLOOD is intricately built around the collision between intentional and unintentional theatre. One element in the scene is an entertainment, a dance performed by one man who relates through song and movement a moral tale of an ambitious man who tries vainly to escape inevitable self-destructive retribution. Washizu halts this performance – presented through typical Noh conventions – and proceeds to drink in silence. On seeing the ghost of Miki, Washizu launches into a dance whose frantic movements break out of the established context of ritualized control, as he slashes wildly with his sword and then backs away against the wall.

The grotesque choreography which now becomes the centre of attention is an indelible public revelation of Washizu's guilt. It develops out of the preceding deliberate theatre in the same way that Claudius' reaction to the staging of 'The Mouse-Trap' suddenly becomes a moment of revelatory and unintentional theatre in its disruption of ceremonial occasion. The integration of Noh conventions has enabled Kurosawa to intensify the banquet scene and so to exploit the Shakespearean potential of the theatre-within-theatre as a dramatic turning point, while at the same time enhancing the organic complexity of the film's overall spatial strategy.

Finally, the incorporation of the pervasive Noh devices in characterization and in the film's cyclic structure give the action an amoral universality. Zambrano claims that the ethical roots of the Noh drama are traditionally Buddhist, so that the life of man is seen to be 'a turbulent period, ruled by passions and endured despite continual fear of death'. Its revelation of human nature as a constant, with no redemptive potential for the ambitious man, places it quite clearly outside the medieval Christian universe of Shakespeare's play. A view of life without the implicit spiritual possibilities of redemption or of moral progress necessarily affects the dramatic relation of action to time. Zambrano maintains that Noh concerns itself with an event in the legendary past, and presents a re-embodied spirit which is forced, in human form, to 'symbolically relive its struggle' in terms of its 'decision and commitment made centuries before'.[48] By linking character with spirit, therefore, Noh refuses to consider death an interruption of dramatic issues, and the system of placing events in past, present or future breaks down.

This complexity of the film's time dimensions is important because it strengthens the case for the film's inclusion in the category of Shakespearean film. THRONE OF BLOOD has a spatial strategy which, in its organic integration and complex development of dramatic opposition, is directly related to Welles's OTHELLO and CHIMES AT MIDNIGHT. However, in its relation of spatial manipulation to time, Kurosawa's film has its one truly profound affinity with Olivier's HENRY V. Through the incorporation of their theatrical dimensions, both these latter films transcend simple time structure. While THRONE OF BLOOD (through the implications of its Noh element) connects character with 'spirit' and so links a particular tale with what are seen as universal traits of human nature, HENRY V relates the particular occasion of a performance at the Globe in London with the universal and enduring relevance of Shakespeare's play. Both films deal essentially with the transformation of history into myth and legend; with the fusion of the instant with the imagination.

9   The film actor

As almost any writer on the history of the cinema has pointed out, there were two parallel lines of development in cinematography from the time of its conception (as an entertainment medium): the realistic line initiated by Lumière and the illusionist line explored by Méliès, who 'stamped the theatrical mark on some of his films by lining up his performers at the end of a reel to take a curtain call as if they were appearing on stage'.[1] It was not, however, until the film began to move away from a fixed-position camera recording of a staged entertainment that the cinema took the first steps towards a dramatic language of its own. Edwin S. Porter was the first film maker to explore this new dramatic language by breaking away from the conventions of the theatre and thereby establishing not simply the discontinuity of space as an essence of cinema, but also the dramatic equation of man and object, and the discontinuity of time. In his film THE LIFE OF AN AMERICAN FIREMAN (1902),

he combined outdoor and indoor scenes and evolved the principle of film editing, of making a film by photographing and putting together separate shots, switching the audience's attention from the woman and child in the burning house to the ringing of the fire alarm and the dash of the fire engine to the house . . . It became clear that real time and film time need not coincide. Time could apparently stand still or go backwards while the camera showed what was happening in another area of action.[2]

The distancing effects which the disjunctions of time and space produced were compensated for by an increase of credibility in the selective visualization of real dramatic elements in the story. The camera now revealed the actor unsupported by the conventions which operated in the theatre. The expectation that the drama of the cinema should bear a close relation to events in real life remained powerful, and it became important that the appearance of a screen character should be authentic.

Casting therefore asserts specific and particular priorities for the dramatic film which is conceived as film. 'Because the credibility and acceptability of a screen character is related to the experience viewers have had in judging people in real life, a given character is expected to look like the kind of person he is attempting to portray.'[3] Pauline Kael maintains that the casting of films is more important than the casting of plays because

In the theatre a competent actor can make many roles his own, but in movies what an actor knows and can do is often less important than what he simply *is* – the way he looks, how he photographs, what he inadvertently projects . . . The camera exposes the actor as a man of a certain age, with definite physical assets and liabilities. There he is in close-up, huge on the screen, and if he's trying to play something that is physically different from what he is, he looks like a fool.[4]

The casting priorities for Shakespearean film are of special interest in view of the emphasis which film places on physical types and photogenic appropriateness. The general trend in British and American films of Shakespeare plays is to cast well-established stage actors in the major roles, and often in *all* the roles. The justification for this would seem to be that the performance of experienced actors would give to the films a degree of respectability as adaptations, and that actors who had stage experience would handle Shakespeare's roles and language with an authoritative skill. Well-known theatre actors have not, however, always stood up well before the sustained scrutiny of the camera. The casting of Judith Anderson as Lady Macbeth in George Schaefer's 1960 film was not particularly fortunate, since she was clearly long past the age where her line 'I have given suck, and know how tender 'tis to love the babe that milks me' evokes a visual relevance.[5] The casting of Eileen Herlie as Gertrude in Olivier's HAMLET produced a visual difficulty in view of Olivier's forty-year-old Hamlet, and Jon Finch, Francesca Annis and Nicholas Selby do nothing to enhance the theatrical impact of Polanski's MACBETH.

On the other hand, the fragmentary process of film shooting might allow the inexperienced actor who is visually suitable to make a satisfactory performance without the necessity of sustaining the role in continuous action. While there is much one could criticize in the portrayals of Romeo and Juliet in Franco Zeffirelli's film, the visualization of adolescent love gives to that film a dimension of credibility, despite the gaucheness of Leonard Whiting and Olivia Hussey, which is patently lacking in the more intelligent performances of Leslie Howard and Norma Shearer in Cukor's ROMEO AND JULIET.

Michael Birkett, in speaking of the casting for the Peter Brook KING LEAR, confirms that the major roles were cast from the Royal Shakespeare Company production which preceded the film, and his comment on Paul Scofield's being one of the major *raisons d'être* of KING LEAR reveals the degree of importance which one theatrical actor can hold in the making of a Shakespearean film.[6] Birkett's awareness of the photogenic demands of cinema emerge when he discusses the casting of the less prominent roles.

For the rest of the cast, we suddenly found ourselves rather in sympathy with the Hollywood moguls who are so often maligned for 'type-casting'. On the stage . . . it's possible simply to equate the talents and the variety of an actor with a part that needs casting; it's possible to get away with a fine performance which at close range would not necessarily look convincing. When it comes to the screen, however, it may be that the very first shot of a character carries no dialogue with it but is close and revealing. The very look of the face has to be convincing; the actor must *be* the character, with no other aid than the clothes he wears and the make-up on his face.[7]

It might be inferred from what Birkett has said that the intention of the film is really to record Scofield's performance as Lear with some modification for the camera, and to shift the film out of theatrical confines by casting some of the roles purely according to visual priorities. In any event, the casting of the leading role, by Birkett's admission, determined the possibility of the film.

Diametrically opposed to this was the approach of Kozintsev in his last film, KING LEAR. Kozintsev was not wedded to the idea of securing the commitment of an established stage actor to play the part of Lear. He set out on his quest for the actor who would be suitable, with two ideas in mind. Neither would be priorities in selecting a theatrical Lear. Both are visually important, the one a detail which would be most telling in the camera's close-shots, and one which would be effective in longer-distance shots.

The one aspect of the film actor's expressive resources which Kozintsev repeatedly writes of is the articulacy of an actor's eyes. The actor whom he cast for Lear was Yuri Yarvet, and Kozintsev discovered his particular suitability for the film part when he was watching screen tests for actors who auditioned for small parts. 'Today, after many difficult months, after so many unsuccessful tests, I have at last seen the eyes on the screen: the very eyes.' Of the attempts to find experienced actors who could play the film part of Lear, Kozintsev was dismissive. 'I have not had the good fortune' he writes, 'to glimpse either the bitter irony born of suffering, or the wisdom arising out of madness.' The face and the eyes of Yarvet, reminiscent of Voltaire, 'the bitter irony, the wit of Europe', convinced Kozintsev that he had found the photographic subject for his film, and after a very simple screen test which involved no speaking at all, Kozintsev's diary notes 'I looked at Yarvet and recognized Lear. Yarvet looked like him.'

The other aspect of Yarvet's physical suitability for the part was his shortness of stature. 'I would like Lear to be short and the people surrounding him, the majority of his kingdom enormously tall.' It arises clearly from Kozintsev's notes, however, that insofar as the actor's expressiveness is concerned, the camera work in close-up is of paramount importance. 'The advantage of the cinema over the theatre is not that you can even have horses, but that you can stare closer into a man's eyes; otherwise it is pointless to set up a cine camera for Shakespeare.' While casting for film in general would seem to set its greatest priorities on the mere surface appearance of the actor, this obviously cannot be the case for Shakespearean film. Kozintsev, despite his insistence on visual articulacy, had to have other qualities in his actor, and he distinguishes two approaches to characterization: that of the actor and that of the interpreter. 'The fundamental meanings of these two words define two different kinds of gifts, two dissimilar qualities. An interpreter could not become Lear. The ability to become Lear depends not on a similarity of outward appearance, but on a kinship of spiritual substance, the constitution of the actor's inner world.'[8]

The major difference between casting for a film which is conceived as film, and casting for Shakespearean film, lies in the fact that where material is taken from what has already been artistically constituted for theatrical presentation as a play, the film maker is inevitably working with structured roles. Whereas a film role 'has no separate conceptual existence' outside its performance, theatre roles are generally 'apprehensible as entities . . . because the theatre is a place where actor and role meet and eventually part'.[9] The distinction between role and actor is most clearly demonstrated in the theatre when the actors step forward after the end of a play to acknowledge the audience's applause in their curtain-call. In that brief appearance, they demonstrate their common humanity shared with the audience, and their abandonment of role. The actor on the screen can do no such thing. He remains separate and trapped within the medium of dramatic expression so that even in those quaint moments when Méliès filmed his actors giving a curtain-call to the camera, that curtain-call was inevitably a part of the structured entity of the film.

The fact that a curtain-call on film does not function like a curtain-call on stage illustrates a significant difference between the theatre and cinema. The same action performed with the same intention is transformed into something different by the change in medium alone. In the theatre we are dealing with a concept of a totality structured within, but isolated from, the natural world of biological and organizational necessities, and this is precisely what Bazin said of theatrical presentation of stage space, when he wrote of the stage as an 'aesthetic microcosm'.[10]

Susanne Langer relates this idea of a wholeness or totality to theatrical presentation when she deals specifically with the 'dramatic illusion'.

Dramatic action is a semblance of action so constructed that a whole, indivisible piece of virtual history is implicit in it . . . It is a human destiny that unfolds before us, its unity is apparent from the opening words or even silent action, because on the stage we see acts in their entirety, as we do not see them in the real world except in retrospect, that is, by constructive reflection. In the theatre they occur in simplified and complicated form, with visible motives, directions and ends.

On character in the theatre, she continues,

Because we are not involved with them as real people, we can view each smallest act in its context, as a symptom of character and condition. We do not have to find what is significant; the selection has been made – whatever is there is significant, and it is not too much to be surveyed 'in toto'. A character stands before us as a coherent whole.[11]

For the film actor, even in the cinematic adaptation of a theatrical work, the entire concept of totality is different. In film, it is only the director who is constantly concerned with a sense of totality. The actor is projected in a series of moments that rely heavily upon visual presence rather than dialogue, creating an image that is momentarily central within a very broad context. He works in front of a camera which, because of its voyeuristic nature, intensifies both the detail of the moment when the actor is present and the privacy of those moments when he is absent.

The film actor does not so much perform a role, as he creates a kind of life . . . The stage actor memorises an entire role in proper order, putting it on like a costume, while the film actor learns his part in pieces, often cut out of chronological order, using his personality as a kind of armature, or as painters will let canvas show through to become part of the total effect.[12]

In short, the film actor, the camera and the director are interdependent elements of film, and the cohesiveness of an actor's performance ultimately depends on the ability of the audience to piece together the elements of characterization in the same way as they do in everyday life, 'in retrospect, that is, by constructive reflection'.

The fragmentary nature of the film actor's work in performance is related to the technology of film synthesis. His performance achieves its finished state through a process which is not organic as the theatre actor's must be, but episodic, so that the resultant structure is in the nature of an assembly. Certain elements and relationships within this assembly make the film actor's work distinctive in its nature.

The relation of the actor to the frame and to the space within the frame is constantly varied. Brief moments of action will be shot a number of times, and from this raw material the director will select and edit shots for inclusion in the film. Sequences of action will be shot out of chronological sequence and out of context of dramatic shape. The actor must sometimes even be prepared to speak and act sections of dialogue and close-up action without the physical presence of other actors. Stand-ins are used in long-shot moments or for dangerous moments of action, and dialogue and sound are often mixed into the sound-track after the shooting.

At the time of performance, the film actor can have no conscious apprehension of his own contribution to the finished film, and in the light of the dislocations which are imposed upon him, the question must now arise as to whether the film actor can be considered an artist. The shift of control from the actor to the director, the editor and to the technical exigencies of the medium has prompted many critics to agree with Josef von Sternberg that 'the motion picture actor cannot function as an artist . . . but only as one of the complex materials of our work'.[13] Since control of both space and timing are effectively removed from the film actor, it must be agreed that at best he is only in fractional control of what might be termed 'artistic performance'.

If the theatre is the actor's medium, film is the director's medium, and the particular nature of the relationship between actor and director in cinema depends in the first place on the relation of actor and performance to text, and in the second place on the actor's relation to décor.

The play text is a special kind of text precisely because it is 'conceived with a view to the potentialities of the theatre, [and] these are already embodied in the text. The text determines the mode and style of the production; it is already potentially the theatre.'[14] This is of immense importance in that it makes possible between the theatre actor and the theatre director a relationship which is not possible between their counterparts in the realm of film making. If the text is the primary and overriding determinant of the 'mode and style of the production', then both the actor and director scrutinize the text as equals. The actor is at liberty to justify his ideas in terms of his reading of the text, just as the director will justify his. The director and the actor work as partners in a way that they cannot in the making of the film, for the film text – such as it is – is in its entirety a confidential document known only – and then probably only incompletely – to the director.

An unpublished shooting script of the film RICHARD III carries the following notice at its start: 'Since this script was written there has been a reconception of its form.'[15] This is a clear admission that to a considerable extent the 'text' of a film's shooting script may change quite radically during the shooting of the film – to say nothing of the editing; and the decisions as to changes made may come from a number of quarters, for a number of reasons which may have little to do with a director's conception. Even if a director modifies the actualization of a stage play text, the text as known and published has in the course of its initial run 'become crystallized so to speak as to its essentials'.[16]

In organizing the actor's relationship with the décor, too, the authority of the director must be paramount, for the cinema image demands a spatial treatment which is clearly different from that which operates on the theatre stage. The pre-eminence of the theatre actor arises from 'the eternal and insoluble contradiction between the living actor and the dead scenery, the flesh and blood figure and the painted perspective of the background'.[17] It is essentially a distinction determined by the spatial properties of the theatre stage, which extends backwards from and forwards into the auditorium. The further the stage is thrust out into the auditorium the more complete will be the dislocation of the actor from the structured spatial context of the dramatic action; the more the actor will cease to be an inhabitant of the space world of the play and become a pioneer of the stage's frontier territory, carrying with him the play's language and embodying the play's theatrical energy.

In the theatre then, both the actor and the director work with a clear knowledge of the inevitability that the actor will carry an increasing degree of dramatic responsibility as the play proceeds, simply because the space and the décor which surround the actor remain constant (except after a deliberate scene change). The stage actor is, above all, an accomplished manipulator of space in the theatre. His movement, his gesture, his vocal projection, all are governed by a sense of space which is consistent with the character he portrays, with the size of the auditorium and the stage, and with the sense of that distance between actor and audience which the actor feels. It is the actor who thus controls the *virtual* space relationship between audience and character at any given performance – and at any given moment within a performance. A soliloquy delivered on stage, for instance, implies a closer *virtual* spatial contact than does a royal proclamation – though the *actual* space relationship remains physically identical.

In film, three spatial considerations require the assertion of directorial control over the film actor: firstly, the dramatic equation between actor and inanimate object (arising from the fact that both are pictured); secondly, the spatial discontinuity which is the essence of cinema; and thirdly, the spatial proportions deployed within the cinema frame. The film actor can no longer assert his flesh-and-blood distinction from inanimate décor or selected spatial detail, as Edwin S. Porter's early film showed when it equated the firemen's bell with the waiting woman and child. Nor can the actor exploit on his own terms a growing relationship with a spatial context which is both changing and articulate in its own terms. Lastly, the film actor has no means of apprehending just how the camera is framing him at any moment.

While the theatre director works almost wholly with the actors, the film director has a dual responsibility; both to the actor and to the camera, and in his mediation between the machine and the human actor, he will seem constantly to require the actor to meet the less flexible demands of the machine. It will seem so, but in fact his alliance with the camera and its potential for the specialized manipulation of space is an aesthetic alliance made in terms of his conception of the individual shot and of the film as a whole. 'The scene size is the primary determinant of the actor's interpretation. This is one of the primary reasons for the authority of the director in cinema; he understands the degree of emphasis required in a given performance for a given scene size, and the relationship of that scene to the edited film.'

The relation of the actor's contribution to the finished film as a whole shatters the concept of an actor's artistic performance in three other respects. Firstly, the finished film is an edited version of the material shot. Short time-sections of an actor's performance may be photographed from different angles, with different lighting effects, or they may be taken in full shot, medium, or in close-up. It is the film editor who selects the finally accepted shot, not simply in accordance with the quality of the actor's performance, but more often with 'the exigencies of cinematic technique in editing – logical continuity, intercharacter motivations, suspense, cutting of movements, cutaways, inserts, expanded and contracted cinematic time and distance, and cross-cutting between parallel dramatic sequences'.[18] Editing is done by the film editor in consultation with the director, and it is perhaps that part of film making which has the most to do with the artistic result of the finished film, and has least to do with the artistic input of the actor. It is a process removed, through technological necessity, in time and place from the performance of the actor.

Secondly, the necessity to shoot action out of the dramatic and chronological sequence means that continuity and dramatic shaping must become the responsibility of the director rather than the actor. The continuity of performance from the beginning to the end of a play generates a momentum and sweep which is not part of the film actor's experience. MacLiammóir writes of this:

Snippets! Yet it's true. Hardly a shot has lasted more than fifty seconds; the meticulous inferno of tripping over the rails arriving on the wooden stool, hitting the wooden blocks with one's toes, turning to go, turning back again, twisting the dagger and saying the line, has no sooner begun than it is all over, and one does it again.

He notes that Welles, too, sought the cinematic suggestion of unrehearsed spontaneity:

Sometimes we make a shot four times, sometimes forty, with intervals between each shot for Sartoli to mop up our sweat and Vasco to comb out the dank strands of our wigs, and Orson to say 'That was the one, I think, mechanically it was perfect, but you were becoming a little bit mechanical. You'd lost the freshness of the second shot which you spoiled by falling over the stool; now let's see if you can put back the freshness and keep on your feet.'[19]

Finally, there is in film work a distinct artificiality of dramatic experience for the actor, arising from the necessity for him to work in isolation – sometimes at intense moments in the filmed action. Josef von Sternberg has written of such experiences:

He [the film actor] may be required to throw his arms around another actor and call him his best friend – without having seen this individual two seconds before playing such a scene. He is induced, and sometimes prefers, to play ardent love scenes to a space near the lens which, in the absence of a leading lady, who is reclining in her dressing room, or still emoting in another film, represents her until she can appear. This doesn't bother him at all, for if the woman is present, who for the moment represents the love of his life, she is asked to look beyond him or at his ear, as otherwise the camera, due to the fact that film lovers are not separated by normal distances, makes them both appear to be cross-eyed.[20]

Despite all that has been so far suggested about the necessary authority which the film director must have over the film actor, this is not to say that the relationship itself is counter-artistic. Miss Myrtle Moss, an actress with the Royal Shakespeare Company in 1977 and with experience of film acting, observes the psychological dimension of the actor–director relationship in film to be crucial:

I think it is very important for the film director to know how to work with the psychology of the individual actor. On stage a director can concentrate much more on what impact is being made from the stage, on the audience – or imaginary audience. Film acting is much more an internal process for the actor, and you've no idea how important it is for a film director to know how to reassure an actor. Sometimes we have to do a 'take' time and time again, so that it becomes terribly depressing unless one is reassured that this may be due to a number of technical problems and not the actor's fault at all. If a stage actor is emotionally disturbed, the projection demands of a stage can enable him still to produce a convincing performance. But for the film actor, any emotional disturbance or any loss of confidence will interfere much more seriously with performance because the internal action of feelings and thoughts is so central to what the camera is catching.[21]

The only director who has written at length of his work with film actors in Shakespearean film is Kozintsev. Of his relationship with Yuri Yarvet he said, 'I have little faith in the term "professional" when applied to a director's work with his actor. In struggling with figures such as Lear, one lives the same life, and becomes so close that one even shares the same objects of love and hate.' Clearly in the casting of his film, Kozintsev was not looking for an actor who would conform to Josef von Sternberg's stereotype. 'I was looking for a Lear who would be a kindred spirit, an actor with imagination, a lover of strange decisions. The four arithmetical rules are little help here.'[22] There is an underlying paradox in Kozintsev's comments, for while the director and the actor are separate people with clear responsibilities on the one hand, their work would seem to dissolve the demarcation between their artistic experience.

In the last resort, the issues of *artistry* and *performance* with regard to the film actor and his work come back to the problem of locating a final authority. For a staged play, the text asserts itself as an authority for both actor and director. Yet there lie between the text and the performed play undetermined dimensions of both temporal and spatial control which are the actor's alone. As Appia has pointed out: 'The stage gives him [the dramatist] a space which he has not measured; it remains alien to his MS.' Furthermore he observes that the text of a play is unable to determine, with any precision, duration of time. 'The duration of speech is indeterminate; speech may be uttered slowly or rapidly, it may be broken et cetera, and these variations occur in a lapse of time difficult to span; too much slowness may destroy the connection of ideas; too much rapidity may make them unintelligible; but between these extremes there is a wide margin.'[23] Paradoxically, while the text embodies the potential presentation of the play, it is precisely in those areas where the text is least able to determine exactness that the particular performance of the actor is built. Performance then becomes a totality, which can be isolated from the presented work.

Despite the comparative flexibility of the film script, no artistry of performance is born of that discrepancy between what the shooting script ordains and what the actor ultimately does. Precisely because there is no authoritative text for a film in the making, other kinds of authority inhibit the versatility of the film actor's work. Where the theatre strives for control, the film actually manages to impose it, existing as it does, as a series of juxtapositions structured in time by an authority outside and removed from the actor.

In a film which is primarily conceived as film, the cinema is free to explore its own specific potentials for characterization. Once the film attempts to adapt a work whose characters have already been developed and established as classic theatrical roles, particular problems arise from that inverse correlation between aesthetic distance and realistic presentation. In the theatre where 'real' people act out a drama in 'real' three-dimensional space before a live audience, the presentation will only take on an artistic stature if there are supporting conventions to which both the audience and the actors are party. On the other hand, because the cinema image is distanced from the audience it can compensate by approaching reality without loss of its artistic validity. 'This gulf between the [cinema] audience and the events presented to them will permit a much greater use of realism than the stage may legitimately employ.' The problem for the actor in Shakespearean film lies in that divide between the conventional characterization of the theatre and the realistic characterization which is natural to film.

In classical drama the experience presented to the audience is heightened; the theatrical character is essentially presented through dialogue and achieves a status which elevates him above the normal level of life. The cinematic character, on the contrary, is revealed through fragments of detail as belonging to the same world as the audience. In film adaptations of Shakespearean drama these two approaches may become confused so that there arises the danger of judging 'theatrical characters by reference to individuals with whom we are acquainted' and of cinematically creating a character with whom the heightened poetry of Shakespeare's dialogue is incompatible.

This aesthetic dissonance between the cinema's tendency to characterize in terms of the individual and theatre's tradition of characterizing its protagonists and antagonists in terms of 'the lineaments of universal humanity' highlights the difficulty of reconciling what is shown with what is spoken.[24] The silent cinema, despite its deliberate discontinuities of time and space, was able to retain its theatrical affinities in certain dramatic characterizations. 'Characters in silent films could be iconographic because they were like moving statues, with a solidity and visual continuity that somehow raised them out of their individuality into some timeless image of human nature.' The silence in which such characters were projected still made necessary some artistic conventions which allowed for the emergence of universality. With the arrival of synchronized dialogue there emerged a new and most important dimension of cinematic characterization, the aural dimension. What a film actor did with his voice raised a new difficulty, for vocal intimacy became more important than vocal projection. In turn, the introduction of vocal intimacy gave the close-up image complete articulacy and afforded the cinematic character a new relation with the cinema audience. As Braudy has observed, 'Light may create objects in film, but sound created people.'[25]

The attempt to reconcile the theatrical dialogue of Shakespeare with the naturalistic trends of cinematic characterization presented similar major problems to Kozintsev, using translated dialogue, as it did to Peter Hall and Peter Brook working with the original language. While Kozintsev conceded that 'reality and naturalness' were essential, he was clear (as Castellani would seem not to have been) that what he sought was 'the reality and naturalness of a poetic image, not of mundane character'. He identified, even in the dialogue of a translated text, the nature of the aesthetic dissonance involved in presenting a theatrical character on film. Either a film director in 'fighting for the natural' must 'contrast declamation and pathos with everyday speech' with the resultant evaporation of verbal impact, or he must accept the nature of the character created in and through Shakespeare's dialogue. 'In Shakespeare's plays – Lear, Hamlet, Othello – they are all not only kings, princes, warriors, but also poets. Poetry is in their blood. Here it seems was the difficulty.'[26]

For Brook and Hall, the problem of presenting credible cinematic characterizations did not arise with the same specific dramatic relevance as it had with Kozintsev. One reason for this was the assumption that their respective films (KING LEAR 1971 and A MIDSUMMER NIGHT'S DREAM 1969) would be viewed by people with a knowledge of Shakespeare's language and an expectation based on inherited cultural tradition. Another was the fact that both films grew out of successful, authoritative stage productions with the same actors in the major roles. The work of characterization was therefore done by the actors in preparation for their stage performances. The aesthetic dissonance between theatre and cinema in the speaking of lines emerged more as a technical problem of compatibility between dialogue and image.

Brook concedes that Shakespeare's verse undoubtedly has, in places, a necessary rhetorical dimension, but he sees the problem of reconciling this with film not so much as one of medial incompatibility, as one of change in the idiom of dramatic delivery.

Then comes the problem of how the actors are actually to speak the lines which in many cases were clearly designed for a 'projected' almost rhetorical form of delivery. This is a problem that's not special to the film, it's special I suppose to the year in which one's working, because everybody recognizes the necessity of making what is a very old-fashioned idiom alive and meaningful for a modern audience.

'The verse', he maintains, 'must be spoken for what it is,' and he finds the greatest challenge comes in the close-up shots. 'And if this search for the truth of expression within the verse is important on stage, how much more important is it in a film, where the close-up must be the most revealing form of expression that acting has ever had to encompass.' Brook finds the cinematic compromise an unsatisfactory solution. 'One has two really unfortunate alternatives: either to allow the screen to bend under the weight of what seems a quite unnatural and operatic delivery, or to withdraw the camera to extra longshot where one isn't embarrassed by what otherwise might appear as overacting.'[27]

Peter Hall, on the other hand, claims that the rhetorical delivery of Shakespeare in the theatre is largely a residual style which stubbornly persists from the nineteenth century. 'I think words tend to be over-projected in theatres. We confuse energy and meaning . . . I like things to be kept cool, flexible, "witty" in the eighteenth-century sense of the word. I like drama in the clash of ideas rather than the noise.' Shakespeare, Hall claims, is not rhetorical in the sense that opera is, and he substantiates this by suggesting that Shakespeare's theatre was not designed to encompass operatic projection. 'Shakespeare had to deal with close-packed theatres, a huge audience compressed into a small space and stationed all round the actors, really on top of them. And he wrote so that the actors could talk literally to them, not boom away over their heads.' Defending his insistent use of the close shot in his film of A MIDSUMMER NIGHT'S DREAM, Hall maintains that if the acting is not necessarily overblown, the cinema can accommodate it and enforce the text's subtleties 'better than theatre'.

So when one is filming, the closeness of the camera is no embarrassment. It is in fact a support. It insists on thoughtful speech! My company working in THE DREAM already appreciated this because of the work they had done with me in the theatre. All we had to do was make sure the faces did nothing excessive in expression during the close shots.[28]

What emerges from the differences between the approaches of Kozintsev on the one hand and Brook and Hall on the other is the issue of just where the responsibility for characterization lies. For Kozintsev it is an organic part of the making of the film. For Brook and Hall characterization is more dependent on the actor's preparation in the theatre, and this latter approach would seem inevitable where a stage actor plays an established theatrical role on film. Michéal MacLiammóir's characterization of Iago in Welles's OTHELLO was the result of elaborate discussion between director and actor, during which the conceptual entity of Iago's role clearly emerged. As MacLiammóir recorded in his diary:

Iago, he [Welles] went on to say (had heard him on this last visit and was in agreement), was in his opinion impotent; this secret malady was, in fact, to be the keystone of the actor's approach. Realised as the talk grew more serious that I was more in agreement than ever ... 'Impotent,' he roared in (surely somewhat forced) rich bass baritone, 'that's why he hates life so much – they always do.'

In a later entry in the diary, MacLiammóir reveals the nature of the character development as it takes shape.

Find myself almost entirely in agreement with O's ideas of our characters; no single trace of mephistophelean Iago is to be used; no conscious villainy; a common man, clever as a waggon-load of monkeys, his thought never on the present but always on the move after the move after next; a business man dealing in destruction with neatness, method, and a proper pleasure in his work: the honest, honest Iago reputation is accepted because it has become almost the truth.

... 'And out of her goodness make the net that shall enmesh them all', to be spoken simply, happily, and logically. One must feel as the cat does with the mouse: think of Rachel [MacLiammóir's cat] – what to her is evil about killing a mouse? And Cyprus is full of mice ...

Any tendency to passion, even the expression of the onlooker's delight at the spectacle of disaster, makes for open villainy and must be crushed ...

Monotony may perhaps be avoided by remembering the underlying sickness of the mind, immemorial hatred of life, the secret isolation of impotence under the soldier's muscles, the flabby solitude gnawing at the groins, the eye's untiring calculation.[29]

The length of time spent on the development of character, the animal suggestions to objectify behavioural traits and the level of psychological identification to offset the danger of 'monotony', all indicate that this is the mind of a stage actor working on a characterization in the context of completely viewed dramatic work.

The readiness with which audiences and critics tend to hold the film actor responsible for a 'performance' on the screen is largely a legacy of cinema's early reputation as 'canned theatre'. Shakespearean film can be made to accommodate a theatrical process of characterization, but the delineation and presentation of a character on the screen must clearly depend upon acting techniques which differ from those used within the relative constancy of theatrical space.

The final question in this consideration of the specific contribution of the actor to film – and more especially to Shakespearean film – is that of whether or not the film actor can be said to have specialized techniques for which he as a performer is ultimately responsible when he acts before the camera. From his experience in Welles's OTHELLO, Michéal MacLiammóir has drawn some general conclusions about the film actor's work. He has claimed that 'one's first job is to forget every single lesson one ever learned on stage', and that the actor before the camera must learn the specific ability 'to express oneself just *below* the rate of normal behaviour'. Despite MacLiammóir's claim that he accepted the need for 'blind, unquestioning obedience' to the director, he does seem here to imply that the film actor has in fact to develop the technique of *concealing technique*. For him the film actor's technique would seem essentially to be to create a certain kind of tension between himself and the viewer by means of suppression and understatement. 'Far from finding one has nothing to do, one is confronted with a complete and bewildering set of new and rigorously negative tasks.'[30]

Myrtle Moss, drawing on her own stage and film experience, sees the film actor's technique more positively as a specifically temporal relation of thought processes to their physical expression:

Firstly, one has to learn to think unselfconsciously. One's movements and gestures have to be not only much more restrained but also much slower. A gesture, or the turning of the head, or a smile must suggest the birth and development of a thought or feeling. Quick, impulsive movements or gestures do not look at all good through the camera.[31]

The critic Robin Wood finds the identification of film acting technique more difficult. He accepts that the nature of the film actor's work will depend very much upon the relationship between director and actor and between camera and actor. Any technique which an actor may develop for one film – or for a limited part of one film – will in all probability be ephemeral. Writing of Charles Laughton's work in Renoir's film THIS LAND IS MINE, Wood asserts that the uninterrupted takes of the trial scene rely wholly on Laughton's own creativity as an actor for their effect. There are no distractions from the décor; Laughton is held in medium shot throughout with the camera static. 'The slightly low angle chosen more to reveal the actor than for rhetorical effect allows him a freedom unusual in a film to build a speech whose effect depends primarily on his own timing rather than on the rhythms of editing.'[32] What Wood is suggesting, in fact, is that the less intervention arises from camera movement and from editing, the more theatrical can be the technique of the actor.

Madsen takes a more specific view of the film actor's particular aptitudes in the context of distinctive cinematic demands. Firstly, he suggests that the actor must develop the capacity to adjust the scale of action and response in terms of the spatial demands of the camera.

Acting for films and television requires specialized techniques on the part of the performer, based upon the proximity of the lens and camera and the scene size being photographed. As a rule, the nearer the camera and focus of the lens, the closer the size, and the lower and more restrained must be the performance of the actor.

Madsen's implication here is considerable, for one of cinema's most important and distinctive dramatic resources is the independent mobility of the camera to intensify dramatic statement. The camera may increase or close the distance between itself and the actor during the uninterrupted process of action or dialogue, or a zoom lens may be used to vary the spatial relation of the actor's face to the cinema frame. Where the actor has access to the director's intention in this regard, Madsen suggests that the actor himself is responsible for adjusting his articulation as a continuous progression harmonized with the dramatic flow of the action. Secondly, Madsen claims for the film actor a specific technical ability to assume with conviction and apparent continuity his dramatic character at short notice and for brief out-of-sequence moments in accordance with the demands of a shooting schedule quite unrelated to the context of dramatic development.

This 'out-of-context' requirement necessitates not only that the actor adapt his performance to the demands of the lens and scene size, but also that he interrupt his role without any sense of continuity and often without any interaction with other actors . . . To give a convincing performance under such scrambled conditions, the actor must understand his role so deeply that he becomes that character under all dramatic circumstances, and knows intuitively how that character would react to any given crises. Only thus can the actor 'turn it on' for a brief roll of the camera.[33]

The technical resources of the film actor would seem then to be distinguished from those of the stage actor by the rigour of demands which the director's overall concept and the exigencies of cinematic synthesis impose upon him. Because the dramatic effectiveness of cinema has come to depend so much upon advanced credibility, the film actor cannot rely on a framework of quasi-operatic conventions, and Skoller rightly claims that 'photographic realism . . . will always find potentially much greater performances in the ordinary human being whose tendency before the camera is behavioural rather than histrionic'. Yet clearly there is no technique in spontaneous behaviour, nor can there be sustained spontaneous behaviour in the context of an established dramatic role. Film acting must encompass some degree of 'interpretation', which 'implies that the actor has developed a definite point of view with regard to the role, but that in the execution of it, primary energies, shaping unplanned nuances of expression are liberated'.[34]

The extent to which any particular film acting techniques are relevant to Shakespearean film will depend upon the kind of Shakespearean film being made. Kurosawa, working on the *Macbeth* narrative, was free to separate the realism of exterior action from the rigorous theatrical discipline of his interior scenes, because a Japanese audience would find acceptable a film comprising so composite a style. Kozintsev sought a more consistently realistic acting style from Yarvet in his KING LEAR, and so had to strive to reconcile the poetic dimensions of character with spatial realism by the dramatic characterization of spatial detail and landscape. Brook's KING LEAR is a film with strong theatrical priorities in the acting technique of Paul Scofield, because the film emerged from a theatre production of the play, and because Brook's cinematic interest lay less in a harmonic integration of theatre and cinema than in a deliberate strategy of alienation and a consequent insistence that the audience be aware of the medium itself.

The distinction which can be drawn between the acting techniques of Laurence

Olivier and Orson Welles in their respective Shakespearean trilogies throws significant light on the whole issue of the actor's contribution to Shakespearean film. Both Olivier and Welles directed and acted the main roles in their Shakespearean adaptations. This meant that as actors they were in the privileged position of knowing the details of the director's adaptive strategies. However, as we have seen, Olivier's theatrical allegiance underlies much of his acting technique. In 1965 he told Roger Manvell that little valid distinction existed between acting in the theatre and acting before the camera, despite the aesthetic differences between cinematic and theatrical dramatization.

The film climax is a close-up; the Shakespearean climax is a fine gesture and a loud voice. I remember going to George Cukor's ROMEO AND JULIET. As a film director he did what seemed the right thing when he took the potion scene with Norma Shearer – he crept right up to a huge head, the ordinary film climax. But it was in fact a mistake. She, being a good technician in film making, cut the power of her acting down as the camera approached her for the climax of the speech leading up to taking the potion – 'Romeo, I come! This do I drink to thee.' At the moment of climax she was acting very smally, because the camera was near. That was not the way it should have been. So the very first test I made for HENRY V I tried to see how it would work in reverse. It was in the scene with the French ambassador, and as I raised my voice, the camera went back – the exact opposite technique to that in ROMEO AND JULIET – and I have done that ever since. There are moments when you want to be in the front row of the stalls seeing every line of the actor's face, and there are moments when you say, 'I wish I was at the back of the gallery for this scene.' These are the only moments when you use the top shot, or so it should be. I think there is far less difference between film acting and stage acting than people think – much less. If you are a long way off in the dress circle you are really no further away than in a long shot. The exception, perhaps, is the big head – the ordinary close-shot is rarely much closer than the front row of the stalls. Your acting should be just as careful on the stage as it is on the screen, because there are always people who can see it.[35]

Olivier is making three significant assertions here. Firstly, the accomplished film director is not necessarily the accomplished director of Shakespearean film. Secondly, the human being, the actor, is more important than the machine. The camera must be used to make the best of what the actor instinctively feels to be right, be it a big gesture and 'a loud voice' or be it whatever the actor and director in their interpretation of the Shakespeare play decide. For Olivier, the actor's relationship with the lines would seem to be sacrosanct: the camera's relationship with the actor is secondary. Finally, the camera must be the ideally mobile member of the theatre audience, sometimes in 'the front row of the stalls', sometimes 'in the back of the gallery'.

This last point is of considerable interest, for it suggests that Olivier does not merely conceive of cinema as a means of enhancing the presented performance of a play in terms of spectacle, but rather as a means of enriching the spatial potential of the auditorium by giving it fluidity. The primacy of Olivier's theatrical allegiance emerges very clearly from the fact that he appears to consider the camera as concentrating on only one side of the action. Its movement is confined to the norms implied in the traditions of theatrical architecture. The actor would seem to be part of a pictorial composition which invites the viewer to explore different viewing points from outside, but whose internal space is inaccessible. In theory at any rate, Olivier seems here to disregard a dimension of cinema which is of major importance in distinguishing the essence of dramatic film: the dissolution of the spatial separation – in *virtual* terms – between picture and percipient. Béla Balázs rightly recognizes this capability as both a justification for – and a barrier to – cinema's claim to autonomous artistic stature. In deliberately creating 'the illusion in the spectator that he is in the middle of the action reproduced in the fictional space of the film', it runs counter to a traditional view of the space of a work of art as 'inaccessible, guarded by its own self-sufficient composition'.[36]

The capacity of the cinema to place the camera within the space of the action naturally has the most profound effects on the nature of the actor's technique, and here there arises an ironic inconsistency between Olivier's theory and his practice. While he seems to suggest in his interview with Roger Manvell that cinema does not create anything new of the material, that it is subservient to and an extension of theatre, one has only to examine his camera work in HAMLET and RICHARD III to observe that the camera is not only within the space of action, but often – in HAMLET – in the mind of a character. HAMLET, particularly, is a most significant cinematic achievement, precisely because of its camera movement within the Elsinore architecture. Furthermore, the subtle modulations in Olivier's acting before the camera suggest that he understood very well the need for that specific capacity to adjust the scale of performance in accordance with the variation of scene size.

The approaches of Welles and Olivier to the work of acting in Shakespearean film are profoundly different in a way which highlights the distinction between the stage actor and the film actor. One is aware, in watching Olivier on film, that he is Olivier the actor, playing Henry V or Hamlet or Richard III. The actor is separated from the role by certain deliberate disguises which give visual dimensions to the actor's subordination of himself to the character. For Welles, on the other hand, the external trappings – the costume and the make-up – are less a disguise than a projection of the character from within himself. Welles and Macbeth do not, in Welles's film, have distinct and separate identities as Olivier and Hamlet do. Welles's fusion of his own personality with the dramatic character and his instinct for the medium together displace the text from its primacy of place. This is in line with the natural priorities of cinema, for in film, performance is, as a rule, superior to the script. 'The tendency in stage acting', asserts Braudy, 'is to subordinate oneself to the character, while the great film actor is generally more important than the character he plays.'[37]

Whatever generalizations can legitimately be made about the nature of the film actor's work in a film which is primarily conceived as a film, there must remain an ineradicable dimension of theatricality about the Shakespearean film. Since Shakespeare's plays are theatrical expressions – even in their texts – of profound human experience, the human actor must retain a greater measure of dramatic responsibility in a Shakespearean film than he might in a film which is not an adaptation of theatrical material. Nevertheless, in any film, the actor's work is substantially changed from its theatrical nature. The actor on the screen is part of a flat image, and as such, his work contributes a relatively small measure to the film's composite method of dramatic expression, which also comprises camera movement and the editing of the film. The photographic image will often give to objects a dramatic equality with the actor. The modern versatility of lenses and sound amplification will render much of the actor's projecting technique redundant, and finally, the lack of an accessible authoritative text which means the same to the actor as it does to the director will give to the film director an authority which his theatrical counterpart does not require. In short, the actor on the cinema screen becomes a part of manipulated pictorial space, for in imaging a Shakespeare play on a screen, the director's essential concern is less with the objects pictured in the image, but rather with the way space is organized. 'There's something about the twist and turn and the dramatic fall of light, and about the spirals and mobility of space, which can give you a way of expressing the turmoil of a play.'[38]

Conclusion

To consider Shakespearean film is essentially to consider the accommodation of Shakespeare's plays in cinematic space, for it is primarily a distinction in spatial terms which makes the dramatic language of cinema different from that of theatre. Apart from its discontinuity, the most significant property of cinematic space is its centrifugality. A Shakespearean film cannot satisfactorily remain confined to the theatre stage. Neither can it abandon that intrinsic theatricality which beats in the heart of Shakespearean drama. Therein lies the challenge, and what emerges from a detailed study of different directors' work is that there are no rules. Film makers achieve dramatic effectiveness in their own ways, and not infrequently, the particular nature of one film's achievement makes it quite distinct from that of another.

Each of the eight films which have been discussed in close detail has managed, to a remarkable degree, to meet the challenge of reconciling theatrical resonance and centripetality with the fluidity, the discontinuity and the centrifugality of cinematic space.

In HENRY V, Olivier's camera moves the action out of the Globe, but throughout the film, there remain clear reminders of theatricality. In HAMLET, too, the fluidity of the camera's movement inside Elsinore is counterpoised with clear theatrical reminiscences. The staging of 'The Mousetrap' photographed by the camera moving on its wide arc is an instance which illustrates the language of the whole film. RICHARD III treats the cinema audience as a theatre audience in the sequences where Richard addresses monologues directly to the camera, yet the camera's selection of detail and the realism of battle are clearly cinematic. The settings for Welles's MACBETH are in fact made of stagey cardboard, but the camera's treatment of this substance gives it a bizarre organic realism. The characterization of Iago in Welles's OTHELLO is both theatrically and cinematically developed, and the location of Mogador is often treated to afford dramatic resonance. Yet the camera angles, the vigour of the juxtapositions and the powerful tracking shot linking Iago and Othello with sky, sea and stone are effects which only cinema can achieve. CHIMES AT MIDNIGHT is theatrical in the extent to which it allows the actor to shape delivery, but clearly filmic in its relation of actor to décor. Brook's KING LEAR is really the extension of a theatre production into film. Character portrayal is essentially theatrical, as is the stress on dialogue. Yet Brook sought particular locations for this film in order 'to do what theatre can never do well – to give a concrete reality to the world in which the story unfolds'.[1] Kurosawa's strategy in THRONE OF BLOOD is to reduce dialogue to a minimum, and to articulate the drama through the manipulation of spatial reality. Yet an emphatic strand of Noh theatricality runs through the film.

The first film discussed, HENRY V, employed the devices of cinema to move the action out of the confines of the Globe playhouse as a distinct basis of its strategy. The last film, Kurosawa's THRONE OF BLOOD, with its clear sequences of Noh stylization, once again establishes the significance of a theatrical dimension in Shakespearean film, so completing a circle in this survey of spatial strategies.

While the film actor is indisputably a part of manipulated space on the screen, no discussion of Shakespearean film can fail to take some account of the specific contribution of the actor. While well-established stage actors have been cast in Shakespearean films and the names of Olivier, Gielgud, Richardson and Scofield have made Shakespearean film respectable, the virtuosity of the actor is inevitably curtailed within the dramatic impact of the cinematic image. The authority of the director, the treatment by the camera and the scissors of the film editor determine, beyond all doubt, the dramatic impact of the film.

This study has not set out to evaluate individual Shakespearean films in relation to others, but inevitably the response of the viewer will be to judge some films more effective than others. In evolving his spatial strategy for a Shakespearean film, a film maker might derive his ideas from the dramatic and poetic images of the play, or he might create new and original cinematic images. An effective Shakespearean film is both derivative and creative, and this is most clearly evident in the three Olivier films, Welles's OTHELLO and CHIMES AT MIDNIGHT, in Brook's KING LEAR and in Kurosawa's THRONE OF BLOOD. HENRY V uses the shifts of time and place implicit in the play, but Olivier also develops the visual imagery from medieval manuscript plates, carefully photographed models and real landscape for its spatial articulations. HAMLET visualizes action and detail described in the dialogue, but it is filmically creative in associating vertiginous heights with Hamlet, arches and natural light with Ophelia, deep-focus distance with character relationships and the camera with a narrator-persona. RICHARD III is derivative in its visualization of the crown as a symbol and object, in its placing Richard in a world whose order was changing, in the shadow images which underscore Richard's rise to power and in its depiction of seasonal change. It is creative in associating the natural voyeurism of cinema with the compulsive voyeurism of Richard as he watches action framed by doors and windows, in its unifying devices and its relation of Richard to his victims in deep focus. Welles's OTHELLO derives its images and motifs from the recurrent allusions to the 'snare' which pervade the play, and it also visualizes the infective energy of Iago's evil in its photographic style. OTHELLO's creativity lies in the means by which its spatial motifs are dynamically developed and in its extension of the opposition of light and darkness, with Iago finally exposed to the sun, and Othello entombed in darkness. CHIMES AT MIDNIGHT is derivative in its visualization of character and creative in its imaging of the alienation of Falstaff from Hal and from the ethos of

Bolingbroke's England. Brook's KING LEAR derives its images of cruelty, bleakness and hostile nature from the play, while it is creative in visualizing Lear's journey from darkness into light. Finally, THRONE OF BLOOD is derivative in its spatial projection of the protagonist's moral confusion and in the relationship of man to nature. It is dynamically creative in developing the dramatic conflict through linear and geometric opposition, and in its expansion of Birnam Wood to a forest which assumes the dramatic stature of a character.

Like any other film, Shakespearean films are primarily visual articulations. Unlike most other films, they are adaptations of classic plays whose texts have become crystallized and widely known. It is unlikely, therefore, that Shakespearean film could ever have been born in a state of original innocence, for the judgement of a film primarily in terms of an assumed authority of the text must inevitably find the film wanting. To a considerable extent, however, it is right to weigh the dramatic effectiveness of a Shakespearean film against the potential of the text, for film is not so autonomous an art form that traditional ways of looking at the actualization of Shakespeare must be wholly discarded. Eisenstein is right when he maintains that 'cinema is not altogether without parents and without pedigree, without a past, without the traditions and rich cultural heritage of past epochs. It is only very thoughtless and presumptuous people who can erect laws and an aesthetic for cinema, proceeding from premises of some incredible virgin-birth of this art'.[2] The effective articulation of the dramatic potential of the text is what both the film director and the stage director set out to achieve. The text, however, is not the authority for the film as it is for the staged play. The difference between theatre and film in this specific respect has been acutely perceived by Peter Brook. Theatre, says Brook, starts with ideas encoded in a printed text. These ideas are given general articulation in performance. Film, on the other hand, starts with some kind of performance, a spatial articulation, which is photographed and encoded on a roll of celluloid.[3] The authority for the cinema, therefore, is not a text, but the organization and control of the cinematic image.

If few Shakespearean films can be judged good cinema as well as good Shakespeare, fewer still of those adaptations made since Olivier's HENRY V are wholly bad in both intention and execution. Most Shakespearean films merit detailed and serious consideration because they are part of the twentieth century's response to Shakespeare, and because many people all over the world have derived – and continue to derive – their most vivid impressions of Shakespeare's dramatic stature from them. To want to establish just where the dramatic success or failure of a Shakespearean film lies is to want to know something more about the dramatic genius of Shakespeare.

The trilogies of Olivier and Welles stand as monuments to the high tide of Shakespearean cinema. Even within the spectrum of films covered in these chapters, the change of the cinema's status in our society becomes clear. The kind of audience which Olivier's HENRY V sought to reach was very different in size and receptivity from that which continues to dissect the stark intellectual experience of Peter Brook's

KING LEAR. The challenge of putting Shakespeare's plays on the big screen in the movie palaces has been overtaken by that of bringing the whole canon into the living rooms of nations. It is without doubt a more urgent contemporary challenge, and it is an endeavour more in line with the social habits and economic thrust of the 1980s. Nevertheless, the contention implicit in this study is that Shakespearean film continues to justify its place as a valid, vigorous and necessary dimension of the contemporary encounter with the world's greatest dramatist.

Notes

INTRODUCTION

1. Charles Marowitz, 'Reconstructing Shakespeare: Harlotry in Bardolatry', a paper delivered at the Twenty-Second International Shakespeare Conference (1986) at Stratford-upon-Avon.
2. Frank Kermode, 'Shakespeare in the Movies' in *Film Theory and Criticism*, first edition, ed. Gerald Mast and Marshall Cohen (New York, 1974), pp. 322–32 (pp. 323–4, 332).

1   THEATRICAL AND CINEMATIC SPACE

1. André Bazin, *What Is Cinema?*, I, trans. Hugh Gray (Berkeley, California, 1967), p. 105.
2. Hugo Münsterberg, *The Film: A Psychological Study (The Silent Photoplay of 1916)* (New York, 1970), p. 64.
3. Bazin, *What Is Cinema?*, I, p. 104.
4. Bazin, *What Is Cinema?*, I, p. 105.
5. Rudolph Arnheim, *Film as Art* (London, 1958), p. 15.
6. Münsterberg, p. 23.
7. John Russell Brown, *Effective Theatre* (London, 1969), p. 31.
8. Bazin, *What Is Cinema?*, I, p. 104.
9. Nicholas Vardac, *Stage to Screen* (New York, 1968), p. xxv.
10. Bazin, *What Is Cinema?*, I, p. 102.
11. Béla Balázs, *Theory of the Film: Character and Growth of a New Art* (London, 1952), p. 90.
12. Bazin, *What Is Cinema?*, I, p. 102.
13. Balázs, pp. 93, 96.
14. Grigori Kozintsev, *KING LEAR: The Space of Tragedy* (London, 1977), p. 26.
15. James E. Fisher, 'Olivier and the Realistic OTHELLO', *Literature Film Quarterly*, 1 (1973), 325, and Jack J. Jorgens, *Shakespeare on Film* (Bloomington, 1977), p. 192.
16. Jorgens, *Shakespeare on Film*, p. 193.
17. Anthony Havelock-Allan in Roger Manvell, *Shakespeare and the Film* (London, 1971), p. 117.
18. *Othello*, I. 3. 410.
19. Donald Skoller, 'Problems of Transformation in the Adaptations of Shakespeare's Tragedies from Playscript to Cinema' (unpublished Ph.D. dissertation, New York University, 1968), p. 413.
20. Skoller, pp. 414, 415.
21. Constance Brown, 'Olivier's OTHELLO', *Film Quarterly*, 19 (1966), 48–50 (p. 49).
22. Jorgens, *Shakespeare on Film*, p. 193.
23. Bazin, *What Is Cinema?*, I, p. 106.
24. The film is held in the National Archives, London.
25. Manvell, p. 28.

26. John Fuegi, 'Explorations in No Man's Land', *Shakespeare Quarterly*, 23 (1972), 37–49 (pp. 42, 45).
27. Manvell, p. 97.
28. Peter Brook in Gerald Camp, 'Shakespeare on Film', *Journal of Aesthetic Education*, 3 (1969), 107–20 (p. 114).
29. Vardac, pp. 42, 131.
30. Bazin, *What Is Cinema?*, I, pp. 105–7.
31. Fuegi, p. 45.
32. John Reddington, 'Film, Play and Idea', *Literature Film Quarterly* 1, no. 4 (1973), 367–71 (pp. 368, 370).
33. Manvell, p. 16.
34. Bazin, *What Is Cinema?*, I, p. 112.
35. Manvell, pp. 107, 104.
36. John Blumenthal, '*Macbeth* into THRONE OF BLOOD' in *Film Theory and Criticism*, ed. Mast and Cohen, pp. 340–51 (pp. 342–3).
37. Bazin, *What Is Cinema?*, I, p. 112.
38. Kozintsev, *Space of Tragedy*, pp. 137, 141.
39. Grigori Kozintsev, *Shakespeare: Time and Conscience* (London, 1967), p. 266.
40. Geoffrey Reeves, 'Finding Shakespeare on Film: From an Interview with Peter Brook' in *Film Theory and Criticism*, ed. Mast and Cohen, pp. 316–21 (pp. 316–17).
41. Kozintsev, *Time and Conscience*, pp. 265–9.
42. Kozintsev, *Space of Tragedy*, p. 80.
43. Kozintsev, *Time and Conscience*, p. 265.
44. Kozintsev, *Space of Tragedy*, p. 123.
45. Balázs, pp. 92, 96–7.
46. Kozintsev, *Space of Tragedy*, p. 128.
47. Ralph Stephenson and J.R. Debrix, *The Cinema as Art*, second edition (London, 1976), p. 14.
48. Kozintsev, *Space of Tragedy*, pp. 129, 131, 230.
49. Bazin, *What Is Cinema?*, I, p. 69.
50. Bazin, *What Is Cinema?*, I, p. 111–12.

2   LAURENCE OLIVIER'S HENRY V

1. Marsha McCready, '*Henry V* on Stage and on Film', *Literature Film Quarterly*, 5, no. 4 (1977), 316–21 (p. 318).
2. Ibid.
3. *Shakespeare on Film Newsletter*, 4 (1982), 1.
4. Gorman Beauchamp, 'HENRY V: Myth, Movie, Play', *College Literature*, 5 (1978), 228–38 (p. 230).
5. Harry Geduld, *Film Guide to HENRY V* (Bloomington, 1973), pp. 29, 27.
6. Manvell, p. 34.
7. Geduld, p. 37.
8. Beauchamp, p. 232.
9. Beauchamp, p. 234.
10. Anne Barton, 'The King's Two Bodies', Royal Shakespeare Company Programme for *Richard II* (1973).
11. Sandra Sugarman Singer, 'Laurence Olivier Directs Shakespeare: A Study in Film Authorship' (unpublished Ph.D. dissertation, North Western University, 1978), p. 58.
12. *Henry V*, III. 1. 1–3.

13. *Henry V*, III. 1. 13–15.
14. Singer, p. 60.
15. Geduld, pp. 30–1.
16. Reeves, pp. 317–18.
17. *Henry V*, I. Prologue. 19.
18. Schlegel cited in Beauchamp, p. 236.
19. *Henry V*, IV. 3. 110–111.
20. Peter Wollen, 'Counter Cinema: vent d'este', *After Image*, 4 (1972), 4–5.
21. Singer, p. 80.
22. Jorgens, *Shakespeare on Film*, p. 124.
23. Geduld, p. 35.
24. Jorgens, *Shakespeare on Film*, pp. 132–3.
25. Geduld, pp. 54–5.
26. James E. Phillips, 'Adapted From a Play by Shakespeare', *Hollywood Quarterly*, 2 (1946), 82–90 (p. 87).
27. Bazin, *What Is Cinema?*, II, pp. 140–8.
28. Bazin, *What Is Cinema?*, II, p. 147.
29. Ibid.
30. Stephenson and Debrix, p. 156.

3   LAURENCE OLIVIER'S HAMLET

1. Robert A. Duffy, 'Gade, Olivier, Richardson: Visual Strategy in *Hamlet* Adaptation', *Literature Film Quarterly*, 4, no. 2 (1976), 141–52 (p. 141).
2. Duffy, p. 142.
3. R. Herring, 'HAMLET: Sir Laurence Olivier's Picture', *Life and Letters*, 57 (1948), 183–92 (pp. 183–4).
4. Manvell, p. 44.
5. Singer, p. 121.
6. Laurence Olivier, 'An Essay in *Hamlet*', in *The Film HAMLET: A Record of Its Production*, ed. Brenda Cross (London, 1948), pp. 11–15 (p. 11).
7. Singer, p. 122.
8. Herring, p. 184.
9. Duffy, pp. 146, 147.
10. Bernice Kliman, 'Olivier's HAMLET: A Film-Infused Play', *Literature Film Quarterly*, 5, no. 4 (1977), 305–14 (pp. 305–6).
11. Susan Sontag, 'Film and Theatre' in *Film Theory and Criticism*, ed. Mast and Cohen, pp. 249–67 (p. 256).
12. Kliman, p. 306.
13. Duffy, p. 149.
14. Duffy, p. 147.
15. Ibid.
16. Duffy, pp. 147, 148.
17. *Hamlet*, V. 1. 127 and 215.
18. In his autobiography, Olivier confirms his earlier justification for the use of monochromatic film. See Manvell, p. 45, and Laurence Olivier, *Confessions of an Actor* (London, 1982), p. 122.
19. J.L. Styan, 'Sight and Space: The Perception of Shakespeare on Stage and Screen' in *Shakespeare, Pattern of Excelling Nature*, ed. David Bevington and Jay L. Halio (Newark, 1978), pp. 198–209 (pp. 205–6).

20. Styan, p. 202.
21. Styan, p. 203.
22. Foster Hirsch, *Laurence Olivier* (Boston, 1979), pp. 81–2.
23. *Hamlet*, I. 2. 114.
24. Hirsch, p. 82.
25. *Hamlet*, IV. 7. 156.
26. The repetition of this spatial articulation of camera movement, conspiratorial situation and architectural detail – but without the physical presence of Hamlet in the frame – is comparable to the function of a *leitmotiv* in the orchestra of a Wagnerian opera, associated with a particular character who is not actually on stage.
27. *Hamlet*, V. 2. 326.
28. *Hamlet*, III. 1. 56–88. Olivier places this after the Polonius/Claudius conspiracy.
29. Hirsch, p. 85.
30. Jorgens, *Shakespeare on Film*, p. 211.
31. Roger Furse, 'Designing the Film HAMLET' in *HAMLET, the Film and the Play*, ed. Alan Dent (London, 1948), unpaged.
32. Don Cook, Review of HAMLET, *New York Herald Tribune*, 9 May 1948, section V, pp. 1–2.
33. Furse, 'Designing the Film HAMLET', unpaged.
34. Jorgens, *Shakespeare on Film*, p. 217.
35. Furse, 'Designing the Film HAMLET', unpaged.
36. Jorgens, *Shakespeare on Film*, pp. 210, 214.
37. Mary McCarthy, 'A Prince of Shreds and Patches' in *Focus on Shakespearean Film*, ed. Charles W. Eckert (New Jersey, 1972), pp. 63–7 (p. 66).
38. Jorgens, *Shakespeare on Film*, p. 215.
39. Kenneth McGowan, *Behind the Screen: The History and Techniques of the Motion Picture* (New York, 1965), p. 436.
40. George Barbarow, '*Hamlet* through a Telescope', *Hudson Review*, 2 (1949), 98–117 (pp. 99–103).
41. F.E. Sparshott, 'Basic Film Aesthetics' in *Film Theory and Criticism*, ed. Mast and Cohen, pp. 209–32 (pp. 214–17).
42. Furse, 'Designing the Film HAMLET', unpaged.
43. *Hamlet*, I. 4. 90.
44. Singer, pp. 124–5.
45. *Hamlet*, III. 2. 285.
46. Jorgens, *Shakespeare on Film*, p. 123.
47. Hirsch, p. 81.
48. Skoller, p. 63.
49. Singer, p. 144.
50. Bazin, *What Is Cinema?*, I, p. 84.

4   LAURENCE OLIVIER'S RICHARD III

1. Jorgens, *Shakespeare on Film*, p. 139.
2. Singer, p. 185.
3. Singer, p. 188.
4. Hirsch, p. 98.
5. Constance Brown, 'Olivier's RICHARD III: A Revaluation' in *Focus on Shakespearean Film*, ed. Eckert, pp. 131–45 (pp. 133, 134).
6. Singer, p. 191.
7. *Richard III*, II. 1. 43–4.

8. *Richard III*, III. 4. 19–20.
9. Laurence Olivier quoted in Roger Manvell, 'Filming Shakespeare', *Journal of the British Film Academy* (Autumn 1955), 2–5 (p. 5).
10. Brown, 'Olivier's RICHARD III', p. 142.
11. Henry Hart, Review of RICHARD III, *Films in Review*, 7 (1956), 124–6 (pp. 124–5).
12. Bazin, *What Is Cinema?*, I, p. 100.
13. Brown, 'Olivier's RICHARD III', p. 143.
14. Hirsch, p. 98.
15. Brown, 'Olivier's RICHARD III', p. 141.
16. Hirsch, p. 99.
17. *Richard III*, II. 2. 150.
18. *Richard III*, III. 7. 95–6.
19. *Richard III*, I. 4. 57.
20. Brown, 'Olivier's RICHARD III', p. 135.
21. John Cottrell, *Laurence Olivier* (London, 1975), p. 268.
22. Interpolation.
23. *Richard III*, V. 3. 294.
24. Singer, p. 206.
25. See Jorgens, *Shakespeare on Film*, p. 212.
26. Laurence Olivier and Alan Dent (unpublished shooting script of RICHARD III, held in the British Film Institute Library, London).
27. Hirsch, p. 100.
28. *3 Henry VI*, V. 6. 84. Oxford Standard Author's edition gives 'sort' instead of 'plan'.
29. Brown, 'Olivier's RICHARD III', pp. 134–5.
30. Hirsch, pp. 97–8.
31. Jorgens, *Shakespeare on Film*, pp. 143 and 139, p. 146.
32. *Richard III*, IV. 2. 108–12.
33. Brown, 'Olivier's RICHARD III', p. 138.
34. *Richard III*, IV. 2. 117.
35. Jorgens, *Shakespeare on Film*, p. 137.
36. Brown, 'Olivier's RICHARD III', p. 139.

5 ORSON WELLES'S MACBETH

1. Charles W. Eckert, ed., *Focus on Shakespeare Film* (New Jersey, 1972), p. 3.
2. André Bazin, *Orson Welles: A Critical Review* (London, 1978), p. 101.
3. Claude Beylie, 'MACBETH, or The Magical Depths' in *Focus on Shakespearean Film*, ed. Eckert, pp. 72–5 (p. 95).
4. Peter Cowie, *A Ribbon of Dreams: The Cinema of Orson Welles* (South Brunswick, 1973), p. 110.
5. Richard France, 'The Voodoo *Macbeth* of Orson Welles', *Yale Theatre*, 5, no. 3 (1974), 66–78 (p. 67).
6. France, p. 69.
7. France, p. 76.
8. France, p. 67.
9. Ibid.
10. John Willett, *Expressionism* (London, 1970), p. 202.
11. Eduard Schmid quoted in Willett, p. 116.
12. See Willett, p. 241.
13. Voice-over prologue to MACBETH.

14. Joseph McBride, *Orson Welles* (London, 1972), p. 114.
15. S.S. Prawer, *Caligari's Children: The Film as Tale of Terror* (Oxford, 1980), p. 271.
16. Robert Sklar, quoted in Prawer, p. 45.
17. McBride, p. 112.
18. Beylie, p. 72.
19. Bazin, *Orson Welles*, p. 101.
20. Ibid.
21. McBride, p. 110.
22. Welles quoted in McBride, p. 111.
23. Skoller, p. 435.
24. Charles Higham, *The Films of Orson Welles* (Berkeley, 1970), p. 125.
25. Skoller, p. 434.
26. McBride, p. 114 and Skoller, p. 430.
27. Maurice Bessy, *Orson Welles: An Investigation into His Films and Philosophy* (New York, 1971), p. 98.
28. *Macbeth*, v. 5. 19. Welles's technique here would seem to offer an interesting solution to the problem Peter Brook encountered and agonized over twenty years later in the making of KING LEAR. See Manvell, p. 138.
29. Cowie, p. 113.
30. *Macbeth*, II. 1. 33.
31. *Macbeth*, III. 4. 89–91. Welles amended the dialogue.
32. Skoller, p. 430.
33. Cowie, pp. 113–14.
34. Skoller, p. 432.
35. *Macbeth*, III. 4. 106.
36. Juan Cobos, Miguel Rubio and J.A. Pruneda, 'A Trip to Don Quixoteland: Conversations with Orson Welles', *Cahiers du Cinéma in English*, 5 (1966), 35–47 (p. 36).
37. Bazin, *Orson Welles*, p. 101.

6 ORSON WELLES'S OTHELLO

1. Bosley Crowther, Review of OTHELLO, *New York Times*, 13 September 1955, p. 27.
2. Donald Phelps, Review of OTHELLO, *Film Culture*, 1, no. 1 (1955), p. 32.
3. Eric Bentley, '*Othello* of Film and Stage', *New Republic*, 3 October 1955, pp. 21–2 (p. 22).
4. Skoller, p. 359.
5. See Prefatory note on the variations in available film prints.
6. Welles himself points out that he worked with many different cameramen in the making of OTHELLO, and sometimes different cameramen were behind the camera for different parts of the same sequence (THE MAKING OF OTHELLO, a documentary film by Orson Welles, 1978).
7. Bentley, '*Othello* of Film and Stage', pp. 21–2.
8. *Othello*, I. 2. 59.
9. *Titus Andronicus*, II. 4. 22–5.
10. André Bazin, Review of OTHELLO, reprinted in *Film Theory and Criticism*, ed. Mast and Cohen, pp. 337–9 (p. 337).
11. Cowie, p. 118.
12. Skoller, p. 350.
13. Orson Welles, THE MAKING OF OTHELLO, a documentary film made in 1978.
14. Skoller, p. 362.
15. Jorgens, *Shakespeare on Film*, p. 175.

16. See chapter 5.
17. G. Wilson Knight, *The Wheel of Fire*, fourth edition (London, 1961), pp. 97–119.
18. Wilson Knight, *The Wheel of Fire*, pp. 116 and 119.
19. Jorgens, *Shakespeare on Film*, pp. 176–7.
20. James Naremore, 'The Walking Shadow: Welles's Expressionist MACBETH', *Literature Film Quarterly*, 1 (1973), 360–6 (pp. 365–6).
21. Susanne K. Langer, *Feeling and Form: A Theory of Art* (London, 1953), p. 96.
22. Jorgens, *Shakespeare on Film*, pp. 179–80.
23. Jorgens, *Shakespeare on Film*, p. 180.
24. Welles quoted in Cobos, Rubio and Pruneda, 'A Trip to Don Quixote-Land', p. 38.
25. Jorgens, *Shakespeare on Film*, p. 180.
26. Skoller, p. 351.
27. The duration of this shot varies slightly in the two versions viewed. See Prefatory note on variations of film prints.
28. *Othello*, III. 3. 129.
29. *Othello*, III. 3. 130–3.
30. Jorgens, *Shakespeare on Film*, p. 181.
31. Skoller, p. 355.
32. It recalls the shot of Macbeth hearing the witches' prophecy in Welles's MACBETH.
33. Cowie, p. 125.
34. Skoller, p. 356.
35. Jorgens, *Shakespeare on Film*, p. 184.
36. McBride, p. 122.
37. Jorgens, *Shakespeare on Film*, p. 184.
38. Skoller, p. 352.
39. Michéal MacLiammóir, *Put Money in Thy Purse: The Filming of Orson Welles's OTHELLO* (London, 1952), *passim*.
40. David Robinson, Review of OTHELLO, *Sight and Sound*, 25 (1956), 196–7 (p. 196).
41. Cowie, p. 119.
42. McBride, p. 120.
43. Ibid.
44. *Othello*, V. 2. 248. Shakespeare's line reads, 'Moor, she was chaste; she lov'd thee, cruel Moor'.
45. *Othello*, II. 1. 168.
46. *Othello*, II. 3. 369–71.
47. *Othello*, III. 3. 358.
48. *Othello*, IV. 1. 210.
49. Cowie, pp. 124–5.
50. *Othello*, II. 3. 375–7.
51. Bazin, Review of OTHELLO, p. 339.
52. Bazin, Review of OTHELLO, p. 338.

7   ORSON WELLES'S CHIMES AT MIDNIGHT

1. Mike Prokosch, 'Orson Welles', *Film Comment*, 7 (1971), 28–37 (p. 29).
2. Welles in McBride, p. 149.
3. Welles in J.A. Cobos and Miguel Rubio, 'Welles and Falstaff: An Interview', *Sight and Sound*, 35 (Autumn 1966), 158–63 (p. 160).
4. Prokosch, p. 30. It is not clear whether the reference is to Welles's original version of the film, or to the later studio version.

5. James Naremore, *The Magic World of Orson Welles* (New York, 1978), pp. 257–8.
6. Robin Wood, *Personal Views: Explorations in Film* (London, 1976), pp. 137–8.
7. See chapter 6, p. 118.
8. McBride, p. 148.
9. Ibid.
10. Pierre Billard, 'CHIMES AT MIDNIGHT', *Sight and Sound*, 34 (Spring 1965), 64–5 (p. 64).
11. Welles in Bessy, *Orson Welles*, p. 103. The film was also released as FALSTAFF.
12. Billard, p. 65.
13. Bessy, *Orson Welles*, p. 103.
14. Prokosch, p. 29.
15. *2 Henry IV*, v. 5. 48–51.
16. Ann Birstein, 'FALSTAFF, a Curiously Mixed Bag', *Vogue*, 1 January 1967, p. 53.
17. *2 Henry IV*, ii. 4. 535–6.
18. Higham, p. 168. The film credits, however, give the location as a monastery.
19. Prokosch, p. 35.
20. James Price, Review of CHIMES AT MIDNIGHT, *Sight and Sound*, 36 (Summer 1967), 146–7 (p. 147).
21. Naremore, p. 265.
22. Naremore, p. 262.
23. *2 Henry IV*, i. 2. 217–39.
24. Prokosch, p. 35.
25. Kozintsev, *Time and Conscience*, p. 203.
26. *2 Henry IV*, iii. 2. 237. Welles has selected from and emended Shakespeare's original dialogue.
27. Naremore, p. 278.
28. *2 Henry IV*, v. 5. 53.
29. *2 Henry IV*, v. 5. 96.
30. *Henry V*, ii. 3. 26–8.
31. Higham, p. 171.
32. Naremore, p. 273.
33. *1 Henry IV*, v. 4. 77.
34. Naremore, p. 276, and Cowie, p. 180.
35. Welles in Cobos and Rubio, 'Interview', p. 159.
36. Higham, p. 170.
37. Cowie, p. 185.
38. Jorgens, *Shakespeare on Film*, p. 110.
39. Welles in Cobos and Rubio, 'Interview', p. 161.
40. Pauline Kael, *Kiss Kiss, Bang Bang* (Boston, 1968), p. 202.
41. Welles quoted in Naremore, p. 274.
42. Birstein, p. 53.
43. Kael, *Kiss Kiss*, p. 202.
44. Cowie, p. 187.
45. *2 Henry IV*, iii. 1. 30–1.
46. Jorgens, *Shakespeare on Film*, p. 115.
47. William Johnson, 'Orson Welles: Of Time and Loss', *Film Quarterly*, 21 (1967), 13–24 (p. 19).
48. *2 Henry IV*, iii. 2. 231–2.
49. *Henry V*, ii. 2. 40–2.
50. Johnson, 'Orson Welles', p. 16.
51. Cowie, p. 183.

52. Naremore, p. 266.
53. Review, 'Body English', *Time*, 24 March 1967, p. 42.
54. Naremore, p. 266.
55. Johnson, 'Orson Welles', p. 16.
56. Jorgens, *Shakespeare on Film*, p. 115.
57. Higham, p. 170.
58. Naremore, p. 277.
59. Bessy, *Orson Welles*, p. 103.
60. Welles in Cobos and Rubio, 'Interview', p. 160.

8   BROOK'S KING LEAR AND KUROSAWA'S THRONE OF BLOOD

1. *King Lear*, III. 4. 27.
2. 'Kell', Review of KING LEAR, *Variety*, 17 February 1971, p. 18.
3. William Johnson, Review of KING LEAR, *Film Quarterly*, 25, no. 3 (1972), 41–8 (p. 42).
4. Michael Birkett in Manvell, p. 137.
5. Manvell, p. 138.
6. Manvell p 140
7. Ibid.
8. Kozintsev, *Space of Tragedy*, p. 25.
9. William Chaplin, 'Our Darker Purpose: Peter Brook's KING LEAR', *Arion*, 1 (Spring 1973), 168–87 (p. 171).
10. *King Lear*, I. 1. 38.
11. Chaplin, pp. 173 and 176.
12. Lilian Wilds, 'One KING LEAR for Our Time: A Bleak Vision by Peter Brook', *Literature Film Quarterly*, 4, no. 2 (1976), 159–64 (p. 160).
13. Kermode, 'Shakespeare in the Movies', pp. 332, 324 and 328.
14. Pauline Kael, *Deeper into Movies* (Boston, 1973), pp. 354–7 (p. 355).
15. Johnson, Review of KING LEAR, pp. 43–4.
16. Kael, *Deeper into Movies*, p. 354 and Johnson, Review of KING LEAR, p. 46.
17. See chapter 1.
18. Johnson, Review of KING LEAR, pp. 46–7.
19. Reeves, p. 320.
20. Wilds, p. 163.
21. Paul Acker, 'Conventions for Dialogue in Peter Brook's KING LEAR', *Literature Film Quarterly*, 8, no. 4 (1980), 219–24 (p. 220).
22. Acker, p. 221.
23. Robert A. Hetherington, 'The *Lears* of Peter Brook', *Shakespeare on Film Newsletter*, 6, no. 1 (January 1982), p. 7.
24. Kael, *Deeper into Movies*, p. 335.
25. Charles Eidsvik, *Cineliteracy: The Film Among the Arts* (New York, 1978), pp. 259–62.
26. Tom Milne, 'Crime and Punishment', *Sight and Sound*, 55, no. 2 (1986), 133–4 (p. 133).
27. Peter Ackroyd, 'An Oriental Lear', *Spectator*, 15 March 1986 (p. 37).
28. Reeves, p. 316.
29. Kermode, 'Shakespeare in the Movies', p. 328.
30. Bosley Crowther, 'Screen: Change in Scene', *New York Times*, 23 November 1961 (p. 50 L).
31. Blumenthal, p. 350.
32. John Gerlach, 'Shakespeare, Kurosawa and *Macbeth*: A Response to J. Blumenthal', *Literature Film Quarterly*, 1, no. 4 (1973), 352–9 (p. 357).
33. Donald Richie, *The Films of Akira Kurosawa* (Berkeley, 1965), p. 123.
34. Richie, pp. 122–3.

35. Film sub-titles.
36. Richie, p. 118.
37. Marsha Kinder, 'THRONE OF BLOOD: A Morality Dance', *Literature Film Quarterly*, 5, no. 4 (1977), 339–45 (p. 340).
38. Richie, p. 117.
39. Kinder, p. 340.
40. A.L. Zambrano, 'THRONE OF BLOOD: Kurosawa's *Macbeth*,' *Literature Film Quarterly*, 2, no. 3 (1974), 262–74 (p. 265).
41. Kinder, p. 343.
42. Kinder, p. 340.
43. Kinder, p. 343.
44. Zambrano, p. 274.
45. Richie, p. 117.
46. Richie, p. 118.
47. Zambrano, p. 274.
48. Zambrano, p. 273.

9 THE FILM ACTOR

1. D.J. Wenden, *The Birth of The Movies* (London, 1975), p. 20.
2. Wenden, p. 21.
3. Roy Paul Madsen, *The Impact of Film* (New York, 1974), p. 220.
4. Kael, *Kiss Kiss*, p. 74.
5. *Macbeth*, I. 7. 54–5.
6. See chapter 8.
7. Manvell, p. 141.
8. Kozintsev, *Space of Tragedy*, pp. 74–6, 60–1.
9. Stanley Kauffmann, 'Notes on Theatre and Film' in *Focus on Film and Theatre*, ed. James Hurt (New Jersey, 1974), pp. 67–77 (p. 75).
10. See chapter 1.
11. Langer, *Feeling and Form*, pp. 49–51, 320, 310.
12. Leo Braudy, *The World in a Frame* (New York, 1976), p. 194.
13. Josef von Sternberg, 'Acting in Film and Theatre' in *Focus on Film and Theatre*, ed. Hurt, pp. 80–98 (p. 97).
14. Bazin, *What Is Cinema?*, I, pp. 83–5.
15. Shooting script of RICHARD III, British Film Institute Library, London.
16. Bazin, *What Is Cinema?*, I, p. 83.
17. Balázs, p. 96.
18. Madsen, pp. 241, 242.
19. MacLiammóir, pp. 101, 242.
20. Sternberg, p. 92.
21. Myrtle Moss (Royal Shakespeare Company), interview, 15 August 1977.
22. Kozintsev, *Space of Tragedy*, pp. 41 and 47.
23. Adolphe Appia, 'The Future of Production', *Theatre Arts Monthly*, 16 (August 1932), 649–66 (pp. 652 and 650).
24. Allardyce Nicoll, 'Film Reality: The Cinema and the Theatre' in *Focus on Film and Theatre*, ed. Hurt, pp. 29–50 (pp. 45–9).
25. Braudy, pp. 187 and 189.
26. Kozintsev, *Space of Tragedy*, pp. 67 and 60. The translation is possibly imprecise here. 'Contrast . . . with' would seem to mean 'Reduce . . . to'.
27. Manvell, pp. 141–2.

28. Manvell, pp. 121–2.
29. MacLiammóir, pp. 26–8.
30. MacLiammóir, pp. 96–100.
31. Myrtle Moss, interview, 15 August 1977.
32. Robin Wood, 'Acting Up', *Film Comment*, 12, no. 2 (1976), 20–5 (p. 21).
33. Madsen, pp. 241–2.
34. Skoller, pp. 143–5.
35. Manvell, pp. 37–8.
36. Balázs, p. 50.
37. Braudy, p. 199.
38. Tim Hallinan, 'Interview: Jonathan Miller on the Shakespeare Plays', *Shakespeare Quarterly*, 32 (1981), 134–45 (p. 138). Miller here relates the dramatic quality of pictorial space with the nature of a play's dramatic substance.

CONCLUSION

1. Peter Brook, personal letter, 11 February 1982.
2. Edward Ruhe, 'Film: The Literary Approach', *Literature Film Quarterly*, 1, no. 1 (1973), 76–83 (p. 76).
3. Peter Brook, public lecture, London, 20 January 1982.

Select filmography

CHIMES AT MIDNIGHT

Spain/Switzerland. 1966. 119 minutes. International Films Espagnola Alpine Productions, released in US by Peppercorn–Wormser, Inc., U–M Film Distributors. Black and White. 35mm.
Producers: Emiliano Piedra and Angel Escoloano. **Executive Producer:** Alessandro Tasca.
Director and Screenwriter: Orson Welles. **Photographer:** Edmond Richard. **Art Directors:** Jose Antonio de la Guerra and Mariano Erdorza. **Editor:** Fritz Muller. **Music:** Angelo Francesco Lavagnino, conducted by Pierluigi Urbini.
Cast: Orson Welles (Sir John (Jack) Falstaff); Jeanne Moreau (Doll Tearsheet); Margaret Rutherford (Hostess Quickly); John Gielgud (King Henry IV); Keith Baxter (Prince Hal, later King Henry V); Marina Vlady (Kate Percy); Norman Rodway (Henry Percy, called Hotspur); Alan Webb (Justice Shallow); Walter Chiari (Mr Silence); Michael Aldridge (Pistol); Tony Beckley (Poins); Fernando Rey (Worcester); Beatrice Welles (Falstaff's page); Andrew Faulds (Westmoreland); Jose Nieto (Northumberland); Jeremy Rowe (Prince John); Paddy Bedford (Bardolph); Ralph Richardson (Narrator).
Note: running time – 115 minutes in version released in USA.

HAMLET

Great Britain. 1948. 153 minutes. Two Cities Films, released by J. Arthur Rank Organization. Black and White. 35mm.
Producer and Director: Laurence Olivier. **Photographer:** Desmond Dickerson. **Art Director:** Carmen Dillon. **Editor:** Helga Cranston. **Music:** William Walton, played by the Philharmonia Orchestra, conducted by Muir Mathieson and John Hollingsworth. **Sound:** John W. Mitchell and Harry Miller.
Cast: Laurence Olivier (Hamlet); Eileen Herlie (The Queen); Basil Sydney (The King); Jean Simmons (Ophelia); Felix Aylmer (Polonius); Norman Wooland (Horatio); Terence Morgan (Laertes); Harcourt Williams (First Player); Patrick Troughton (Player King); Tony Tarver (Player Queen); Peter Cushing (Osric); Stanley Holloway (Gravedigger); Russell Thorndike (Priest); John Laurie (Francisco); Esmond Knight (Bernardo); Anthony Quayle (Marcellus); Niall MacGinnis (Sea Captain).

HENRY V

Great Britain. 1944. 137 minutes. A Two Cities Film, released by United Artists. Technicolor. 35mm.
Producer and Director: Laurence Olivier. **Screenplay:** Alan Dent and Laurence Olivier.
Photographer: Robert Krasker. **Art Director:** Paul Sheriff. **Editor:** Reginald Beck. **Music:** William Walton, played by the London Symphony Orchestra, conducted by Muir Mathieson.
Sound: John Dennis and Desmond Dew.

Cast: Laurence Olivier (King Henry V); Robert Newton (Ancient Pistol); Leslie Banks (Chorus); Renee Asherson (Princess Katharine); Esmond Knight (Fluellen); Leo Genn (The Constable of France); Felix Aylmer (Archbishop of Canterbury); Ralph Truman (Montjoy, the French Herald); Harcourt Williams (King Charles VI of France); Ivy St Helier (Alice, Lady-in-Waiting); Ernest Thesiger (Duke of Beri); Max Adrian (The Dauphin); Frances Lister (Duke of Orleans); Valentine Dyall (Duke of Burgundy); Russell Thorndike (Duke of Bourbon); Michael Shepley (Captain Gower); Morland Graham (Sir Thomas Erpingham); Gerald Case (Earl of Westmoreland); Janet Burnell (Queen Isabel of France); Nicholas Hannen (Duke of Exeter); Robert Helpman (Bishop of Ely); Freda Jackson (Mistress Quickly); Jimmy Hanléy (Williams); John Laurie (Captain Jamie); Niall MacGinnis (Captain MacMorris); George Robey (Sir John Falstaff); Roy Emerton (Lieutenant Bardolph); Griffith Jones (Earl of Salisbury); Arthur Hambling (Bates); Frederick Cooper (Corporal Nym); Michael Warre (Duke of Gloucester).

KING LEAR

Great Britain/Denmark. 1970. 137 minutes. Filmways, Inc. in association with the Royal Shakespeare Company, released by Columbia Pictures. Black and White. 35mm.
Producer: Michael Birkett. **Director and Screenplay:** Peter Brook. **Photographer:** Henry Kristiansen. **Editor:** Kasper Schyberg.
Cast: Paul Scofield (King Lear); Irene Worth (Goneril); Jack MacGowran (Fool); Alan Webb (Duke of Gloucester); Cyril Cusack (Duke of Albany); Patrick Magee (Duke of Cornwall); Robert Lloyd (Edgar); Tom Fleming (Earl of Kent); Susan Engel (Regan); Annelise Gabold (Cordelia); Ian Hogg (Edmund); Barry Stanton (Oswald); Soren Elung Jensen (Duke of Burgundy).

MACBETH

USA. 1948. 105 minutes. A Mercury Production, released by Republic Pictures. Black and White. 35mm.
Producer, Director and Screenplay: Orson Welles. **Photographers:** John L. Russell and William Bradford. **Art Director:** Fred Ritter. **Editor:** Louis Lindsay. **Music:** Jacques Ibert, conducted by Efrem Kurtz. **Sound:** John Stransky, Jr, and Garry Harris.
Cast: Orson Welles (Macbeth); Jeanette Nolan (Lady Macbeth); Dan O'Herlihy (Macduff); Roddy McDowell (Malcolm); Edgar Barrier (Banquo); Alan Napier (A Holy Father); Erskine Sanford (Duncan); John Dierkes (Ross); Keene Curtis (Lennox); Peggy Webber (Lady Macduff); Lionel Braham (Siward); Archie Heugly (Young Siward); Jerry Farber (Fleance); Christopher Welles (Macduff Child); Morgan Farley (Doctor); Lurene Tuttle (Gentlewoman); Brainerd Duffield (First Murderer); William Alland (Second Murderer); George Chirelio (Seyton); Brainerd Duffield, Lurene Tuttle, Peggy Webber (The Three Witches).

OTHELLO

USA. 1952. 91 minutes. Mercury Productions, released by United Artists. Black and White. 35mm.
Producer and Director: Orson Welles. **Photographers:** Anchise Brizzi, G. Araldo, George Fanto. **Editors:** Jean Sachs, with Renzo Luoidi and John Shepridge. **Music:** Francesco Lavagnino, Alberto Barberis, conducted by Willi Ferrero.
Cast: Orson Welles (Othello); Michéal MacLiammóir (Iago); Suzanne Cloutier (Desdemona); Robert Coote (Roderigo); Hilton Edwards (Brabantio); Michael Lawrence (Cassio); Fay Compton (Emilia); Nicholas Bruce (Lodovico); Jean Davis (Montano); Doris Dowling (Bianca).

OTHELLO

Great Britain. 1965. 166 minutes. BHE Productions, released by Warner Brothers Pictures. Technicolor. 35mm Panavision.
Producers: Anthony Havelock-Allan and John Brabourne. **Director:** Stuart Burge. **Stage Director for National Theatre of Great Britain:** John Dexter. **Photographer:** Geoffrey Unsworth. **Film Art Director:** William Kellner. **Editor:** Richard Marden. **Music:** Richard Hampton.
Cast: Laurence Olivier (Othello); Frank Finlay (Iago); Maggie Smith (Desdemona); Robert Lang (Roderigo); Anthony Nicolls (Brabantio); Dereck Jacobi (Cassio); Harry Lomax (Duke of Venice); Terence Knapp (Duke's Officer); Joyce Redman (Emilia); Stella Reid (Bianca); Roy Holder (Clown); Michael Turner (Gratiano); Kenneth Mackintosh (Lodovico); Edward Hardwicke (Montano).

RAN

Japan. 160 minutes. A Serge Silberman Production for Greenwich Film Production/Herald Ace Inc./Nippon Herald Films Inc. Color. 35mm.
Producers: Serge Silberman and Masato Hara. **Director:** Akira Kurosawa. **Screenplay:** Akira Kurosawa, Hideo Oguni, and Masato Ide. **Photographers:** Takao Saito and Masaharu Ueda. **Art Director; Editor; Music:** Toru Takemitsu.
Cast: Tatsuya Nakadai (Lord Hidetora Ichimonji); Akira Terao (Taro); Jinpachi Nezu (Jiro); Daisuke Ryu (Saburo); Mieko Harada (Lady Kaede); Yoshiko Miyazaki (Lady Sué); Masayuki Yui (Tango); Kazuo Kato (Ikoma); Peter (Kyoami); Hitoshi Ueki (Fujimaki); Jun Tazaki (Ayebe); Norio Matsui (Ogura); Hisashi Ikawa (Kurogane); Kenji Kodama (Shirane); Toshiya Ito (Naganuma); Takeshi Kato (Hatakeyama); Takeshi Nomura (Tsurumaru).

RICHARD III

Great Britain. 1956. 155 minutes. Presented by Laurence Olivier in association with London Films, released by Lopert Films Distribution Corporation. Technicolor. 35mm VistaVision.
Producer and Director: Laurence Olivier. **Photographer:** Otto Heller. **Art Director:** Carmen Dillon. **Editor:** Helga Cranston. **Music:** William Walton.
Cast: Laurence Olivier (Richard III); Ralph Richardson (Buckingham); John Gielgud (Clarence); Claire Bloom (Lady Anne); Cedric Hardwicke (King Edward IV); Alex Clunes (Hastings); Pamela Brown (Jane Shore); Mary Kerridge (Queen Elizabeth); Norman Wooland (Catesby); Helen Hayes (Duchess of York – Queen Mother); George Woodbridge (Lord Mayor of London); John Phillips (Norfolk).

THRONE OF BLOOD

Japan. 1957. 105 minutes. Brandon Films, Inc. Black and White. 35mm.
Producer and Director: Akira Kurosawa. **Screenplay:** Akira Kurosawa, Shinobu Hashimoto, Ryuzo Kikushima and Hideo Oguni.
Cast: Toshiro Mifune (Washizu); Isuzu Yamada (Asaji); Takashi Shimura (Odagura); Minoru Chiaki (Miki); Akira Kubo (Yoshiteru); Takamaru Sasaki (Tsuzuki); Yoichi Tachikawa (Kunimaru); Chieko Naniwa (The Weird Woman).

Bibliography

GENERAL

Ackroyd, Peter, 'An Oriental Lear', *Spectator*, 15 March 1986, pp. 38–9
Agate, James, *Around Cinemas* (London, 1948)
Alexander, Peter, *Hamlet: Father and Son* (Oxford, 1955)
Allais, Jean-Claude, 'Orson Welles: Itinéraire d'un poète maudit', *Les Cahiers de la Cinématique*, 20 (Summer 1976), 47–65
Alpert, Hollis, *The Dreams and the Dreamers* (New York, 1962)
  'Movies Are Better than the Stage', *Saturday Review*, 23 July 1955, pp. 5–6, 31 a
Alvarez, A., 'Williamson: I Hate Intellectual Actors', *New York Times*, 27 April 1969, p. 1D
Anderegg, Michael A., 'Shakespeare on Film in the Classroom', *Literature Film Quarterly*, 4, no. 2 (1976), 165–75
Andrew, Dudley, *André Bazin* (New York, 1978)
Armes, Roy, *Film and Reality: An Historical Survey* (London, 1974)
Arnheim, Rudolph, *Film as Art* (London, 1958)
Appia, Adolphe, 'The Future of Production', translated from the French by Ralph Roder, *Theatre Arts Monthly*, 16 (August 1932), 649–66
Balázs, Béla, *Theory of the Film: Character and Growth of a New Art* (London, 1952)
Ball, Robert Hamilton, *Shakespeare on Silent Film* (London, 1968)
Barber, Lester E., 'This Rough Magic: Shakespeare on Film', *Literature Film Quarterly*, 1, no. 4 (1973), 372–6
Barnes, Clive, 'Stage: Midlands *Hamlet*', *New York Times*, 2 May 1969, p. 38
Barton, Anne, 'The King's Two Bodies', Royal Shakespeare Company Programme for *Richard II* production, 1973
Bawden, Liz Anne, ed., *The Oxford Companion to Film* (London, 1976)
Bazin, André, *Orson Welles: A Critical Review* (London, 1978)
  What is Cinema?, trans. Hugh Gray, 2 vols. (Berkeley, California, 1967)
Bazin, André, Charles Bitsch, and Jean Domarchi, interview with Orson Welles, translated and reprinted by the British Film Institute, from *Cahiers du Cinéma*, 87 (1968), unpaged
Beckerman, Bernard, 'The Flowers of Fancy, the Jerks of Invention, or, Directorial Approaches to Shakespeare' in *Shakespeare 1971*, ed. Leech and Margeson (Toronto, 1972), 200–14
  'Shakespeare's Industrious Scenes', *Shakespeare Quarterly*, 30 (1979), 138–50
Benedek, Laslo, 'Play into Picture', *Sight and Sound*, 22 (Autumn 1952), 82–4, 96
Bentley, Eric, *What is Theatre?* (London, 1969)
Berlin, Normand, '*Macbeth*: Polanski and Shakespeare', *Literature Film Quarterly*, 1, no. 4 (1973), 290–8
Bessy, Maurice, 'Les vertes statues d'Orson Welles', *Cahiers du Cinéma*, 11, no. 12 (1952), 28–32
  Orson Welles: An Investigation into His Films and Philosophy (New York, 1971)
Bingham, Robert, 'Movies: The Shakespeare Boom', *The Reporter*, 17 November 1955, pp. 34–7

Bluestone, George, *Novels Into Film* (Berkeley, California, 1973)

Booth, Michael R., 'Shakespeare as Spectacle and History: The Victorian Period', *Theatre International Research*, 1, no. 2 (1976), 99–112

Bordwell, David, and Kristin Thompson, *Film Art: An Introduction* (Reading, Massachusetts, 1979)

Brace, Keith, 'Spectacular Realism, a Heresy', *Birmingham Post*, Shakespeare Quatercentenary Supplement, 17 April 1964, p. xx

  '76 Shakespeare Films . . . But So Few at Oscar Level', *Birmingham Post*, Shakespeare Quatercentenary Supplement, 17 April 1964, p. xxi

Bradley, A.C., *Shakespearean Tragedy* (London, 1965)

Bradbrook, Muriel C., 'The Triple Bond: Audience, Actors, Author in the Elizabethan Playhouse' in *The Triple Bond*, ed. Joseph G. Price (University of Pennsylvania, 1975), pp. 50–69

Braudy, Leo, *The World in a Frame* (New York, 1976)

Brook, Peter, *The Empty Space* (London, 1968)

Brosnan, John, *Movie Magic* (London, 1977)

Brown, John Russell, *Discovering Shakespeare: A New Guide to the Plays* (London, 1981)
  Drama (London, 1968)
  Effective Theatre (London, 1969)
  Free Shakespeare (London, 1974)
  Shakespeare's Plays in Performance (London, 1966)

Brown, John Russell, ed., *Drama and the Theatre, with Radio, Film and Television* (London, 1968)

Burgess, Anthony, 'Stars Without Their Glitter', *Sunday Times*, 20 April 1980, pp. 45–51

Byrne, M. St Clare, 'Dramatic Intention and Theatrical Realization' in *The Triple Bond*, ed. Joseph G. Price (University of Pennsylvania, 1975), pp. 30–49

Cameron, Kenneth, and Theodore J.C. Hoffman, *The Theatrical Response* (London, 1969)

Camp, Gerald, 'Shakespeare Alive!', *Media and Methods*, 5 (October 1968), 42–5
  'Shakespeare on Film', *Journal of Aesthetic Education*, 3 (1969), 107–20

Clair, René, *Cinema Yesterday and Today* (New York, 1972)

Clay, J.H. and D. Krempel, *The Theatrical Image* (New York, 1967)

Clayton, Thomas, 'Aristotle on Shakespearean Film', *Literature Film Quarterly*, 2 (1974), 183–4

Composers' Symposium, 'Music in Films', *Films*, 1 (Winter 1940), 5–24

Cook, Judith, *Director's Theatre* (London, 1974)

Cook, Page, 'The Sound Track: Music from Great Shakespearean Films', *Films in Review*, 16 (1975), 359–61

Cottrell, John, *Laurence Olivier* (London, 1975)

Cowie, Peter, *A Ribbon of Dreams: The Cinema of Orson Welles* (South Brunswick, 1973)

Darlington, W.A., *Laurence Olivier*, Great Contemporaries Series (London, 1968)

David, Richard, *Shakespeare in the Theatre* (Cambridge, 1978)

Dehn, Paul, 'The Filming of Shakespeare' in *Talking of Shakespeare*, ed. John Garrett (London, 1954), pp. 49–72

Durgnat, Raymond, *A Mirror for England* (London, 1970)
  'Canned Theatre Comes Alive', *Films*, 1, no. 11 (1981), 10–14

Dworkin, Martin S., 'Stay Illusion: Having Words about Shakespeare on Screen', *Journal of Aesthetic Education*, 11, no. 1 (1977), 51–61

Eberwein, Robert T., *A Viewer's Guide to Film Theory and Criticism* (New Jersey, 1979)

Eckert, Charles W., ed., *Focus on Shakespearean Film* (New Jersey, 1972)

Eidsvik, Charles, *Cineliteracy: The Film among the Arts* (New York, 1978)
  'Soft Edges: The Art of Literature and the Medium of Film', *Literature Film Quarterly*, 2, no. 1 (1974), 16–21

Eisenstein, S., *The Film Sense* (London, 1943)

Elley, Derek, 'RAN', *Films and Filming* (February 1986), 36
Elliott, Eric, *Anatomy of Motion Picture Art* (London, 1928)
Faure, Elie, *The Art of Cineplastics*, trans. Walter Pach (Boston, 1923)
Fairweather, Virginia, *Cry God for Larry* (London, 1969)
Felheim, Marvin, 'Criticism and the Films of Shakespeare's Plays', *Comparative Drama*, 9
    (1975), 147–55
France, Richard, *The Theatre of Orson Welles* (New Jersey, 1968)
Fuegi, John, 'Explorations in No Man's Land: Shakespeare's Poetry as Theatrical Film',
    Shakespeare Quarterly, 23 (1972), 37–49
Furness, R.S., *Expressionism*, Critical Idiom Series, 29 (London, 1973)
Gerdes, Peter R., 'Film and/or Theatre: Some Introductory Comments', *Australian Journal of
    Screen Theory*, 7 (1980), 4–17
Gianetti, Louis D., *Understanding Movies* (New Jersey, 1976)
Gielgud, Sir John, *An Actor and His Time* (London, 1979)
Gielgud, Val, 'Much Ado About Nothing – II', *The Listener*, 10 March 1937, p. 450
Gillett, John, 'King Lear on a Throne of Blood', *The Guardian*, 3 November 1984, p. 10
Godfrey, Lionel, 'It Wasn't Like That in the Play', *Films and Filming* (August 1967), 4–8
Goldwasser, Noe, 'Film Diary for a Film Version of Shakespeare's *Macbeth*', *Cinéaste*, 2 (1968),
    9–12
Gottesman, Ronald, ed., *Focus on Orson Welles* (New Jersey, 1976)
Gourlay, Logan, ed., *Olivier* (London, 1973)
Granville-Barker, Harley, 'Alas, Poor Will', *The Listener*, 3 March 1937, pp. 387–9, 425–6
Greenspun, Roger, 'Williamson as Hamlet: Richardson Film Based on Debated Version', *New
    York Times*, 22 December 1969, p. L43
Gregory, R.L., *Eye and Brain: The Psychology of Seeing* (London, 1966)
    The Intelligent Eye (London, 1970)
Griffin, Alice, 'Shakespeare Through the Camera's Eye', *Shakespeare Quarterly*, 7 (1956), 235–8
Grossvogel, David I., 'When the Stain Won't Wash: Polanski's MACBETH', *Diacritics*, 2 (1972),
    46–51
Halio, Jay L., 'Zeffirelli's ROMEO AND JULIET: The Camera versus the Text', *Literature Film
    Quarterly*, 5, no. 4 (1977), 322–5
Hallinan, Tim, 'Interview: Jonathan Miller on the Shakespeare Plays', *Shakespeare Quarterly*, 32
    (1981), 134–45
Handzo, Stephen, 'The Producer's Signature: An Interview with John Houseman', *Film
    Comment*, 11 (1975), 18–21
Harcourt, Peter, *Six European Directors* (London, 1974)
Harrison, Carey, 'THE TAMING OF THE SHREW', *Sight and Sound*, 36 (Spring 1967), 97–8
Hatch, Robert, 'Films', *The Nation*, 10 March 1956, pp. 206–7
Hawkes, Terence, *Shakespeare's Talking Animals* (London, 1973)
Hayman, Ronald, 'Shakespeare on the Screen', *TLS*, 26 September 1968, pp. 1081–2
Henderson, Elaine, 'Only Fools and Horses', *Stills*, no. 25 (March 1986), 43
Hennedy, Hugh, 'Shakespeare on the Screen', *Commonweal*, 95 (1971), 134–5
Herring, Robert, 'Shakespeare on the Screen', *Life and Letters Today*, 16, no. 7 (1937), 125–30
Heston, Charlton, *The Actor's Life* (New York, 1976)
Higham, Charles, *The Films of Orson Welles* (Berkeley, California, 1970)
Hirsch, Foster, *Laurence Olivier* (Boston, 1979)
Hitchcock, Alfred, 'Much Ado About Nothing – I', *The Listener*, 10 March 1937, pp. 448–50
Hodgdon, Barbara, 'Kozintsev's KING LEAR: Filming a Tragic Poem', *Literature Film Quarterly*,
    5, no. 4 (1977), 291–8
Holderness, Graham, 'Radical Potentiality and Institutional Closure: Shakespeare in Film and

Television' in *Political Shakespeare*, ed. J. Dollimore and A. Sinfield (Manchester, 1985), pp. 182–201

Homan, Sydney R., 'A Cinema For Shakespeare', *Literature Film Quarterly*, 4, no. 2 (1976), 176–86

'Criticism for the Filmed Shakespeare', *Literature Film Quarterly*, 5, no. 4 (1977), 282–90

Houseman, John, *Run-Through: A Memoir* (New York, 1973)

Houston, Penelope, 'Orson Welles', *Times Saturday Review*, 8 March 1980, p. 6

Hurt, James, ed., *Focus on Film and Theatre* (New Jersey, 1974)

Hurtgen, Charles L., 'Film Adaptation of Shakespeare's Plays' (unpublished Ph.D. dissertation, University of California, 1962)

'The Operatic Character of Background Music in Film Adaptations of Shakespeare', *Shakespeare Quarterly*, 20 (1969), 53–64

Huss, R., and N. Silverstein, *The Film Experience* (New York, 1968)

Jackson, Peter, 'Shakespeare: Stage versus Screen', *Plays and Players*, 6 (December 1958), 8–9

Jacobs, Lewis, ed., *Introduction to the Art of the Movies* (New York, 1960)

Johnson, William, Review of Polanski's MACBETH, *Film Quarterly*, 25, no. 3 (1972), 41–8

Jorgens, Jack J., 'Image and Meaning in the Kozintsev HAMLET', *Literature Film Quarterly*, 1, no. 4 (1973), 307–15

'The Cinematic Bard', *The Washingtonian* (May 1976), 272–7

'The Opening Scene of Polanski's MACBETH', *Literature Film Quarterly*, 3, no. 4 (1975), 277–8

Shakespeare on Film (Bloomington, 1977)

Jorgenson, Paul A., 'Castellani's ROMEO AND JULIET: Intention and Response', *Film Quarterly*, 10, no. 1 (1955), 1–10

Kael, Pauline, *Deeper into Movies* (Boston, 1973)

I Lost It at the Movies (Boston, 1965)

'Is There a Cure for Film Criticism?', *Sight and Sound*, 31 (Spring 1962), 56–64

Kiss Kiss, Bang Bang (Boston, 1968)

Kauffmann, Stanley, *Figures of Light: Film Criticism and Comment* (New York, 1971)

'Notes on Theatre and Film' in *Focus on Film and Theatre*, ed. James Hurt (New Jersey, 1974), pp. 67–77

Kermode, Frank, Review of THE TEMPEST, *TLS*, 16 May 1980, p. 553

'Shakespeare in the Movies' in *Film Theory and Criticism*, ed. Gerald Mast and Marshall Cohen (New York, 1974), pp. 322–32

Kiernan, Thomas, *Olivier: The Life of Laurence Olivier* (London, 1981)

Knight, G. Wilson, *Shakespeare's Dramatic Challenge* (London, 1977)

Shakespearean Production (London, 1968)

The Wheel of Fire, fourth edition (London, 1961)

Knights, L.C., *Explorations* (London, 1964)

Knoll, Robert F., Review of Polanski's MACBETH, *Western Humanities Review*, 27 (Winter 1973), 85–9

Koltai, Ralph, personal interview on stage design, Stratford, 18 June 1980

Kott, Jan, *Shakespeare Our Contemporary* (London, 1965)

Koval, Francis, 'Interview with Welles', *Sight and Sound*, 19 (Winter 1950), 314–16

Kozintsev, Grigori, 'HAMLET and KING LEAR: Stage and Film' in *Shakespeare 1971*, ed. Clifford Leech and J.M.R. Margeson (Toronto 1972)

KING LEAR: The Space of Tragedy (London, 1977)

Shakespeare: Time and Conscience (London, 1967)

'The HAMLET within Me', *Films and Filming* (September 1962), 20

Kracauer, Siegfried, *Theory of Film: The Redemption of Reality* (London, 1960)

Lambert, J.W., 'Shakespeare and the Russian Soul', *Drama*, 126 (1977), 12–19
Langer, Susanne K., *Feeling and Form: A Theory of Art* (London, 1953)
    Philosophy in a New Key (Cambridge, Massachusetts, 1980)
Levaco, I., ed., *Kuleshov on Film* (London, 1974)
Lindgren, Ernest, *The Art of the Film* (London, 1950)
Lindsay, Vachel, *The Art of the Moving Picture* (New York, 1922)
Litton, Glen, 'Diseased Beauty in Tony Richardson's H A M L E T', *Literature Film Quarterly*, 4, no.
    2 (1976), 108–22
Lumet, Sydney, 'Colour and Concepts', *Films and Filming*, 24, no. 8 (1978), 13–16
McGowan, Kenneth, *Behind the Screen: The History and Techniques of the Motion Picture* (New
    York, 1965)
    'The Film Director's Contribution to the Screen', *English Journal*, 40 (1951), 127–34
MacLiammóir, Micheál, 'Orson Welles: A Pen-Portrait', *Sight and Sound*, 24 (Summer 1954),
    36–8
McBride, Joseph, *Orson Welles* (London, 1972)
McClellan, Kenneth, *Whatever Happened to Shakespeare?* (London, 1978)
McConnell, Frank D., *The Spoken Seen: Film and the Romantic Imagination* (Baltimore, 1975)
McDonald, Neil, 'The Relationship Between Shakespeare's Stage-craft and Modern Film
    Technique', *Australian Journal of Screen Theory*, 7 (1980), 18–23
McLuhan, Marshall, *Understanding Media* (London, 1974)
McNeir, W.F., 'Grigori Kozintsev's K I N G L E A R', *College Literature*, 5 (1978), 239–47
Madsen, Roy Paul, *The Impact of Film* (New York, 1974)
Manchel, F., *Film Studies: A Resource Guide* (New Jersey, 1973)
Manvell, Roger, *Shakespeare and The Film* (London, 1971)
Manvell, Roger and John Huntley, *The Technique of Film Music*, revised and enlarged by
    Richard Arnell and Peter Day (New York, 1975)
Marienstras, Richard, 'Orson Welles, interprète et continuateur de Shakespeare', *Positif*, 167
    (1975), 37–44
Mason, Pamela, 'Olivier's Shakespeare' (unpublished Ph.D. dissertation, University of Bir-
    mingham, 1978)
Mast, Gerald and Marshall Cohen, eds., *Film Theory and Criticism*, first edition (New York,
    1974)
Millard, Barbara C., 'Shakespeare on Film: Towards an Audience Perceived and Perceiving',
    Literature Film Quarterly, 5, no. 4 (1977), 352–7
Miller, Jonathan, 'To Be or Not To Be a Producer', *Radio Times*, 18 October 1980, pp. 90–1
Milne, Tom, 'Crime and Punishment', *Sight and Sound*, 55, no. 2 (1986), 133–4
Monaco, James, *How to Read a Film* (New York, 1981)
Morris, Peter, 'Shakespeare on Film', *Films in Review*, 24 (1973), 132–63
Muir, Kenneth, 'The Critic, the Director and Liberty of Interpreting' in *The Triple Bond*, ed.
    Joseph G. Price (University of Pennsylvania, 1975), pp. 20–9
Mullin, Michael, '*Macbeth* on Film', *Literature Film Quarterly*, 1, no. 4 (1973), 332–42
    'Peter Hall's *A Midsummer Night's Dream* on Film', *Education Theatre Journal*, 27 (1975),
    529–34
    'Tony Richardson's H A M L E T: Script and Screen', *Literature Film Quarterly*, 4, no. 2 (1976),
    123–33
Münsterberg, Hugo, *The Film: A Psychological Study (The Silent Photoplay of 1916)* (New York,
    1970)
Murray, Edward, ed., *Nine American Film Critics: A Study of Theory and Practice* (New York,
    1975)
Murray, Edward, *The Cinematic Imagination* (New York, 1972)

Narboni, Jean, 'Sacher & Masoch', *Cahiers du Cinéma in English*, 11 (September 1967), 23

Naremore, James, *The Magic World of Orson Welles* (New York, 1978)

Nicholls, Bill, ed., *Movies and Methods* (Berkeley, California, 1976)

Nicoll, Allardyce, *Film and Theatre* (London, 1936)

'Film and Reality: The Cinema and the Theatre' in *Focus on Film and Theatre*, ed. James Hurt (New Jersey, 1974), pp. 29–50

Noble, Peter, *The Fabulous Orson Welles* (London, 1956)

Olivier, Laurence, *Confessions of an Actor* (London, 1982)

Ornstein, Robert, 'Interpreting Shakespeare: The Dramatic Text and the Film', *University of Daytona Review*, 14 (1979), 55–61

Parker, Barry M., *The Folger Shakespeare Filmography* (Folger Books, 1979)

Pascal, Valerie, *The Disciple and His Devil* (London, 1970)

Pasolini, P.P., 'The Cinema of Poetry', *Cahiers du Cinéma in English*, 6 (1966), 34–43

Pechter, William S., *Twenty-Four Times a Second* (New York, 1971)

Perkins, Victor, *Film as Film* (London, 1972)

Potter, Henry C., George Roy Hill and Gene Saks, 'Stage to Film', *Action*, 3, no. 5 (1968), 12–14

Prawer, S.S., *Caligari's Children: The Film as a Tale of Terror* (Oxford, 1980)

Prior, Moody E., 'Page versus Stage: The Province of the Critic of Shakespeare', *University of Denver Quarterly*, 10, no. 2 (1975), 75–81

Pudovkin, V.I., *Film Technique and Film Acting* (London, 1974)

Pursell, Michael, 'Zeffirelli's Shakespeare: The Visual Realization of Tone and Theme', *Literature Film Quarterly*, 8, no. 4 (1980), 210–18

Ray, Satyajit, *Our Films, Their Films* (Calcutta, 1976)

Raynor, Henry, 'Shakespeare Filmed', *Sight and Sound*, 22 (Summer 1952), 10–15

Rayns, Tony, 'RAN', *Monthly Film Bulletin*, 53, no. 627 (1986), 115–16

Reddington, John, 'Film, Play and Idea', *Literature Film Quarterly*, 1, no. 4 (1973), 367–71

Reilly, Charles P., Review of Polanski's MACBETH, *Films in Review*, 23 (1972), 111–12

Richardson, Jack, 'Relevant Shakespeare', *Commentary*, 53, no. 4 (1972), 85–7

Richardson, Robert, *Literature into Film* (Bloomington, 1973)

Richmond, Hugh M., 'The Synergistic Use of Shakespearean Film and Video-tape', *Literature Film Quarterly*, 5, no. 4 (1977), 362–4

Robinson, David, 'King Lear Gets the Royal Touch', *The Times*, 5 November 1984, p. 10. xi

Rose, T.J. 'Shakespeare among the Nations: The Tragedies in the International Cinema', *Literary Review*, 22 (1979), 381–2

Rotha, Paul, *Rotha on the Film* (London, 1958)

Rothwell, Kenneth, 'Appreciating Shakespeare on Film', *Literary Film Quarterly*, 5, no. 4 (1977), 365–7

'Hollywood and Some Versions of ROMEO AND JULIET', *Literature Film Quarterly*, 1, no. 4 (1973), 343–51

'Roman Polanski's MACBETH: Golgotha Triumphant', *Literature Film Quarterly*, 1, no. 1 (1973), 71–5

'Zeffirelli's ROMEO AND JULIET: Words into Picture and Music', *Literature Film Quarterly*, 5, no. 4 (1977), 326–31

Ruhe, Edward, 'Film: The Literary Approach', *Literature Film Quarterly*, 1, no. 1 (1973), 76–83

Sarris, Andrew, *Interviews with Film Directors* (New York, 1967)

Schwarz, Daniel, 'The Present and the Future of Shakespeare', *New York Times*, 12 May 1946, pp. 22–3, 58

Shakespeare, William, *The Complete Works of William Shakespeare*, Oxford Standard Authors edition, ed. W.J. Craig (London, 1974)

Shelley, Frank, *Stage and Screen*, Film Quarterly Series (London, 1946)

Silverstein, M., and Kenneth Rothwell, 'The Opening Shot of Roman Polanski's MACBETH', *Literature Film Quarterly*, 11, no. 1 (1974), 88–90

Silviria, Dale, *Laurence Olivier and the Art of Film Making* (Rutherford, 1985)

Singer, Sandra Sugarman, 'Laurence Olivier Directs Shakespeare: A Study in Film Authorship' (unpublished Ph.D. dissertation, North Western University, 1978)

Skoller, Donald, 'Problems of Transformation in the Adaptation of Shakespeare's Tragedies from Playscript to Cinema' (unpublished Ph.D. Dissertation, New York University, 1968)

Sontag, Susan, 'Film and Theatre' in *Film Theory and Criticism*, ed. Gerald Mast and Marshall Cohen (New York, 1974), 249–67

Sparshott, F.E., 'Basic Film Aesthetics' in *Film Theory and Criticism*, ed. Gerald Mast and Marshall Cohen (New York, 1974), pp. 209–32

Staton, Shirley F., 'Shakespeare Redivivus: Supplementary Techniques for Teaching Shakespeare', *Literature Film Quarterly*, 5, no. 4 (1977), 358–61

Stearn, G.E., ed., *McLuhan: Hot and Cool* (London, 1968)

Stein, Elliott, 'The Art of Art Direction', *Film Comment*, 2, no. 3 (1975), 32–4

Steiner, George, *The Death of Tragedy* (London, 1961)

Stephenson, Ralph, and J.R. Debrix, *The Cinema as Art*, second edition (London, 1976)

Sternberg, Joseph von, 'Acting in Film and Theatre' in *Focus on Film and Theatre*, ed. James Hurt (New Jersey, 1974), pp. 80–98

Stoll, Michael John, 'A Village Production of *Hamlet*', *Film Quarterly*, 19, no. 4 (1976), 51–4

Styan, J.L., 'Sight and Space: The Perception of Shakespeare on Stage and Screen' in *Shakespeare, Pattern of Excelling Nature*, ed. David Bevington and Jay L. Halio (New Jersey, 1978), 198–209

The Shakespeare Revolution (Cambridge, 1977)

Taylor, John Russell, 'Shakespeare in Film, Radio and Television' in *Shakespeare: A Celebration, 1564–1964*, ed. T.J.B. Spencer (London, 1964), pp. 97–113

Thorp, Margaret Farrand, 'Shakespeare and the Movies', *Shakespeare Quarterly*, 9 (1958), 357–66

Time, 'Elsinore of the Mind', Review of Richardson's HAMLET, 12 January 1970, p. 46

Trewin, J.C., *Peter Brook: A Biography* (London, 1971)

Tudor, Andrew, *Theories of Film* (London, 1971)

Tyler, Parker, *Classics of the Foreign Film* (New York, 1962)

Tynan, Kenneth, 'Interview: Orson Welles', *Playboy*, 14 March 1967, pp. 53–64

The Sound of Two Hands Clapping (London, 1971)

Vardac, Nicholas, *Stage to Screen* (New York, 1968)

Walker, George Graham, 'Film as Fine Art', *Sight and Sound*, 17 (Winter 1948), 173–4

Walker, Roy, 'In Fair Verona', *Twentieth Century*, 156 (1954), 464–71

Wall, John, 'Shakespeare's Aural Art: The Metaphor of the Ear in *Othello*', *Shakespeare Quarterly*, 30 (1979), 358–66

Watts, Richard, 'Films of a Moonstruck World', *Yale Review*, 25 (1935), 311–20

Webster, Margaret, 'The Interpretation of Shakespeare Today', *Wisdom*, 17 July 1956, pp. 23–35

Welles, Orson, 'The Third Audience', *Sight and Sound*, 23 (Winter 1954), 120–2

Wells, Stanley, *Literature and Drama* (London, 1970)

'Television Shakespeare', *Shakespeare Quarterly*, 33 (1982), 261–77

'Reunion with Death', *TLS*, 14 March 1986

Welsh, James M., 'Shakespeare with – and without – Words', *Literature Film Quarterly*, 1, no. 1 (1973), 84–8

'To See It Feelingly: KING LEAR Through Russian Eyes', *Literature Film Quarterly*, 4, no. 2 (1976), 153–8

Wenden, D.J., *The Birth of the Movies* (London, 1975)
Wilders, John, 'Adjusting the Set', *THES*, 10 July 1981, p. 13
Wilds, Lilian, 'On Film: Maximilian Schell's Most Royal Hamlet', *Literature Film Quarterly*, 4, no. 2 (1976), 134–40
Willett, John, *Expressionism* (London, 1970)
Williams, Raymond, *Drama in Performance* (London, 1968)
  Television: Technology and Cultural Form (London, 1974)
Williams, W.E., 'Film and Literature', *Sight and Sound*, 4 (Winter 1935), 164–5
Winnington, Richard, *Drawn and Quartered* (London, 1949)
Wood, Robin, 'Acting Up', *Film Comment*, 12, no. 2 (1976), 20–5
  Personal Views: Explorations in Film (London, 1976)
Young, Vernon, 'Fat Shakespeare, Fat City, Lean Wilderness', *Hudson Review*, 26, no. 1 (1973), 170–1
Yutkevitch, S., 'The Conscience of the King', *Sight and Sound*, 40 (Autumn 1971), 192–6
Zitner, Sheldon, 'Wooden O's in Plastic Boxes: Shakespeare and Television', *University of Toronto Quarterly*, 51, no. 1 (1981), 1–12

LITERATURE RELEVANT TO THE FILMS UNDER DISCUSSION

CHIMES AT MIDNIGHT, directed by Orson Welles (1966)

Archer, Eugene, 'Welles Captures Cannes', *Saturday Review*, 23 July 1966, pp. 62–3
Billard, Pierre, 'CHIMES AT MIDNIGHT', *Sight and Sound*, 34 (Spring 1965), 64–5
Birstein, Ann, 'FALSTAFF, a Curiously Mixed Bag', *Vogue*, 1 January 1967, p. 53
Brendan, Gill, Review of CHIMES AT MIDNIGHT, *The New Yorker*, 25 March 1967, p. 152
Cobos, Juan and Miguel Rubio, 'Welles and Falstaff: An Interview', *Sight and Sound*, 35 (Autumn 1966), 158–63
Cobos, Juan, Miguel Rubio, and J.A. Pruneda, 'A Trip to Don Quixoteland: Conversations with Orson Welles', *Cahiers du Cinéma in English*, 5 (1966), 35–47
Comolli, Jean-Louis, 'Jack le Fataliste', *Cahiers du Cinéma in English*, 11 (September 1967), 21
Crowl, Samuel, 'The Long Goodbye: Welles and Falstaff', *Shakespeare Quarterly*, 31 (1980), 369–80
Crowther, Bosley, 'Cannes Film Festival', *New York Times*, 12 May 1966, p. 54
  'Cannes of Worms', *New York Times*, 29 May 1966, section 2, p. 1
  Review of CHIMES AT MIDNIGHT, *New York Times*, 20 March 1967, section 2, p. 26
Daney, Serge, 'Welles in Power', *Cahiers du Cinéma in English*, 11 (September 1967), 17
Duboeuf, Pierre, 'The Other Side', *Cahiers du Cinéma in English*, 11 (September 1967), 21
Houston, Penelope, Review of CHIMES AT MIDNIGHT, *Sight and Sound*, 35 (Summer 1966), 125–7
Johnson, William, 'Orson Welles: Of Time and Loss', *Film Quarterly*, 21 (1967), 13–24
Price, James, Review of CHIMES AT MIDNIGHT, *Sight and Sound*, 36 (Summer 1967), 146–7
Prokosch, Mike, 'Orson Welles', *Film Comment*, 7 (Summer 1971), 28–37
Review, 'Body English', *Time*, 24 March 1967, p. 42
Welles, Orson, Dialogue Script for CHIMES AT MIDNIGHT (English translation), unpublished, Library of the Shakespeare Institute, University of Birmingham
Zimmerman, Paul D., 'Falstaff as Orson Welles', *Newsweek*, 27 March 1967, pp. 50–2

HAMLET, directed by Laurence Olivier (1948)

Agee, James, 'Olivier's HAMLET', *Time*, 29 June 1948, pp. 28–31
Aiken, Frederick, 'Shakespeare on the Screen', *Screen Education*, 21 (1963), 33–6

Ashworth, John, 'Olivier, Freud and *Hamlet*', *Atlantic Monthly*, 183 (May 1949), 30–3
Babcock, R.W., 'George Lyman Kittredge, Olivier, and the Historical *Hamlet*', *College English*, 11 (1950), 256–65
Barbarow, George, '*Hamlet* Through a Telescope', *Hudson Review*, 2 (1949), 98–117
Barnes, Howard, Review of HAMLET, *New York Herald Tribune*, 30 September 1948, p. 21
Bayley, John, '*Hamlet* as a Film', *National Review*, 131 (December 1948), 603–6
Brown, John Mason, 'Seeing Things: Olivier's HAMLET', *Saturday Review of Literature*, 2 October 1948, pp. 26–8
Chappel, Connery, 'Olivier's HAMLET', *Kinematograph Weekly*, 6 May 1948, p. 6
Cook, Alton, 'Olivier's HAMLET', *New York World Telegram*, 30 September 1948
Cook, Don, Review of HAMLET, *New York Herald Tribune*, 9 May 1948, section v, pp. 1–2
Cross, Brenda, ed., *The Film HAMLET* (London, 1948)
Crowther, Bosley, Review of HAMLET, *New York Times*, 3 October 1948, section 2, p. x
'Discussing HAMLET', *New York Times*, 7 November 1948, section 2, p. x
'The Screen: A Trio of Newcomers Arrives', *New York Times*, 30 September 1948, p. 32L
Dent, Alan, 'HAMLET and CALIGARI', *Illustrated London News*, 15 May 1948, p. 562
'Text-Editing Shakespeare – with Particular Reference to HAMLET' in *HAMLET, The Film and The Play*, ed. Alan Dent (London, 1948), unpaged
Duffy, Robert A., 'Gade, Olivier, Richardson: Visual Strategy in *Hamlet* Adaptation', *Literature Film Quarterly*, 4, no. 2 (1976), 141–52
Furse, Roger, 'Designing the Film HAMLET' in *HAMLET, the Film and The Play*, ed. Alan Dent (London, 1948), unpaged
Halio, Jay L., 'Three Filmed *Hamlets*', *Literature Film Quarterly*, 1, no. 4 (1973), 316–20
Harper's Magazine, 'Citizen Dane' (September 1948), 116–17
Hart, Henry, Review of HAMLET, *Films in Review*, 17 (1966), 251–2
'HAMLET Revisited', *Films in Review*, 5 (1954), 144–5
Hartung, Philip, Review of HAMLET, *Commonweal*, October 1948, p. 596
Hatch, Robert, Review of HAMLET, *New Republic*, 4 (October 1948), 28–30
Herring, R., 'HAMLET: Sir Laurence Olivier's Picture', *Life and Letters*, 57 (June 1948), 183–92
Hift, Fred, 'Honours for HAMLET', *New York Times*, 14 May 1950, p. x5
Hollywood Quarterly, 'HAMLET: The Play and the Screenplay', 3 (Spring 1948), 293–300
Hopkins, Arthur, 'HAMLET and Olivier', *Theatre Arts*, 32 (Summer 1948), 30–1
Huntley, John, 'The Music of HAMLET and OLIVER TWIST' in *The Penguin Film Review* (London 1949), 110–16
Kliman, Bernice, 'Olivier's HAMLET: A Film-Infused Play', *Literature Film Quarterly*, 5, no. 4 (1977), 305–14
Lesser, Simon O., 'Freud and Hamlet Again', *American Imago*, 12 (1955), 207–20
McCarthy, Mary, 'A Prince of Shreds and Patches', reprinted in *Focus on Shakespearean Film*, ed. Charles Eckert (New Jersey, 1972), 63–7
McCarten, John, 'Olivier's HAMLET', *The New Yorker*, 2 October 1948, pp. 90–1
McManaway, James G., 'The Laurence Olivier HAMLET', *Shakespeare Association of America Bulletin*, 24 (January 1949), 3–11
Marshall, Margaret, 'Notes By The Way', *Nation*, 23 October 1948, p. 468
Newsweek, 'HAMLET Triumph', 27 September 1948, pp. 87–8
New York Times, 'Olivier HAMLET Acclaimed in London', 5 May 1948, p. L29
Olivier, Laurence, Foreword in *HAMLET, The Film and The Play*, ed. Alan Dent (London, 1948)
Olivier, Laurence, and Alan Dent, Shooting Script for HAMLET, unpublished, Library of the British Film Institute
Powell, Dilys, '*Hamlet* on the Screen', *Britain Today*, 147 (July 1948), 18–21
Ramsaye, Terry, 'Britain's HAMLET is Presented to American Reviewers', *Motion Picture Herald*, 3 July 1948, p. 17

Time, 'Better Than the Play', 15 May 1948, p. 38
Tyler, Parker, 'HAMLET and Documentary', *Kenyon Review*, 11 (Summer 1949), 527–32
Vesselo, Arthur, 'British Films of the Quarter', *Sight and Sound*, 17 (Summer 1948), 99–100
Wyatt, Euphemia, Review of HAMLET, *Catholic World*, 168 (December 1948), 243–4

HENRY V, *directed by Laurence Olivier (1944)*

Agee, James, Review of HENRY V, *Time*, 8 April 1946, p. 58
Beauchamp, Gorman, 'HENRY V: Myth, Movie, Play', *College Literature*, 5 (1978), 228–38
Brown, John Mason, 'Seeing Things: The Old Vic and HENRY V', *Saturday Review of Literature*, 25 May 1946, pp. 24–6, 28
Clearing House, 'HENRY V', 33 (September 1958), 59
Crowther, Bosley, Review of HENRY V, reprinted in *Focus on Shakespearean Film*, ed. Charles Eckert (New Jersey, 1972), pp. 57–62
Farber, Manny, Review of HENRY V, *New Republic*, 8 July 1946, p. 14
G.B., 'The Film of HENRY V', *English*, 5 (1945), 107–8
Geduld, Harry, *Film-Guide to HENRY V* (Bloomington, 1973)
Hartung, Philip T., Review of HENRY V, *Commonweal*, 21 June 1946, pp. 238–9
Herzberg, Max J., 'Olivier as Henry V', *Scholastic Teacher*, 14 October 1946, p. 6T
Huntley, John, *British Film Music*, reprint of the 1948 edition (New York, 1972)
Le Jeune, C.A., 'This Wider Cockpit' in her *Chestnuts in Her Lap* (London, 1947), pp. 134–5
Life, 'Movie of the Week: HENRY V', 20 May 1946, pp. 38–42
McCarten, John, Review of HENRY V, *The New Yorker*, 22 June 1946, pp. 40–2
McCready, Marsha, 'Henry V on Stage and on Film', *Literature Film Quarterly*, 5, no. 4 (1977), 316–21
McLean, Andrew M., 'God for Harry! England and Saint George', *Literature Film Quarterly*, 1, no. 4 (1973), 377–80
Merton, James, 'Shakespeare Comes to the Films', *Christian Science Monitor*, 30 March 1946, p. 7
Mosdell, D., Review of HENRY V, *Canadian Forum*, 26 (1946), 161
Newsweek, 'Great King Henry', 17 June 1946, p. 102
New York Herald Tribune, 'Olivier Found England at War No Place to Film Battle of 1415', 2 June 1946, p. 3
Norton, Elliott, 'Drama and Politics Mingled Expertly in Film HENRY V', *Boston Post*, 7 April 1946, p. 22x
Olivier, Laurence, and Reginald Beck, 'Screenplay for HENRY V', in *Film Scripts One*, ed. G.P. Garrett, O.B. Hardison, and Jane R. Gelfman (New York, 1971)
Phillips, James E., 'Adapted From a Play by Shakespeare', *Hollywood Quarterly*, 2 (October 1946), 82–90
Shakespeare on Film Newsletter, 'Homage to Olivier's HENRY V', 4, no. 1 (1982), 1
Vogue, 'Recreates Medieval Paintings', 1 September 1946, pp. 218–19
Wyatt, Euphemia, Review of HENRY V, *Catholic World*, 163 (1946), 457

KING LEAR, *directed by Peter Brook (1971)*

Acker, Paul, 'Conventions for Dialogue in Peter Brook's KING LEAR', *Literature Film Quarterly*, 8, no. 4 (1980), 219–24
Andrews, Nigel, Review of KING LEAR, *Sight and Sound*, 40 (Autumn 1971), 223–4
Berlin, Normand, 'Peter Brook's Interpretation of *King Lear*: Nothing Will Come of Nothing', *Literature Film Quarterly*, 5, no. 4 (1977), 299–303
Braun, Eric, Review of KING LEAR, *Films and Filming*, 18 October 1971, pp. 54–6

Brook, Peter, Draft Shooting Script for KING LEAR, 5 December 1968, unpublished, Library of the Shakespeare Institute, University of Birmingham
Catholic Film Newsletter, 'Peter Brook's Bold Homage to Shakespeare's Dark and Dire Tragedy', 15 December 1971, p. 117
Chaplin, William, 'Our Darker Purpose: Peter Brook's KING LEAR', *Arion*, 1 (Spring 1973), 168–87
Film Maker, Review of KING LEAR, 5 (December 1971), 56
Hetherington, Robert A., 'The *Lears* of Peter Brook', *Shakespeare on Film Newsletter*, 6, no. 1 (1982), 7
Johnson, William, Review of KING LEAR, *Film Quarterly*, 25, no. 3 (1972), 41–8
Kell, Review of KING LEAR, *Variety*, 17 February 1971, p. 18
Knoll, Robert F., Review of KING LEAR, *Western Humanities Review*, 27 (Winter 1973), 85–9
Reeves, Geoffrey, 'Finding Shakespeare on Film: From an Interview with Peter Brook' in *Film Theory and Criticism*, ed. Gerald Mast and Marshall Cohen (New York, 1974), pp. 316–21
Reilly, Charles P., Review of KING LEAR, *Films in Review*, 22 (1971), 637–8
Wilds, Lilian, 'One KING LEAR for Our Time: A Bleak Vision by Peter Brook', *Literature Film Quarterly*, 4, no. 2 (1976), 159–64
Wolf, William, Review of KING LEAR, *Cue*, 27 November 1971, p. 76

MACBETH, directed by Orson Welles (1948)

Beylie, Claude, 'MACBETH, or The Magical Depths', translated and reprinted in *Focus on Shakespearean Film*, ed. Charles W. Eckert (New Jersey 1972), 72–5
France, Richard, 'The Voodoo *Macbeth* of Orson Welles', *Yale Theatre*, 5, no. 3 (1974), 66–78
Hatch, Robert, 'Bloody, Bold and Resolute!', *New Republic*, 15 January 1951, 30–1
Hope-Wallace, Phillip, Review of MACBETH, *Sight and Sound*, 21 (Summer 1951), 22–3
Knight, Arthur, 'Violence on a Low Budget', *Saturday Review*, 3 February 1951, p. 25
Le Maître, Henri, 'Shakespeare, the Imaginary Cinema and the Pre-Cinema', translated and reprinted in *Focus on Shakespearean Film*, ed. Charles W. Eckert (New Jersey, 1972), pp. 27–36
Leonard, Harold, 'Notes on MACBETH', *Sight and Sound*, 19 (Spring 1950), 15–17
McCarten, John, 'Orson's Cauldron', *The New Yorker*, 30 December 1951, p. 51
Mullin, Michael, 'Orson Welles' MACBETH: Script and Screen' in *Focus on Orson Welles*, ed. R. Gottesman (New Jersey, 1976), pp. 136–45
Naremore, James, 'The Walking Shadow: Welles's Expressionist MACBETH', *Literature Film Quarterly*, 1, no. 4 (1973), 360–6
Newsweek, 'Scotch Broth', 18 October 1948, pp. 109–10
Senior Scholastic, Review of MACBETH, 27 March 1948, p. 29
Time, Review of MACBETH, 13 November 1948, p. 90
Wilson, Richard, 'Macbeth on Film', *Theatre Arts*, 33 (June 1949), 53–5

OTHELLO, directed by Stuart Burge (1965)

Birstein, Ann, 'OTHELLO, a Gorgeous Blackness', *Vogue*, 1 March 1966, p. 95
Brendan, Gill, 'Black and White', *The New Yorker*, 19 February 1966, p. 145
Brown, Constance, 'OTHELLO', *Film Quarterly*, 19, no. 4 (1966), 48–50
Coffey, Warren, 'Double Feature', *Commentary*, 41 (April 1966), 79–81
Crist, Judith, 'The Role or the Star?' in her *The Private Eye, the Cowboy and the Very Naked Girl* (Chicago, 1968), pp. 168–9
Davies, Brenda, 'OTHELLO', *Sight and Sound*, 35 (Summer 1966), 149

D.W. 'OTHELLO, Great Britain 1965', *Monthly Film Bulletin*, 33 (June 1966), 90
Fisher, James E., 'Olivier and the Realistic OTHELLO', *Literature Film Quarterly*, 1, no. 4 (1973), 322–31
Gow, Gordon, 'OTHELLO', *Films and Filming*, 12 (May 1966), 6
'The Struggle: John Dexter in Interview with Gordon Gow', *Plays and Players*, 27, no. 2 (1979), 58–62
Kenner, Hugh, Review of OTHELLO, *National Review*, 22 March 1966, pp. 281–3
Kuhn, Weldon, 'OTHELLO', *Films in Review*, 17 (January 1966), 52–3
Nelson, Harland S., 'OTHELLO', *Film Heritage*, 2 (1966), 18–22
Sarris, Andrew, 'OTHELLO', *Village Voice*, 17 February 1966, pp. 21–3
Time, 'One Man's Moor', 4 February 1966
Tynan, Kenneth, 'Olivier's OTHELLO', *The Observer*, 12 December 1966, Supplement pp. 8–14, 17–18, 21
'Olivier: The Actor and the Moor' in his *The Sound of Two Hands Clapping* (New York, 1975), pp. 127–40

OTHELLO, directed by Orson Welles (1952)

Bazin André, Review of OTHELLO, reprinted in English in *Film Theory and Criticism*, ed. Gerald Mast and Marshall Cohen (New York, 1974), 337–9
Bentley, Eric, 'OTHELLO of Film and Stage', *New Republic*, 3 October 1955, pp. 21–2
Bingham, Robert, Review of OTHELLO, *The Reporter*, 13 (November 1955), 34–7
Crowther, Bosley, Review of OTHELLO, *New York Times*, 13 September 1955, p. 27
Downing, Robert, 'OTHELLO', *Films In Review*, 6 (1955), 341–2
Goldstein, R.M., 'OTHELLO', *High Points*, 37 (October 1955), 46–50
Hamburger, Phillip, 'The Moor', *The New Yorker*, 17 September 1955, p. 132
Hatch, Robert, Review of OTHELLO, *The Nation*, 1 October 1955, p. 290
MacLiammóir, Mícheál, *Put Money in Thy Purse: The Filming of Orson Welles's OTHELLO* (London, 1952)
Phelps, Donald, Review of OTHELLO, *Film Culture*, 1, no. 1 (1955), 32
Plotkin, Frederick, 'Othello and Welles: A Fantastic Marriage', *Film Heritage*, 4 (Summer 1969), 9–15
Robinson, David, Review of OTHELLO, *Sight and Sound*, 25 (Spring 1956), 196–7
Whitebait, William, 'Big Brother', *New Statesman and Nation*, 10 March 1956, pp. 210–12

RICHARD III, directed by Laurence Olivier (1955)

Appleton, William, Review of RICHARD III, *Films in Review*, 7 (1956), 122–3
Benson, Harold, 'Shakespeare in Vista-Vision', *American Cinematographer*, 37 (February 1956), 94–5, 119–22
Brinson, Peter, 'The Real Interpreter', *Films and Filming*, 1 (April 1955), 4–5
Brown, Constance, 'Olivier's RICHARD III: A Revaluation', reprinted in *Focus on Shakespearean Film*, ed. Charles W. Eckert (New Jersey, 1972), pp. 131–45
Diether, Jack, 'RICHARD III: The Preservation of Film', *Hollywood Quarterly and Quarterly of Film, Radio and Television*, 11 (1957), 280–93
Downing, Robert, Review of RICHARD III, *Films in Review*, 7 (1956), 123–4
English, Review of RICHARD III, by 'Thespis', 11 (1956), 19–20
Furse, Roger, 'Middle Ages Through Modern Eyes', *Films and Filming*, 1 (May 1955), 10–11
Hart, Henry, Review of RICHARD III, *Films in Review*, 7 (1956), 124–6
Hatch, Robert, Review of RICHARD III, *The Nation*, 10 March 1956, pp. 206–7

Henning, T.H., 'Sir Laurence Olivier: Triumph in Shakespeare's Great Year', *Newsweek*, 19 March 1956, pp. 105–6

Knight, Arthur, 'Sir Laurence and the Bard', *Saturday Review*, 10 March 1956, pp. 26–8

Leyda, J., 'The Evil That Men Do . . .', *Film Culture*, 2, no. 1 (1956), 21–3

Manvell, Roger, 'Laurence Olivier on Filming Shakespeare', *Journal of The British Film Academy* (Autumn 1955), 2–5

Miller, Don, 'Films on TV', *Films In Review*, 7 (1956), 179–80

Olivier, Laurence, and Alan Dent, Shooting Script for RICHARD III, unpublished, Library of the British Film Institute

Phillips, James E., 'RICHARD III: Some Glories and Some Discontents', *Film Quarterly*, 10, no. 3 (1956), 339–407

Prouse, Derek, Review of RICHARD III, *Sight and Sound*, 25 (Winter 1956), 144–5

Schein, Harry, 'RICHARD III: A Magnificent Fiasco?', *Film Quarterly*, 10 (1956), 407–15

Theatre Arts, 'At Home and Abroad with RICHARD III', 40 (March 1956), 22–4

Time, 'The New Pictures', 12 March 1956, pp. 52–3

Walker, Roy, 'Bottled Spider', *Twentieth Century*, 159 (January 1956), 58–68

THRONE OF BLOOD, directed by Akira Kurosawa (1957)

Barnet, Sylvia, 'Kurosawa's THRONE OF BLOOD' in *A Short Guide to Writing About Literature* (Boston, 1971), pp. 225–51

Bazerman, Charles, 'Time in Play and Film: *Macbeth* and THRONE OF BLOOD', *Literature Film Quarterly*, 5, no. 4 (1977), 332–8

Blumenthal, J., '*Macbeth* into THRONE OF BLOOD' in *Film Theory and Criticism*, ed. Gerald Mast and Marshall Cohen (New York, 1974), pp. 340–51

Crowther, Bosley, 'Screen: Change in Scene', *New York Times*, 23 November 1961, p. 50

Gerlach, John, 'Shakespeare, Kurosawa and *Macbeth*: A Response to J. Blumenthal', *Literature Film Quarterly*, 1, no. 4 (1973), 352–9

Keene, D., *Noh: The Classical Theatre of Japan* (Tokyo, 1966)

Kinder, Marsha, 'THRONE OF BLOOD: A Morality Dance', *Literature Film Quarterly*, 5, no. 4 (1977), 339–45

Koval, Francis, 'Venice 1957', *Cue*, 8 (October 1957), 375–82

Richie, Donald, *The Films of Akira Kurosawa* (Berkeley, California, 1965)
  'Kurosawa on Kurosawa', *Sight and Sound*, 33 (Autumn 1964), 200–3

Scott, A.C., *The Theatre in Asia* (London, 1972)

Vasey, Ruth, 'Ozu and The Noh', *Australian Journal of Screen Theory*, 7 (1980), 88–102

Zambrano, Ana Laura, 'THRONE OF BLOOD: Kurosawa's *Macbeth*', *Literature Film Quarterly*, 2, no. 3 (1974), 262–74

Index